MW00534113

100 Spiritual Movies
to See Before You Die

Christmas 2023 —
Fun to share
remotely!
Enjoy.
Jan

P.S. Don't miss *Home Alone*
which was filmed in
Winnetka, Illinois

100
SPIRITUAL MOVIES
TO SEE BEFORE
YOU DIE

JOHN A. ZUKOWSKI

the pilgrim press

The Pilgrim Press, 1300 East 9th Street
Cleveland, Ohio 44114
thepilgrimpress.com

© 2023 John A. Zukowski

All rights reserved. No part of this book may be used or reproduced in any manner whatsoever without written permission.

Published 2023.

In-text artwork and photographs used by permission. Scripture quotations, unless otherwise noted, are from the New Revised Standard Version of the Bible, © 1989 by the Division of Christian Education of the National Council of Churches of Christ in the United States of America. Used by permission. Changes have been made for inclusivity.

Printed on acid-free paper.

Library of Congress Cataloging-in-Publication Data on file.
LCCN: 2023932467

ISBN 978-0-8298-0044-9 (paper)
ISBN 978-0-8298-0045-6 (ebook)

Printed in The United States of America.

For Kim,

forever a bright morning star in my life.

CONTENTS

CONTENTS

CONTENTS

CONTENTS

INTRODUCTION

Like many others during the COVID lockdown, I watched movies. A lot of them.

During a time of uncertainty and isolation, the movies that gave me the most consolation were what I called spiritual movies, including *Tree of Life* (2011), *Tender Mercies* (1983), and *The Book of Eli* (2010); films series such as *Lord of the Rings*, *The Hunger Games*, and *Harry Potter*; as well as classic films from *The Tokyo Story* (1953) to *Groundhog Day* (1993).

Watching these movies raised a question that became the basis for this book: What makes a film a spiritual movie?

Some movies, and art in general, are informed by a concept of a higher spiritual self. Other art comes from more worldly, materialistic, or commercial motives. So not all films are spiritual. Moreover, the association of spirituality solely with ethics generates confusion. Characters in all films display some sort of ethical behavior, whether good, bad, or ugly. But not all films contain a sense of spirituality.

Some define spiritual movies as those that feature religious characters, such as Biblical figures, saints, or clergy members. But this is too narrow. Spirituality is not limited to religious figures. Movies with religious figures can be spiritual films, but they do not define the entire genre. And putting a religious figure in a film does not necessarily make it a spiritual film.

Some might say a spiritual film needs to be inspirational. Film critic Roger Ebert said *Ikiru* (1952), a movie about a man with terminal cancer deciding how to spend his last days, is "one of the few movies that might actually be able to inspire someone to lead their life a little differently."[1] The American Film Institute compiled a list of the Top 100 Inspirational Films, including *Mr. Smith Goes to Washington* (1939), *The Sound of Music* (1965), and *Rocky* (1976). Most of these films feature characters conquering great odds to accomplish something substantial. But some of these movies are more about individual achievement than the spiritual life.

To define a spiritual film, I turned to how religion scholar William James succinctly describes religious experience: good comes from recognizing and responding to a transcendent reality.[2]

How the transcendental manifests in films varies. Sometimes it is expressly supernatural, as in a heavenly visitation from an angel in *It's A Wonderful Life* (1946) or a glimpse of an afterlife as in *Soul* (2020). But it also can come through in movies with no references to the divine, such as *The Wizard of Oz* (1939) and *The Devil Wears Prada* (2006), two films that follow the spiritual narrative of the hero's journey.

The most common outcome in the spiritual film genre, regardless of whether it constitutes a full-fledged redemption story or not, is a character progressing from an individualistic lower self to a holier higher self. The flawed self desires individualistic sensations, is often restless, and is self-centered,[3] while the higher self contains grace, peace, and is other-focused.[4] Spiritual films, in short, feature a redemptive transformation from ego-based narcissism into altruism.[5]

This differs from most films, whose narrative formulas often glorify a character implementing their individualistic will into the world. As Pema Lhaki explains to a Westerner in *Seven Years in Tibet* (1997), "You admire the man who pushes his way to the top in any walk of life, while we admire the man who abandons his ego."

In non-spiritual films, a character's sense of control is their salvation, while a misguided attempt to control is often the central problem in the spiritual film.[6] *Bruce Almighty* (2003) shows how salvation comes from relinquishing control. In one key scene, the exhausted protagonist falls to his knees and prays to God, "I want you to decide what's right for me. I surrender to your will."

The psychological film shares some attributes of the spiritual film. These films show damaged characters who must change to become more complete. Forces outside of the conscious individual's life must be corrected.[7] Psychologists even take on roles of guru-like liberators in *Good Will Hunting* (1997) and *Antwone Fisher* (2002). In some psychological films, characters uncover the original source of trauma that wounded them and are liberated by exploring it and accepting it. In other psychological films, the narrative revolves around the protagonist's need to overcome a particular manifestation of their psychological condition. Although some psychological films integrate spirituality, they generally show how the mind responds, not necessarily the spirit. What makes the spiritual film different is that it acknowledges a force beyond psychology and individual personality that stems from the transcendental or divine.[8]

While psychology focuses on internal obstacles, films once called social problem films, and now called social justice films, are directed at external difficulties. From some perspectives, social justice requires a more heightened spirituality because it demands characters become other-focused. And it adheres to the prophetic tradition of speaking out against inequity and acknowledging a collective sense of sin. However, the prophetic tradition always comes from transcendental insight. In keeping with that tradition, films such as *Gandhi* (1982) and *Malcolm X* (1992) are spiritual social justice films because social movement leaders are driven by spiritual ideals and principles rather than by secular definitions of justice.

An interesting but more ambiguous category of films are those that show an absent or misplaced sense of the divine. This happens in *Citizen Kane* (1941), often considered the best film of all time by critics. Newspaper tycoon Charles Foster Kane dares to take on a god-like role and thus demonstrate that secular power guides modern society, not faith.[9] This idea carries through in some crime films in which a criminal assumes the role of a misplaced God-like authority. However, just because these films engaged with a misplaced or absent spirituality does not necessarily make them spiritual movies.

The psychological film, social justice film, and misplaced/absent sense of God films at least make a social statement or indicate something significant about the human condition. Many other non-spiritual films are more escapist and, as a result, non-spiritual. Some escapist films contain a sanitized version of reality that reinforces secular social norms or taboos. Others celebrate a lack of morality through charismatic anti-heroes. Still others manipulate viewers into emotions such as fear, suspense, and anger, which is particularly true of horror movies, thrillers, and special-effects driven films.

Recent years have witnessed a significant decrease in the number of spiritual films produced. One explanation might be found in cultural religious trends, such as a decline in church attendance, growing distrust of social institutions including the church, and rising polarization in both religion and politics. With such distrust and division, filmmakers avoid religion so they can, in their view, maximize the commercial appeal of their movies.

This may explain why there are fewer movies about institutional religion. But films that are more spiritual than religious have also become uncommon. The spiritual but not religious movement is increasingly associated with New Age ideology which young people are increasingly criticizing and rejecting.[10] Another factor is that movies are in danger of becoming anachronistic or obsolete. With the rise of streaming services emphasizing television shows and limited series, creativity is shifting away from movies toward television shows.

Despite these trends, the films in this book demonstrate that spiritual films are an important part of film history and have impacted popular conceptions of spirituality. I have learned there is no one approach to making a spiritual film. However, after several years of watching movies, I identified consistent patterns within spiritual films. While I cannot define one overall spiritual film format, spiritual films fall into one of the following twelve categories.

BIBLICAL AND CLERGY FIGURES

Biblical figures, clergy, or spiritual leaders begin with a higher sense of a spiritual self. They show the difficulties of manifesting holiness in a world that resists their level of godliness.

The film most associated with this category is the Bible epic. It thrived in the silent era, re-emerged after the Second World War, and peaked in popularity in the 1950s and early 1960s.

Bible epics fall into three categories:

1. Old Testament stories, including *David and Bathsheba* (1951), *The Ten Commandments* (1956), and *The Story of Ruth* (1960).

2. Films about the life of Jesus, such as *King of Kings* (1961) and *The Greatest Story Ever Told* (1965).

3. Films about early Christians, such as *Quo Vadis* (1951), *The Robe* (1953), and *Ben Hur* (1959). They occur either in Jesus's lifetime or just after it. Later came gladiator films set either before the birth of Christ (*Spartacus*) or more than a century after his death (*The Fall of the Roman Empire* and *Gladiator*).[11]

By the 1970s, Old Testament stories and Roman Christian films largely disappeared. But the "Jesus film" was reconfigured. Jesus became a symbol of each era's spiritual preoccupations.

Christ represents the contemporary counterculture in *Godspell* (1973), a questionable messiah in *Jesus Christ Superstar* (1973), and a victim of zealous followers in *Life of Brian* (1979), while *The Last Temptation of Christ* (1988) emphasizes the human aspects of Christ. Partly because these alterations became increasingly controversial, the Christ film, too, largely vanished.

Occasionally, a successful Bible epic has appeared like *The Passion of the Christ* (2004) and *Noah* (2014). But these films didn't ignite a full-fledged Bible epic revival.

Other films in this category feature saints, including *Song of Bernadette* (1943), *The Flowers of St. Francis* (1950), and the numerous films about Joan of Arc. These films emphasize the asceticism, temperance, and mystical experiences of saints. Their great desire for moral consistency and purity leads them to withdraw as much as possible from secular life.[12]

Hollywood was generally more comfortable with a character that did the opposite of withdrawing from the world. The streetwise heroic clergy figures in movies such as *Boys Town* (1938), *Going My Way* (1944), and *The Bells of St. Mary's* (1945) feature amiable surrogate parental figures confronting social problems. A deeper and more mature version of this figure came in Karl Malden's priest willingly entangling himself in danger against corruption in *On the Waterfront* (1954).

However, a turning point came with Audrey Hepburn's character in *A Nun's Story* (1959), who ultimately feels the demands of pacifism and obedience are too confining. Portrayals of clergy after this film often show unrealistic expectations of the religious life or the turmoil a clergy member feels between divine and worldly impulses. These films include the troubled monsignor in *True Confessions* (1981), the imperialistic Jesuit missionary in *Black Robe* (1991), and a shunned gay priest in *Priest* (1994). By *Sister Act* (1992), the Catholic cloistered life is shown as irrelevant. A convent is trapped in apathy and fear until an outsider played by Whoopi Goldberg modernizes the convent by adding variations on pop songs to the Catholic Mass and integrating the nuns more into the community.

The socially conscious Catholic religious figure reemerges occasionally. In *Romero* (1989), El Salvador's archbishop Oscar Romero helps the oppressed against a corrupt government. *Dead Man Walking* (1995) features a nun trying to find humanity in a killer on death row, and *Entertaining Angels* (1996) chronicles the life of social activist Dorothy Day. But the Catholic priest abuse scandals shifted the image of the priest to one of suspicion in *Doubt* (2008) and led filmmakers to portray the church as a corrupt institution in works like *Philomena* (2013) and *Spotlight* (2015).

Protestant ministers aren't featured in spiritual films as prominently as Catholic clergy. They are often secondary or minor characters. However, exceptions are the small-town minister played by Joel McRae in *Stars in My Crown* (1950), a minister helping a rape victim in Ida Lupino's *Outrage*

(1950), and James Earl Jones as a South African pastor in *Cry the Beloved Country* (1995). Perhaps Protestant ministers aren't as visually appealing because they don't have the signifier of the Catholic priest's collar or nun's habit dramatically setting them apart. And perhaps there is curiosity about the cloistered lifestyle of Catholic religious orders.

In *The Night of the Hunter* (1955), Robert Mitchum's performance as a murderous itinerant country minister ushered in portrayals of dangerous evangelicals. This trope was solidified by the release of *Elmer Gantry* (1960), which features a preacher played by Burt Lancaster who hoodwinks worshippers at evangelistic tent revivals. The stereotype continued for decades with other sham preachers like Steve Martin's character in *Leap of Faith* (1992) and a sinister evangelist in *There Will Be Blood* (2007). A more complex variation is found in *The Apostle* (1997) and *First Reformed* (2017), both featuring Protestant ministers with conflicting spiritual and criminal tendencies.

This category also features spiritual leaders of social movements in *Gandhi* (1982) and *Malcolm X* (1992) and spiritual authors such as C.S. Lewis in *Shadowlands* (1993).

CHRIST FIGURES

Lloyd Baugh identifies ten common characteristics of the Christ figure on the screen:

1. Mysterious origins
2. Attracts followers
3. A commitment to justice
4. The working of miracles, wonders, or unexpected events
5. Is at conflict with authority
6. Redeems other characters
7. At a crucial moment withdraws to a deserted place where the character communes with the mystical

8. Suffers for his actions/beliefs

9. Experiences a trip to the cross in some way

10. Undergoes some form of a resurrection (if not a bodily resurrection, the spirit of the individual carries on in other characters).[13]

Anton Kozlovic extends the list to twenty-five attributes with additional traits, including a betrayer associate, a relationship of some kind with a Mary Magdalene-type figure, a crucifix-like pose at a crucial moment, and even sharing the same initials "J.C." like John Coffey (Michael Clark) in *The Green Mile*, James Cole (Bruce Willis) in *Twelve Monkeys*, or John Connor (Edward Furlong) in *The Terminator* and *Terminator 2: Judgment Day*.[14]

Whether there are ten or twenty-five, Christ figures do not possess all of these traits, but they have enough to draw parallels with Jesus's life in the gospels. However, there's a difference between characters with multiple qualities of the Christ figure and characters with fewer such traits. Many non-spiritual films include characters who are at odds with authority or who are committed to justice but are not full-blown Christ figures.

In some ways, the Christ figure involves an imaginative exercise in how Christ would act in contemporary society. In other ways, it shows how a follower of Christ acquires attributes of Christ. But like portrayals of Biblical figures, clergy members, and saints, Christ figures begin in a redeemed state. So, the tension occurs externally, because their spirituality clashes with a misunderstanding secular world.

One trait that perhaps signifies a Christ figure the most is self-sacrifice for others, which is often portrayed as the highest form of altruism. Another common trait is unjust suffering. Movies like *Cool Hand Luke* (1967), *The Shawshank Redemption* (1994), and *The Green Mile* (1999) imprison the Christ figure as a metaphor for a misunderstood savior figure trapped in an unjust confining world. The seminal influential films linking prisons to spiritual confinement are *Strange Cargo* (1940), with a Christ figure guiding an escape, and Bresson's *A Man Escaped* (1956), in which an escape from prison represents spiritual release.

Other Christ figures emphasize the messianic aspect of Christ and receive special designation as liberators, such as Katniss in *The Hunger Games* (2012) and Neo in *The Matrix* (1999), referred to repeatedly as "the one."

Christ figures are extra-terrestrials in *The Day the Earth Stood Still* (1951) and *E.T.* (1982), a misunderstood Gothic artist in *Edward Scissorhands* (1990), and a female Christ figure offering a communion-like meal in *Babette's Feast* (1987). Perhaps the most innovative Christ figure is the donkey in Bresson's movie *Au Hasard Balthazar* (1966), who is a figure of both adoration and suffering. Aslan in *The Lion, The Witch, and the Wardrobe* (2005) is another significant animal Christ figure.

THE REDEMPTION STORY

The redemption story is a clear illustration of the spiritual movie's movement from a lower self to a higher self. These films portray conversion experiences where a flawed character spiritually awakens and longs to escape sin and embrace positive qualities such as peace, altruism, and tenderness.[15]

These epiphanies can come dramatically and suddenly or gradually with small change over a period of time.[16] In Kurosawa's *Ikiru* (1952), an epiphany occurs more suddenly when Kanji Watanabe realizes he can perform a philanthropic action in his otherwise meaningless job. In *Groundhog Day* (1993), the process of realization is gradual, with Phil Connor undergoing a laborious process of trial and error to be a better person.

Redemption advances in three stages:

1. Ignorance of one's damaged non-spiritual state

2. Conflict between an old self and an emerging self

3. Embracing a new spiritually oriented self

This replicates what William James describes as three spiritual conditions: The sick soul, the divided self, and conversion.

It also mirrors Kierkegaard's three stages of spiritual development: The aesthetic, the ethical, and the religious.

These stages also connect to justification and sanctification in Christianity. The second act of the redemption story embodies justification by moving someone out of sin, while the third phase shows sanctification as the redeemed sinner progressively becomes more purified.

Redemption radically differs from self-improvement.

Redemption is deliverance from a destructive, sinful condition. It is an overhaul, a drastic change of living and alteration of character. The redemption story replicates the Christian theology of overcoming original sin—a tendency in the human condition toward sin and selfishness. Before conversion, the character is immersed in estrangement, alienation, and meaninglessness.[17] The isolation of Kanji Watanabe's deadening routine as a bureaucrat in *Ikiru* and Phil Connor's egoism and emotional detachment in *Groundhog Day* are both important examples.

This differs from the secular self-help influenced film, in which characters overcome a lack of assertion against oppressive external forces or internal self-doubts. Those films are a wish fulfillment of escaping pressures and limitations rather than breaking from a flawed self.[18] With no focus on the divine, the goal is to boost self-worth through maximizing personal choice and individual potential.[19]

Westerns often feature redemptive violence that restores moral order. In *Shane* (1953), the violence the eponymous protagonist uses to protect a group of homesteaders ultimately forces him to leave the community. The redemptive violence of Westerns influenced action films like *Die Hard* (1988), in which the protagonist restores his better self and marriage by battling terrorists. *Taxi Driver* (1976) is a complex redemption-through-violence story. Travis Bickle acts to destroy the moral decay surrounding him, but his violent vigilante rampage turns him into an anti-hero character.[20] Anti-heroes are misguided or fail to achieve the deliverance in the third phase of the redemption arc. These films are about an attempt at redemption rather than achieving it. *Taxi Driver* features an ironic redemption story as Travis receives praise for his vigilantism despite appearing not to have changed internally.

Fellini's *La Dolce Vita* (1960) is a variation with the protagonist missing his chance at redemption. The ending scene on the beach with Marcello Mastroianni waving goodbye to a symbol of innocence and redemption shows how redemption is within reach, but the character doesn't have the consciousness to recognize it.

La Dolce Vita is also an example of the existentialist film, where a character drifts through life feeling emptiness and foregoing redemption. Antonioni's films, such as *L'Avventura* (1960) and *La Notte* (1961), are landmark films in this category, as is Stanley Kubrick's *Eyes Wide Shut* (1999).

THE APOCALYPTIC AND POST-APOCALYPTIC FILM

Apocalyptic literature from the Bible, most notably the Book of Revelation, influenced this category of spiritual films, which are usually dystopias, science fiction, or horror films.

Some film and religion scholars believe a true apocalyptic film shows a cosmic force conquering evil forces. They differentiate those films from secular apocalyptic films that depict humans correcting a threat such as disease, environmental disaster, or, in *Armageddon* (1998), an asteroid headed for earth. Non-spiritual apocalyptic films and dystopias are often symbols of contemporary social ills and warn of potential disaster. These films lack a supernatural struggle and do not show a divine will shaping the outcome.[21]

However, even in apocalyptic films without supernatural intervention, religious imagery and themes can elevate them above a secular apocalyptic film. In *The Omega Man* (1971), Charlton Heston dies in a crucifixion-like pose giving a vial of blood to his followers so they can survive. He becomes a Christ figure that provides the film with religious symbolism.

Some films in this category are post-apocalyptic. The action occurs after an apocalyptic battle showing how survivors live afterwards. These films have grown in popularity within past few decades, probably because a post-apocalyptic worldview reflects anxiety that America is in economic and social decline with its better days in the past.

Whether apocalyptic or post-apocalyptic, defining it as a spiritual film depends on the amount of religious imagery or themes that can affirm the transcendental. For example, *The Book of Eli* (2010) shows consistent religious imagery and references, while Pixar's *WALL-E* (2008) features a post-apocalyptic landscape without religious themes or imagery.

DIVINE INTERVENTION

This category always features a supernatural occurrence manifesting in the world. Because a supernatural being directly intervenes, it is the spiritual movie genre's most visible affirmation of the transcendental.

Divine intervention takes place in six different ways:

1. God manifesting in human form

2. An angel intervening in the world

3. A soul reborn in a living body

4. A dead person returning as a ghost

5. Death manifesting in human form

6. Variations on the *Faust* story with a character giving his soul to the devil in exchange for an earthly goal

Some portrayals of God are essentially walk-on roles, such as Ralph Richardson in *Time Bandits* (1981) or Alanis Morissette in *Dogma* (1999), but God plays a larger role imparting wisdom to humans with George Burns in *Oh, God!* (1977), Morgan Freeman in *Bruce Almighty* (2003), and Octavia Spencer in *The Shack* (2017).

Angel interventions are much more common than God manifestations, but they perform the same purpose: providing supernatural aid to a human in need. Most popular are guardian angel figures, including the angel Clarence aiding a troubled small-town man in *It's A Wonderful Life*, a dead pilot returning to help another pilot in *A Guy Named Joe* (1943), and an angel taking human form to help a minister in *The Bishop's Wife* (1947).

Another subcategory shows an afterlife where souls are reborn in other bodies to learn lessons on earth, such as *Here Comes Mr. Jordan* (1941) and its two remakes, *Heaven Can Wait* (1978) and *Down To Earth* (2001). The transmigration of souls has been presented in comedies from *I Married a Witch* (1942) to *Defending Your Life* (1991) and even through the reincarnation of animals in *A Dog's Purpose* (2017). Sometimes these films are informed by a mixture of Eastern and Western theology, as in *What Dreams May Come* (1999).

Death itself assumes human form in films such as Ingmar Bergman's *The Seventh Seal* (1957), *Death Takes a Holiday* (1934), and its loose remake *Meet Joe Black* (1998). Manifestations of Satan also occur, including variations of the Faust story centered on a character selling his soul for some benefit, such as seven years of prosperity in *The Devil and Daniel Webster* (1941) or musicians trading their souls for success in *Angel Heart* (1987) and *Crossroads* (1986).

THE SPIRITUAL HERO'S JOURNEY

Comparative religion and mythology scholar Joseph Campbell examined consistent narrative patterns of heroic figures in religious and mythological texts to define the hero's journey (also known as the monomyth), an adventure that leads to spiritual transformation. In *Hero with a Thousand Faces*, Campbell notes that the majority of people are not heroic adventurers. They choose what he calls civic and tribal routines that generate spiritual meaning out of sacraments, rituals, and rites of passage within a community.[22]

However, Campbell's hero figure pursues a different spiritual path.

In stages, the hero proceeds through a dangerous journey away from his community.[23] After a series of trials, the hero returns and reintegrates into society as a changed and enlightened person.[24]

For example, in *Star Wars*, the first act of the hero's journey includes a call to adventure (Princess Leia's message), refusal of the call (Luke must help with the harvest), supernatural aid in the form of a guide/mentor (Luke meets Obi-Wan Kenobi), and a crossing of the threshold (Luke leaves Tatooine). The second act shows trials as well as a meeting with the goddess (Princess Leia, who wears white) and an important culmination where the hero acquires new abilities and characteristics. In the third stage, the hero receives help from without (Han Solo assists him). After Luke destroys the Death Star using the power of the Force, which shows him as a spiritual person, he reintegrates into the community (receives a medal with his friends Han Solo and Chewbacca).

Like Christ figures that don't have to possess all the traits of a Christ figure, characters don't usually follow all of the stages of the hero's journey. However, they must take an adventure away from the hero's initial community. Sometimes it is a magical place, as in *The Wizard of Oz* (1939), while at other times it is a journey through the temptations of contemporary New York City in *The Devil Wears Prada* (2006) and *Wall Street* (1987).

Other necessary components are a mentor or guide, goddess and tempter figures, and a concluding return home. The hero's journey is a popular film narrative because the affirmation of the transcendental occurs through an action-driven story.

Hero's journeys are often variations of coming-of-age stories, since the protagonist is usually an adolescent or young adult. However, secular coming-of-age stories often end at the conclusion of the first stage: crossing the threshold. A character recognizes limitations and disillusionments and feels a call to adventure. Films such as *I Vitelloni* (1953), *American Graffiti* (1973), *Ghost World* (2001), and *Sing Street* (2016) conclude with a protagonist leaving their confining hometown.

Films usually do not feature the mode of spirituality that Campbell defines as being derived from staying in the community, often because American movies romanticize adventurers. A notable example of a movie that defies this trend is *It's a Wonderful Life* (1946). It elevates sacraments, rituals, and civic responsibilities above adventure. This influenced later films such as Pixar's *Soul* (2020).

An offshoot of the hero's journey is the pilgrimage movie. Sometimes the space that the protagonist defines sacred is a religious site such as the shrine of St. James in *The Way* (2010). Other times it follows out of what a site represents, like in The *Straight Story* (1999), where the endpoint is the home of the protagonist's estranged brother and reaching it signifies forgiveness and reconciliation.

Pilgrimage films show spiritual transformation on a journey rather than revelation at the destination. After separation from a social structure, the pilgrimage acts as a transitional liminal space before eventual reintegration.[25]

The separation is sometimes provoked by a spiritual crisis or death of a loved one, such as in *Wild* (2014), which tells the story of a grieving woman (Reese Witherspoon) who hikes the Pacific Crest trail after the death of her mother, and *The Way* (2010), which follows a father (Martin Sheen) who walks the Camino de Santiago (The Way of St. James) following the death of his son. The pilgrimage is typically provoked by a sense of guilt about sins in the protagonist's life, and the journey with all its dangers becomes an act of penance.[26] During this journey, there is an inner movement of the heart not possible within existing social structures.[27]

Some road films fall into the category of pilgrimages, while more secular variations focus on the rebelliousness of leaving a social structure for the road rather than a sense of penance or meaningful inner transformation.

OLD TESTAMENT INFLUENCED CAUTIONARY TALE

These films are variations on Old Testament narratives in which figures such as Adam and Eve, Cain, and Jonah defy God by enacting sinful traits such as pride, ambition, or disobedience. Although films such as *East of Eden* (1955) create modern versions of Cain and Abel, films in this category do not often explicitly modernize Biblical characters.

Such films can be categorized as cautionary tales because they thwart social taboos about marriage, murder, and crime and expose tragic flaws in the characters. Some are not purely cautionary tales because they do not contain an explicit warning. This stands in contrast to *Treasure of the Sierra Madre* (1948), where an old prospector warns gold miners about greed, and *Gremlins* (1984), in which a shop owner cautions about the danger of neglecting responsibilities.

Due to its depiction of a fallen world, film noir is a genre closely associated with this category. Characters often commit a murder or try to cover up a sinful act.

In *Double Indemnity* (1944), an insurance salesman believes he is smart enough to commit a crime to collect a large sum of insurance money. He suffers from the sin of pride, believing he can outwit morality and the law, as some Biblical characters believed they could outsmart God. In *The Postman Always Rings Twice* (1946), Lana Turner wants a better life than her job as a waitress at a diner offers. Her sin of ambition leads to murder. In *The Woman in the Window* (1944), Edward G. Robinson kills out of self-defense and tries to cover it up, which escalates into more deceit.

In other renditions of this storyline, a character erroneously believes they can leave the corrupt criminal world behind whenever they want. In *Asphalt Jungle* (1950), Sterling Hayden incorrectly hopes he can return to the simplicity of his country home after he commits a bank robbery. In *The Harder They Fall* (1956), Humphrey Bogart believes he can work a public relations job for a prize fighter in rigged boxing matches, but he is unable to back out of the job as planned. In *The Roaring Twenties* (1939), James Cagney cannot leave a life of crime to marry the woman who can free him from his criminal tendencies.

These films illustrate how sin escalates into an inescapable lifestyle. The corrective force of the police, courts, and investigators looms as a god-like moral agent, which was partly due to the Hays Code, which, strictly enforced between 1934 and the early 1960s, prohibited criminals from getting away with crimes.

Crime films made after the classic Hollywood period are more morally ambiguous. They break the pattern of the basically good person corrupted by committing a sin, forced into crime by lack of opportunity, or tempted by the allure of a femme fatale character. Perhaps the point of these films is the lack of self-awareness embodied by characters like the young killers played by Martin Sheen and Sissy Spacek in *Badlands* (1973).

WESTERNER SEEKING EASTERN WISDOM

Since D.W. Griffith's *Broken Blossoms* (1919), the dominant narrative in Western movies featuring Eastern religion involves generalizations that cover over the plurality of Asian religions. The narrative centers on an idealized monk or monk-like Asian character conveying spiritual knowledge to a Westerner.[28] This stereotype in Western cinema is based on a trope of a wise guru correcting faults in the equivalent of a novice disciple, who is damaged or limited by a materialistic, ego-based, and violent Western culture. Although exalting the Eastern sage as a purveyor of spiritual knowledge, this stereotype presents a simplified representation of Eastern religions. In some cases, the guru-like character's identity is based on assisting or rescuing the Westerner rather than an independent spiritual identity.

In these films, Westerners often leave their flawed situations in Western culture to travel to a romanticized religious site or monastery in the East for spiritual wisdom, like in *The Razor's Edge* (1946), *Seven Years in Tibet* (1997), and *Eat Pray Love* (2010). In *Lost Horizon* (1937), the Eastern guru character lives in a remote monastery in the Himalayas called Shangra-La, a utopian-like paradise where inhabitants are so spiritually superior that they can halt the aging process. This movie shows how Asian spirituality is fetishized to present not just a guru but an entire spiritual community and ultimately Asian culture as spiritually advanced. In other versions, the guru educates non-Asians in the West with secret knowledge to help the troubled Westerner overcome adversities including physical threats, as in *The Karate Kid* (1984).

Variations on the Eastern sage have permeated popular culture. One of the most popular is the Jedi Master Yoda in *The Empire Strikes Back* (1980), a hermit-like guru character who speaks his aphorisms with the cadence of an Eastern sage but who also possesses secret knowledge that enables him to manipulate objects. *The Legend of Bagger Vance* (2000) modifies the sacred Hindu Bhagavad Gita by reworking the Arjuna character into a troubled golfer named R. Junuh who receives mystical insights and wisdom from the mysterious guru-like caddy Bagger Vance (Will Smith). In *Peaceful Warrior* (2006), the guru character is reconfigured as a Western gas station worker who possesses a combination of secret spiritual knowledge giving him superhuman physical powers and the sage-like characteristic of dispensing spiritual advice to a restless and spiritually flawed Westerner.

In this category, the affirmation of the transcendental usually comes through the wisdom of the sage figure correcting the flaws of the Western character. A notable exception is *Kundun* (1997), which depicts the young Dalai Lama on his own spiritual journey without having to educate Westerners with spiritual lessons. But generally, as the streetwise Catholic priest declined, the Eastern guru became the cinematic stereotype of spiritual wisdom.

Although the Eastern sage stereotypes dominated this category, another variation is the reincarnation-centered film. Since the 1940s, comedies have been made based on characters reborn into other bodies with little or no solid spirituality. But reincarnation is portrayed more seriously in films such as *Little Buddha* (1993), about a young Western boy who may be the reincarnation of a religious teacher; *Cloud Atlas* (2012), which shows people reappearing in different human forms in different eras; and *I Origins* (2014), which revolves around a scientist seeking scientific proof of reincarnation.

DIFFICULTY LIVING OUT FAITH

In this category, a non-Christ figure character clashes with a secular power structure that doesn't understand a character's religiosity. This generates tension in the film between worldly achievement and religious faith. A notable example is the Olympic athlete who refuses to run a race on the Sabbath in *Chariots of Fire* (1981).

Movies with Amish and Quaker characters often fall under this category because of these groups' belief in non-violence. Pacifism contrasts with the secular view that violence is sometimes necessary. In most films, nonviolence is seldom a viable option.[29] However, films often do criticize culture for being too dominated by violence.

As a result, films often maintain an ambivalence about pacifist characters. They are sometimes idealized as figures of salvation and wisdom, dismissed as unrealistic and overly idealistic, or attributed with both qualities.

Some films place characters in a position in which they are forced to choose between secular and spiritual lives. In *The Angel and the Badman* (1947), the wayward cowboy played by John Wayne marries a Quaker woman to end his life of violence. However, in *Witness* (1985), Harrison Ford is attracted to the peaceful community-oriented life of an Amish woman but chooses to return to his secular life in law enforcement. In *Friendly Persuasion* (1956), the pacifist Quaker family headed by Gary Cooper must decide on how realistic a non-violent life is when their farm is raided during the Civil War.

Other films convert the pacifist to violence as a pragmatic response to threats. The Quaker played by Grace Kelly in *High Noon* (1952) saves her husband's life by shooting a villain. In *Sargent York* (1941), a born-again evangelical (Gary Cooper) refuses to fire a gun in the military. After an officer gives him a book on United States history, however, Cooper's patriotism supersedes his religious beliefs. He not only agrees to fire his gun at enemy soldiers but wins a medal for doing so. *Hacksaw Ridge* (2016) finds a way to uphold both pacifism and violence. An unarmed pacifist medic puts himself in extreme danger to rescue and aid soldiers, which wins the respect of the military.

Contemporary Christian films often fall into this category. They frequently show the Christian believer clashing with a secular world that dismisses their beliefs, as in *God's Not Dead* (2014), where a Christian student battles an atheist college professor.

THE TRANSCENDENTAL FILM STYLE

In some spiritual films, it is the film style itself, rather than the content of the film, that puts it in the spiritual movie category. These transcendental-style films use slow pacing not to create mood, but to direct the viewer into a contemplative state.[30]

Most films advance action, but the transcendental film is about being in the present.[31] This recalls the practice of *Lectio Divina*, the act of reading the Bible by concentrating on revelations gleaned from contemplating details of the text.[32]

To lead the viewer into concentrating on the present, the most distinctive technique transcendental film directors use is the long take (the uninterrupted shot). This allows the viewer to observe visual details they might otherwise overlook. Other transcendental film techniques include a static camera, using ambient sound rather than music, reducing edits, and highlighting the mundane.[33] These techniques reveal how ordinary people, objects, and events possess spiritual qualities.[34] The subject matter does not necessarily have to be overtly religious, as the content takes a back seat to the film's style.[35]

The basis for this category of films is Paul Schrader's book *Transcendental Style in Film* (1971), which outlines the transcendental film techniques of three film directors (Ozu, Bresson, and Dreyer). Ozu's *Tokyo Story* (1953), Bresson's *Diary of a Country Priest* (1951), and Dryer's *Ordet* (1955) are all important examples of this film style, as is Paweł Pawlikowski's *Ida* (2013). Other films use a less severe transcendental style, such as *Tender Mercies* (1983) and *The Straight Story* (1999). "Slow cinema," like the films of Russian director Andrei Tarkovsky, which have unconventional and sometimes confusing narratives, crosses over into the transcendental category.

But whether transcendental or slow cinema, this category usually consists of indie or non-American films. These are considered alternative movies because the delay in action counteracts the more frenetic pace of mainstream cinema.

THE SEARCH FOR GOD

These movies try to prove the existence of God. This is pursued not through a hero's journey or mystical experiences, but often through Western science or logic. *Contact* (1997) and *I Origins* (2014) show characters representing science and religion clashing over about whether God exists. Both films are driven by plots that push atheistic or agnostic scientists toward believing in the possibility of the transcendental even if they cannot obtain the solid verifiable proof that they desire.

However, God is not always defined in scientific terms. In Woody Allen's *Crimes and Misdemeanors* (1989), God is defined as justice and morality. The film's search for God is a moral inquiry into whether suffering and injustice mean there is no God.

Starting in the 1990s, some films with ensemble casts featured a variation on the search for god. People from different social spheres are brought together through what first appears to be an accidental or chance encounter, but the characters wonder if it is instead providential will.

Some of the characters in *Grand Canyon* (1991) believe a spiritual force led them to each other. This contrasts with ensemble films like *21 Grams* (2003) where the characters appear to be thrown together by chance.

The Shack (2017) turns the tables, with God inviting the protagonist to begin a search rather than the protagonist initiating it. *The Da Vinci Code* (2006) and *Angels and Demons* (2009) take this category in yet another direction. A largely non-spiritual academic reveals a flawed definition of God through his search. The secular intellectual protagonist becomes a heroic figure exposing what he believes is the irrationality, oppression, and prejudice of the Catholic Church.

Other films feature a search that unravels into disbelief or agnosticism. In *A Serious Man* (2009), a modern-day Job character is plagued with marriage, career, and health problems. He asks a rabbi why God "makes us feel the questions if he's not going to give us any answers." In *The Truman Show* (1998), the god-like character Christof who controls Truman's life is an oppressive force the protagonist must escape from.

Other films show clergy undergoing a spiritual crisis, such as in Ingmar Bergman's *Winter Light* (1963), Martin Scorsese's *Silence* (2016), and *Doubt* (2008), which concludes with a weeping nun declaring, "I have doubts, I have such doubts." While these films feature religious characters, the end result is not an affirmation of the transcendental, which is an essential component of spiritual films. Instead, it is ambiguity about faith that places them outside of the spiritual film genre, despite their religious themes and characters.

RETAINING INDIGENOUS COMMUNITY AND CULTURE

Unlike many other world religions, many Indigenous religions do not emphasize salvation or a transcendent reality.[36] Cinematic depictions of Indigenous spirituality by non-Indigenous directors often generate cosmic harmony between a tribe and the earth.[37] Movies in this genre show the tribe connecting with both the tradition of ancestors and forces of nature.

As with films inspired by Eastern religion that can generalize about Asian faith traditions, the variety of Indigenous religions are often simplified and stereotyped in Western cinema, even in the best-intentioned and most sympathetic films. And often the narrative is initiated by a dilemma with Westerners, thus making the narratives centered around the actions of Westerners. In the Eastern religion film, the sage-like spiritual elder gives advice to a flawed or troubled Westerner. However, in the Indigenous film, a threat from the West to the Indigenous culture is often the reason a tribe must utilize their spirituality to maintain their tradition and culture.

In *Pocahontas* (1995), a spiritual elder in the form of a talking willow tree gives the protagonist advice before an invasion of Westerners into a Native American community. In *Spirited Away* (2000) and other Japanese anime films, the natural world is a Shinto-inspired realm where spirits assume differing forms. However, in films such as *Spirited Away*, the initiation into the spiritual world occurs not because of a physical invasion from Westerners but because of a cultural invasion. Materialism, individualism, and other qualities associated with the flaws of the West stand to contaminate the Indigenous culture. Other films use totemism, linking a human tribe to an animal that gives them a common life.[38] In *Whale Rider* (2002), a humpback whale and a New Zealand tribe are connected through a myth of the tribe's heritage. This process is also initiated not through a physical invasion from Westerners, but a cultural one in which the allure of individualism and conformity to Western ambitions threatens the tribe.

However, some of the films in this category do feature plots driven by full-fledged invasions from the West and their correction by Indigenous practices and tribal unity. This is often triggered by a clash between an oppressive dominant culture against the Indigenous culture. *Avatar* (2009), *The New World* (2005), and *Pocahontas* show battles with imperialist invaders. However, all three films also draw on a romance between an Indigenous woman and a Western man. This gives these films an element of a tragic love story that takes focus away from the tragedy of the entire tribe being threatened.

Movies such as *Dances with Wolves* (1990) and *The Last Samurai* (2003) don't fall into this category because they depict an outsider assimilating into the tribe. Although the films are empathetic toward the Indigenous cultures, they place emphasis on conversion of someone outside the tribe, not on what the tribe needs to retain their spirituality. These films are closer to the aforementioned works in which a spiritual guru from the East initiates a Westerner, with the tribe substituting for the sage figure.

Although the first prominent modern superhero movie *Superman* (1978) and some of the sequels and remakes portray Superman as a messianic or Christ figure, many superhero films show a neo-paganist worldview, another variation in this category.

Black Panther (2018) features a creation story and its own set of gods. Like films that stereotype Indigenous religion, it requires restoring balance to a tribe, not through connection to nature but through the correct tribal leadership. *Wonder Woman* (2017) also displays rituals reminiscent of a tribal film.

The following hundred spiritual films aren't necessarily the best spiritual films. This isn't a ranking of spiritual films. Rather, they are a canon of films that have endured over the years that demonstrate the range of the spiritual film genre.

Neither is this book anything near a listing of all significant spiritual films. Instead, this book is a starting point for anyone interested in the spiritual movie genre. In their own way, the films in this book can be viewed as spiritual texts to be analyzed and discussed. To encourage that, the discussion questions and Bible quotes/religious terms are a point of entry for group discussion or individual reflection.

2001: A Space Odyssey

1968

2 hours 29 minutes

CATEGORIES: Search for God, cautionary tale

SUMMARY: After the appearance of a mysterious black monolith, an ape is inspired to use a bone as a weapon. Four million years later, members of a space program find another monolith buried under the surface of a moon crater that beams a signal to Jupiter. A spaceship, with the help of the humanlike computer HAL, goes on a mission to Jupiter to find the target of the signal.

2001: A Space Odyssey is a milestone film in the spiritual movie genre because it blends traditional religious allusions with ambiguous spirituality—a combination that influenced massively popular science-fiction films like *Star Wars* (1977) and *The Matrix* (1999). *2001* is also significant because it doesn't have a conventional narrative or sympathetic main character and is instead a type of meditation on the transcendent. This makes it different from most films, which are about characters that achieve goals after overcoming difficulties.[1]

"The God concept is at the heart of *2001*, but not any traditional, anthropomorphic image of God," *2001* director Stanley Kubrick said.[2] The movie's spirituality is instead emphasized through visual symbols and music rather than dramatic conventions.[3] There is less than forty minutes of dialogue in the film's two hours and nineteen minutes. It spends little time on character development and lacks a clear protagonist with which the audience can identify.[4] As a result, the visuals and archetypical symbols become the center of the film, with the most distinct ones being the monolith and the fetus figure at the end of the film.[5]

A monolith—a mysterious, tall, domino-like black object—appears in all four sections of the film: the prehistoric segment, the moon expedition, a mission to Jupiter, and an astronaut's transcendental experience in which he rapidly ages and is reborn as a fetus.

Viewers and critics have interpreted the monolith as an alien device, a symbol of evolution/advancement, and a visual metaphor for human inspiration.[6] However, it can also be understood as a symbol of divine energy. This force connects to a God-like intelligence that produces a progression in the human species.[7] It demonstrates how humans depend upon a higher power for a more meaningful life.[8]

Although the monolith produces an unexplained spiritual effect, the beginning segment of the film recalls the Book of Genesis. The film's opening sequences begin with darkness, evoking the Bible's creation story.[9] The monolith functions as a tree of knowledge that, like its counterpart in the Garden of Eden, brings both a fall and an ascent.[10] Primitive humanity gains godlike potential and a capacity for violence after a tool becomes a weapon, resulting in a killing reminiscent of Cain's murder of his brother.[11] Christian iconography also is depicted through the impulse to touch the monolith, referencing the image of Michelangelo's *Creation of Adam*, with God and Adam reaching toward each other.[12]

Probably the most striking spiritual segment of the film comes after the astronaut Dave reaches out toward the monolith and is transported from earthbound forms through shapes and colors and a series of images.[13] He enters another dimension that transcends matter into pure energy,[14] after which he is reborn as a fetus and transfigured and transformed into a super-being.[15] It shows how man can renew himself and be "born again."[16] He also becomes a Christ figure that moves through a passion, last supper, and transfiguration/resurrection.[17]

Additionally, the film's third segment acts as a cautionary tale. The computer HAL is the result of another creation story in the film, with humanity as the creator.[18] HAL's use of violence allegorizes the fear that humans will lose control of technology. Its capacity for Cain-like violence can make scientific creations destructive.[19] Ironically, HAL is more human and emotional in his words and actions than the astronauts, who are more mechanical and emotionless.[20] Whether HAL's violence is the result of mechanical error or a psychological and spiritual breakdown constitutes one of the film's central ambiguities.[21]

BIBLE PASSAGE

"As the heavens are higher than the earth, so are my ways higher than your ways and my thoughts than your thoughts." (Isaiah 55:9 NIV)

2001: A Space Odyssey shows a higher force operating in the universe, although its meaning and origin is unclear.

DISCUSSION QUESTIONS

1. Is the film's narrative structure innovative or difficult to follow? Why?
2. What is the central conflict in the entities depicted in the film, whether they are apes, humans, or machines? How does this connect to tensions in contemporary society?
3. How does the film show the perils of selfishness? How can people spiritually overcome that impulse?
4. How is the film in some ways a dystopia depicting injustices? Do you see connections to the present day?
5. How do you interpret the ending? What hope does it offer?

ABOUT A BOY

2002

1 hour 41 minutes

CATEGORIES: Redemption story

SUMMARY: Will Freeman (Hugh Grant) is a thirty-something bachelor living in a trendy London neighborhood. A serial dater who tries to find single women with children because he believes they won't commit to a serious relationship, his life is changed after he meets a suicidal single woman Fiona (Toni Colette) with a twelve-year-old boy, Marcus (Nicholas Hoult), who is bullied, lonely, and worried about his mother.

About a Boy is not the first movie to engage with a man whose care for a child jolts him out of self-centeredness. Movies from *Three Man and a Baby* (1987) to *Knocked Up* (2007) use a baby or young child as a catalyst to shift a narcissistic or non-committed man into maturity. What places *About a Boy* in the spiritual movie genre is that Will experiences epiphanies that move him out of nihilism and into a life with meaning. It is a redemption story rather than a transition from prolonged adolescence into adulthood.

Redemption stories feature characters with initial flawed conditions. In Will's defective state, he is a nihilist and sees no meaning in his existence. However, Will views this as an asset. "You have to mean things to help people," Will says. "I didn't mean anything. About anything to anyone. And I knew that guaranteed me a long, pressure-free life." Will believes this lack of meaning is freedom from the messiness of lasting relationships and emotional entanglements with other people.

Will's condition is what Viktor Frankl in *Man's Search for Meaning* calls an existential vacuum: boredom resulting from lack of meaning in life.[1] Will tries to fill this void with pleasure seeking in short-term romantic relationships, consumerism, and the self-indulgence of doing what he wants—largely while alone. He feels he is his own master, a common condition of the pre-redeemed figure.

Defying the romantic comedy movie convention, it is not a single mother Will forms a meaningful relationship with that triggers a redemption story. It is her son Marcus. But, again defying stereotypes in movies, they are mutual mentors to each other. Will learns from Marcus as well.

The second phase of the redemption story is a period of warfare between Will's flawed old self and an emerging new self. The weight of shedding one identity for another is so overwhelming that Will retreats back into isolation in his apartment. At his lowest point, he drops to his knees in prayer-like submission and sums up his existence: "All in all, I had a very full life; it's just that it didn't mean anything."

He has progressed enough to realize this lack of meaning is deadening, which constitutes the turning point in the redemption story toward a new identity. For Will, this means recognizing that life contains meaning because Marcus means something to him. From there, he sees a chain of meaning. Because Marcus means something to him and Marcus's mother means something to Marcus, then he must help her.

Like the Psalmist who often found salvation and hope at the deepest moment of despair, the redemption story features a similar pattern. At a low point, Will undergoes—if not a full-fledged conversion experience—then at least an existentialist recognition that there is meaning in life.

Will's change follows Frankl's theory that neurosis and lack of fulfillment are often caused not by a deep psychological problem, but by a lack of meaning.[2] The primary ways out of this emptiness are meaningful work, positive loving connection to others, and finding meaning in suffering.[3] For Will, connecting with other people generates meaning and ends his self-inflicted cycle of isolation, boredom, and pleasure seeking.

SPIRITUAL CONCEPT AND DISCUSSION TOPIC

Existential vacuum. In *Man's Search for Meaning*, Viktor Frankl says finding meaning is the primary motivational force in a person's life. Without it, people experience an *existential vacuum*, generating boredom, pleasure seeking, and a feeling of emptiness. *Logotherapy* is the process of seeking meaning rather than finding pleasure or avoiding pain.

DISCUSSION QUESTIONS

1. What are some ways Will uses technology and consumerism to isolate himself? How can you overcome reliance on technology and consumerism in your life?

2. Nihilism is the belief that there is an inherent lack of meaning in life. How do you see that manifest in modern life?

3. According to Victor Frankl, an existential vacuum occurs when there's a lack of meaning in someone's life, and it manifests

in boredom and a desire for pleasure. How does this occur in Will's life?

4. How does Will determine what means something to him? What is meaningful in your life and how can you create more meaning?

5. What steps does Will take to create community? What can you do to create more community in your life, particularly among people that aren't family members?

AMAZING GRACE

2006

1 hour 58 minutes

CATEGORIES: Difficulty living out faith

SUMMARY: William Wilberforce (Ioan Gruffudd) is torn between a life of religious contemplation and becoming a political activist. Encouraged by his former pastor, John Newton (Albert Finney), he attempts to merge the two. Wilberforce works over many years to end slavery in the British Empire.

Even without being the main character, the presence and gravitas of the tormented religious figure John Newton towers over this film.

Former slave trader Newton wrote the hymn "Amazing Grace" to express his conversion to Christianity. But Newton, now a cleric, is still anguished. "Twenty thousand slaves live with me in this little church," he laments. "There's still blood on my hands."

At a crucial point, the young politician William Wilberforce asks Newton for advice. A group of activists want Wilberforce to spearhead a campaign to end slavery in England, but he also wants to retreat from secular culture to explore his spirituality.

Can he do both? He says there's been "no bolts of lightning" to help him decide. Newton tells Wilberforce, "God sometimes does his work with gentle drizzle, not storms." After warning him to "just make sure you're in the world, not of the world," Newton urges him to continue his activism in Parliament.

This film shows the difficulty of living out one's faith on two levels. First, Wilberforce must decide if immersing himself in politics will take him away from his faith. Once he resolves that dilemma, the film shifts to the difficulties of implementing moral and spiritual values in the political sphere.

The film explores why public officials are hesitant to correct injustice. *Amazing Grace* outlines four reasons why politicians do not end slavery. Interestingly, they all turn on the effect of slavery on others, not on the enslaved themselves. But they can also apply to contemporary injustices and why they often are not corrected.

The first and primary reason are concerns about disruptions to the economic system. Politicians are beholden to industries dependent on slavery, and the economic web of dependency places the needs of business over the moral and spiritual objections to slavery. Second, reformists want to move very slowly. "Violent storms sink ships," one politician says. But gradualism is an exercise in delay where little of consequence ends up changing.

Third, the will of the majority isn't followed. After a massive petition to end slavery is submitted to Parliament, one politician declares he won't be led by "the rule of the mob," arguing that politicians are the "natural leaders" capable of making decisions, not the people. The fourth reason is that, in times of war or international tension, criticism of the current system is considered seditious and unpatriotic. Supporters of slavery use this to suppress denunciation of slavery.

Like *Gandhi* (1982), another movie about a spiritual person who was also a political figure, *Amazing Grace* focuses on the protagonist's political shrewdness and effectiveness. As with *Gandhi*, the spiritual background of the main character receives less attention. However, some powerful scenes depict Wilberforce's faith as a kind of defiance. After being offered a slave as a bet in a card game, Wilberforce initially flees in disgust but returns and sings a stirring rendition of "Amazing Grace."

Both allies and enemies view Wilberforce as a powerful individual because he is driven by Christianity more than politics or nationalism. "I know you have your loyalties, Wilberforce, but underneath it you're more radical than any of us," his activist friend Clarkson says. "You see, you never doubt you're right." An opposing politician admits Wilberforce is such a threat because he "follows no leader but the preacher in his head."

BIBLE PASSAGE

"So faith by itself, if it has no works, is dead." (James 2:17 NRSV)

William Wilberforce's spiritual struggle in the first part of the film is resolved by realizing he can act as God's instrument through his actions rather than faith alone.

DISCUSSION QUESTIONS

1. What do you think was the main reason the slave trade in Britain didn't end sooner? What is another major injustice that could be corrected that continues in the present day? Why doesn't it end?
2. What does the movie say about religion and social change? How do you believe they can be combined?
3. How does the film show Wilberforce's spiritual beliefs as a foundation for his actions? Is there room in your profession to sometimes express your beliefs?
4. Who are Wilberforce's closest allies in his struggle? Why is it important for people to have like-minded allies in such a situation?
5. How is John Newton affected by his days as a slave trader? How does he try to resolve this pain?

THE APOSTLE

1997

2 hours 14 minutes

CATEGORIES: Religious figure, redemption story

SUMMARY: Texas preacher Euliss F. "Sonny" Dewey (Robert Duvall) realizes his wife Jessie (Farrah Fawcett) is having an affair with youth minister Horace (Todd Allen). Sonny attacks Horace, who later dies. Sonny flees for Louisiana and begins a new life by starting a church.

American cinema generally depicts evangelical Christianity negatively. *Elmer Gantry* (1960), *Leap of Faith* (1992), and *There Will Be Blood* (2007) are examples of films that play on the stereotype of manipulative, dangerous preachers. In the past few decades, films have increasingly come to portray Middle America and rural culture negatively as well. To counteract this, *The Apostle* makes a case for the dignity of marginalized rural religious culture, people whom Hollywood might dismiss as ignorant and lowbrow.[1]

However, *The Apostle* doesn't make the evangelist protagonist a hero. Sonny is not idealized, but the film also never makes him an object of ridicule or forces him into the stereotype of a charlatan preacher. For this reason and others, it represents a turning point in the spiritual movie genre. Sonny's belief that his soul is a battleground between the Holy Spirit and Satan turns him into a complex character.[2]

In some ways, Sonny is reminiscent of King David. He achieves significant successes as a spiritual leader but also commits monumental sins in his personal life. Sonny has an intense and somewhat conflicted emotional life and does not engage in much self-reflection. He is a man of action, and it is sometimes up to the viewer to decipher Sonny's internal life.

Following the standard first act of the spiritual film's redemption story, Sonny begins as a flawed character and a womanizer. But when

33

his wife has an affair, his anger escalates into a violent act that forces him to flee from the police.

The second stage of the redemption story is more of an attempt to seek salvation rather than to escape the law. Sonny symbolically buries his former life by getting out of the car before it descends into a river, leaving both his wallet and identity behind him.[3] Crossing a bridge afterwards symbolizes a transitional passage that foreshadows a later scene when Sonny baptizes himself in a river.[4]

Sonny completes his transformation by taking a new name, the Apostle E. F.[5] The baptism is a resurrection marking transformation from an old self to a new self.[6] During this second stage, he is guided by what he feels is God's will, at one point even asking God to direct his physical steps as he walks through a small town.

In the redemption story's third act, he builds a new church and a new community, further solidifying a new identity. This enables him to fully accept the consequences of his crime. What begins as an individualistic religious pilgrimage with Sonny cut off from family and church becomes a community-filled redemption.[7] The new community completes the transformation.[8] When finally pursued by the law again, he doesn't run away, which reveals that he feels more assured of his redemption.

The Apostle's belief that his moral failure works as part of God's plan poses an interesting theological question.[9] This is confirmed by another preacher's (Brother Blackwell) assertion that God directs people's actions.[10] This evokes a moral dilemma about whether God could use a crime to put the Apostle in a position of ministry or whether the idea of a sovereign God guiding all actions dismisses personal moral responsibility.[11]

Rather than the conventional Hollywood stereotype of a pastor as a predator on others' emotions and finances, the movie engages with the limitations of the protagonist's own nature.[12] He needs grace as much as those who listen to his sermons about grace. Although he has flaws, he remains sincere in his beliefs and devotion to his ministry.[13] And, as the ending of the film shows, no matter what situation he finds himself in, Sonny still evangelizes as part of his ongoing salvation.

BIBLE PASSAGE

"In Him we were also chosen, having been predestined according to the plan of Him who works out everything in conformity with the purpose of his will." (Ephesians 1:11 NIV)

Sonny believes it is the will of God for him to minister wherever he finds himself, because he believes his situation is ordained by God.

DISCUSSION QUESTIONS

1. Does the film make Sonny a well-rounded character? Is he more likeable or unlikeable? Why?
2. What strengths does Sonny have? What weaknesses does he have?
3. While forming Sonny's new church, why is his preaching so appealing to people?
4. How does this film fit into other presentations of religious clergy that you've seen in movies?
5. What does the end of the film show about how Sonny views his role as a preacher?

AU HASARD BALTHAZAR

1966

1 hour 35 minutes (France)

CATEGORIES: Christ figure, transcendental style

SUMMARY: A donkey is born in the French countryside. He passes through a series of owners. A few are kind, but most mistreat him.

Although the film's protagonist is an animal, *Au Hasard Balthazar* is far from an uplifting children's movie. Filmmaker Jean-Luc Godard called it "a dreadful vision of the world and the evil in it."[1] The film's power derives from the atmosphere of pervasive sin and evil that it creates, its innovative use of a Christ figure, and its transcendentalist style.

Many of French director Robert Bresson's films are spiritual movies. *Diary of a Country Priest* (1951) and *The Trial of Joan of Arc* (1962) are two of his best-known films featuring religious figures. In other Bresson films, including *Au Hasard Balthazar*, the protagonists are Christ figures.[2] But Bresson's films are also spiritual because of the director's use of long takes, ambient sound, and the preference of images over dialogue, all of which constitute, in the words of Paul Schrader, a transcendental style that guides the viewer into a contemplative state.[3]

However, *Au Hasard Balthazar* is perhaps best known for its innovative use of a donkey as a Christ figure. Balthazar is baptized by children and named after what tradition says is one of the three wise men visiting Jesus after his birth. Christian folklore placed a donkey at the stable of Jesus's birth in Bethlehem, a donkey carries Christ into Jerusalem on Palm Sunday, and the Old Testament contains the idea of a scapegoat who carries the sins of the people—a tradition related to Jesus Christ in the Epistle to the Hebrews.[4] Some of Balthazar's owners also carry Biblical allusions, including Marie (whose name alludes to the mother of the son of God and who makes for Balthazar a kind of crown of thorns from garland of flowers) and the drunkard Arnold, who becomes a kind of Judas figure.[5]

At times, Balthazar carries the sins of the characters (sometimes literally), offers some small form of comfort, or serves as pure and sympathetic spectator. However, the most dominant Christ figure trait in Balthazar is suffering. He endures assaults and mortifications like a variation on the Stations of the Cross as he goes from owner to owner.[6] Each owner represents a human vice such as drunkenness, laziness, and pride, and Balthazar suffers in a different way from each of these.[7] Because most of the human characters are so flawed, the viewer empathizes and identifies with Balthazar through Bresson's skillful placement of shots of the donkey.

This film is a challenging but distinctive piece in the spiritual movie genre because of its emphasis on the presence of sin and evil. Unlike many films, the narrative is not propelled by virtuous action or positive

One of the most unique Christ figures in the spiritual movie genre is the suffering donkey Balthazar in Robert Bresson's *Au Hasard Balthazar*. His treatment from a series of owners shows how sin is an integral component of the human condition. Photo courtesy Argos Films/Everett Collection

behavior but by immorality.[8] Evil and sin are personified through the flaws of people in a small town, not through charismatic villains.

Although most of Balthazar's owners exhibit spiritual and moral dissolution, Gerard is the primary figure of evil. Wearing a leather jacket and jeans and listening to modern pop music, he represents a modernity that contrasts with Balthazar, who represents a more ancient force. "That antiquated donkey makes us look ridiculous," Marie's father says, one of several comments on the outmoded donkey.

The film offers no psychological or sociological explanation for the evil of Gerard and his delinquent friends,[9] but Gerard is a destructive force affecting all who come into contact with him.[10] This is particularly true for Marie, who is seduced by Gerard, which ultimately leads to her spiritual annihilation and rejection of the good in her life.[11] "I've no more tenderness, no heart, no feelings," she confesses toward the end of the film.

However, underneath the film's sense of evil without underlying cause is the suggestion that, at times, money motivates the characters to sin.[12] A notable example is when Marie asks what the merchant believes in. "I believe in what I own," he says. "I love money, I hate death."

BIBLE PASSAGE

"For all have sinned and fall short of the glory of God." (Romans 3:23 NIV)

Au Hasard Balthazar is one of the few films that strongly emphasizes the universally pervasive nature of sin.

DISCUSSION QUESTIONS

1. What strikes you as most disturbing about the way sin is portrayed in the film? Do you think sin is talked about enough in contemporary society?
2. What are Marie's character flaws? Why is she not stronger morally?
3. How does Gerard represent evil? Does he match how you see evil working in the world?
4. What qualities do you see in Balthazar?
5. How does the film's ending illustrate the resurrection symbolism in the Christ figure film?

BABETTE'S FEAST

1987 (Denmark)

1 hour 43 minutes

CATEGORIES: Christ figure, transcendental style

SUMMARY: A Lutheran dean leads an ascetic group of worshippers in a small Scandinavian village. His two daughters reject suitors to stay with their father and carry on his charitable work after his death. Their lives change after the French refugee Babette (Stephane Audran) asks for a housekeeping job and becomes a devoted member of the household.

This film presents two types of devotion that must merge to form a more complete Christianity.

One is the austerity and piety of two unmarried sisters. Martine is named after Martin Luther and Filippa after Luther's theological collaborator Philip Melanchthon. They continue their father's tradition of reverence, morality, and charitable works. But they are insular, solemn, and deny the sensual.

The French maid Babette conveys another type of spirituality. She carries the weight of worldliness that left her a destitute refugee. However, she expresses a theology of creativity and aesthetics. She so strongly embodies the incarnational joining of the flesh with spirit that she becomes a Christ figure.

The sisters' generosity and self-sacrifice is expressed through their leadership in a religious community and their charitable acts for people in the village. However, the sisters and the other followers focus their attention on the afterlife.[1] They sing as if in exile, saying, "Jerusalem, my heart's true home." The dean represents the Old Testament's chosen people, who are strictly disciplined, ascetic, and protect themselves against outsiders.[2] After the dean's death, however, the community begins to disintegrate. While they are earnest and good-hearted, something is lacking, and the disciples' moral uprightness collapses into pious routine.[3]

Yet, the worldly life outside the village is even more limiting. Babette is saved by the religious community from catastrophes and evils characteristic of the secular world, including a political uprising, the death of her husband and child, and termination of her career.[4] Babette, though, is also shown as a figure of salvation. She arrives at night with signs in the heavens: a strong wind, violent rain, and a mysterious shaft of white light from above.[5] Babette's presence soon begins to have miraculous effects, reversing the sisters' precarious economic position.[6]

The emptiness of the secular world is also portrayed through two men whom the sisters reject. Both the opera singer and the cadet are attracted to the sisters as potential saviors from their unsatisfying existence. Both later lament their choices of career and the hollowness of success. While preparing for Babette's meal, the cadet—now a general— quotes Ecclesiastes that "all is vanity." The opera singer writes to Filippa, "I feel it is you who chose the better part in life," adding, "What is fame? The grave awaits us all." The secular and sacred are divided, and neither achieves fullness.[7]

Babette bridges the divide by putting on a lavish meal with her lottery winnings. Her relationship to the puritanical community is an allegory of Christ's actions on behalf of the church, and her feast is a kind of liberating Eucharist.[8] The meal is a Last Supper where she sacrifices all she has.[9] Twelve people are seated at the table like the twelve apostles.[10] Through this Eucharistic sacrifice, the people of God are given a new covenant, a new way of being with one another and of praising God.[11] They joke about conflicts between them and sing praises in a circle. The general is spiritually rejuvenated, pronouncing: "Grace makes no conditions." This demonstrates that salvation is available no matter what wrong decisions one makes.

The movie also displays the transcendentalist style in film. The lack of accompanying music puts the viewer in a contemplative state and allows them to be more aware of sounds like the waves, wind, and the opening and shutting of doors.[12] The film's scenes and settings underscore this sense of contemplative awareness with the sisters' world a palate of grays, black, and white in a bare seaside landscape.[13] This contrasts with the sumptuous warm tones of Babette's feast.[14]

BIBLE PASSAGE

"Day by day, as they spent much time together in the temple, they broke bread at home and ate their food with glad and generous hearts." (Acts 2:46 NRSV)

The combination of worship and sharing a meal is the climatic segment of *Babette's Feast*.

DISCUSSION QUESTIONS

1. What are the spiritual distinctions between the sisters and Babette? Which of the two spiritual styles do you tend to express more? Why?

2. What do the general and the opera singer find unsatisfying about worldly life? What do the members of the congregation find unsatisfying?

3. Why do you think Babette sacrifices her lottery earnings for the meal?

4. Why does Babette tell the sisters after the meal that "a great artist is never poor"?

5. Why does the general believe grace is infinite? How does that fit your understanding of the Christian concept of grace?

BARABBAS

1961

2 hours 17 minutes

CATEGORIES: Bible epic, redemption story

SUMMARY: To fulfill a Passover season custom, Judean governor Pontius Pilate releases a prisoner. The crowd in Jerusalem demands the criminal Barabbas (Anthony Quinn) be freed, so Jesus is crucified instead. Barabbas is tormented by Jesus taking his place and struggles with guilt and whether to believe in Christianity.

Barabbas features a protagonist with a prolonged and anguished agnosticism.[1] This makes it a fascinating variation on the three-stage redemption story of: a flawed self, a clash between flawed self and emerging self, and a transformed new self.

For most of the film, Barabbas remains lodged in the second stage of the painful conflict between belief and disbelief. For more than two decades, he is enslaved in a sulfur mine, where the harsh physical demands appear to be almost a welcome diversion from his internal spiritual warfare.

Barabbas features a troubled protagonist far different from conventional heroes in other Christian Roman films. Barabbas is a loner, sinner, and doubter afflicted with uncertainty, shame, and moral confusion. The film is also unique in the Christian Roman film category because most of the action takes place in the Jerusalem criminal underground.[2] As a thief, Barabbas is in many ways the genre's original infidel.[3]

However, like other characters in films set at the time of Christ, even a momentary encounter with Jesus is enough to spiritually transform Barabbas.[4] Like Ben-Hur, he is ultimately saved because of a brief encounter with Christ.[5]

Throughout the film, Barabbas recalls the biblical Jonah because he runs away from God. Barabbas first tries to escape his anguish through hedonism, and he uses skepticism to try to prove that Christians are wrong about Jesus's divinity. At the empty tomb of Jesus, he tells Rachel (his former girlfriend and now a follower of Christ) that friends of Jesus took his body away to perpetuate a myth about the risen Christ. During a visit to the apostles, he identifies with the questions of the doubting apostle Thomas. He remains unconvinced even after talking to Lazarus, whom Jesus raised from the dead.

No external evidence can convince Barabbas. Spiritual transformation is something internal that doesn't come from being shown proof. Barabbas cannot commit to Christianity but still feels pursued. "God should make himself plain or leave me alone," he says. This suits a movie dominated by doubt and a persistent sense of suffering.[6]

Barabbas also doesn't repeat the romantic conventions of the Roman Christian film. The protagonist is an elderly hero who, after the beginning of the film, has no romantic life.[7] Usually in the Christian-Roman drama, the primary purpose of Christian women like Lygia in *Quo Vadis* or Esther in *Ben-Hur* is to shape the conversion of the non-believer. Rachel, on the other hand, is a well-developed and independent woman who is not a romantic partner, but a spiritual teacher and martyr.

Later, in Rome, the Christian prisoner Sahak refuses to kill other men for sport in the arena because of his Christian beliefs, while Barabbas becomes a successful gladiator because of his inability to believe.[8]

The arena is a site of sadism, the opposite of Christian virtues and the image of everything Christianity claims to transcend.[9]

Barabbas is distinguished by its emphasis on Barabbas's struggle as being not just a spiritual education, but a mode of experiencing the divine. God is found less in the peace of transformation than in spiritual conflict. Barabbas is an archetypical sufferer who achieves a sort of heroism through endurance and suffering.[10]

After Barabbas finally declares himself a Christian but wonders if he has gotten any closer to God, the Apostle Peter tells him: "There has been a wrestling in your spirit, back and forth in your life, which in itself is knowledge of God." Peter adds in what could be a summary of Barabbas's spiritual journey: "By the conflict you have known him."

BIBLE PASSAGE

"The Lord is not slow in keeping his promise, as some understand slowness. Instead he is patient with you, not wanting anyone to perish, but everyone to come to repentance." (2 Peter 3:9 NIV)

Slowness to change conditions sometimes appears to be God's method of education leading someone toward redemption.

DISCUSSION QUESTIONS

1. Rachel says about Barabbas, "He knows but is afraid to believe it." Why is he afraid? When was a time in your life you were afraid or ran away from the spiritual?
2. How does guilt affect Barabbas? How have you spiritually resolved guilt in your life?
3. How is the imagery of darkness and light used in the film? What scenes does this come through the most?
4. Why is Barabbas's spiritual journey so long and difficult? Has your spiritual journey been arduous at times? When was it particularly difficult?
5. How does the idea of atonement through Christ come across in Barabbas?

BECKET

1964

2 hours 28 minutes

CATEGORIES: Religious figure, redemption story, difficulty living out faith

SUMMARY: A century after the Norman conquest of 1066, King Henry II (Peter O'Toole) rules over the conquered Saxons in England. After the death of the Archbishop of Canterbury, Henry appoints his chancellor and friend Thomas Becket (Richard Burton) as Archbishop, believing that he will serve the king's interests rather than the church's. However, Becket actively defends the church, which enrages the monarch.

After the early 1960s, Bible epic and Roman historical films declined in popularity, as a variation on the religious epic emerged that featured clergy challenging both secular government and the church establishment. Iconoclastic clergy characters echoed the growing anti-establishment youth movement of the 1960s.

The two most prominent of these films were the historical dramas *Becket* (1964), about the clash between King Henry II and Thomas Becket, and *A Man for All Seasons* (1966), about the conflict between Sir Thomas More and King Henry VIII. Other 1960s films set in more modern times feature socially conscious religious figures. *The Shoes of the Fisherman* (1968) highlights a humble pope initiating steps toward world peace during the Cold War era. *The Cardinal* (1963) shows a Catholic clergy member working against both the Ku Klux Klan and Nazi totalitarianism.

In *Becket* and *A Man for All Seasons*, the protagonists face a conflict between serving a higher ideal of honoring God or appeasing a secular government. This conflict puts both films partly in the category of difficulty living out faith. They demonstrate that the central dilemma of those spiritual films is the clash between the ideals of spirituality and the conforming pressures of secularism.

One crucial difference between *Becket* and *A Man for All Seasons* is that *Becket* tracks a spiritual progression, while *A Man for All Seasons* presents Thomas More as a consistent moral force. In the first stage of Becket's redemption story, he lives a self-indulgent existence arranging dalliances for King Henry II, a hedonistic and temperamental extension of the neurotic emperor of Roman Christian epics. The king is a hyperactive force that contrasts with Becket's calm intellectualism.[1]

However, as protagonists sometimes do in the redemption story's first phase, they receive glimmers of insight about their flawed state. "Where honor should be, there is only a void," Becket says in a moment of self-reflection. And in a penetrating insight about Becket, Henry tells him, "So what in most people is morality in you is just an exercise in aesthetics." Becket must realize morality is much more than the exhibition of polished manners and style.

The three key turning points of the film are propelled by heartfelt prayer. The shift into the second act depicting the conflict between an old, flawed self and an emerging new self begins with a penetrating and heartfelt prayer. Becket's prayer contains two main characteristics central to the redemption story. The first is repentance about sin, selfishness, and turning away from God. The second is a longing to receive God's direction. This combination of repentance and guidance to change leads him out of his flawed spiritual condition.

The turning point into the third stage, leading to a full-fledged redemption, comes from a prayer of commitment rather than repentance. After the pope sends Becket to a monastery, he commits to returning to his role as Archbishop, even it if means battling his former friend and the secular power structure.

Becket establishes a dual purpose. The first goal is one of action, as he declares that he will be "a soaring force for what I know to be right." The second is relinquishing control, which he does by saying, "All the rest, thy will be done." Although Becket is not a Christ figure, this is a Garden of Gethsemane moment. His final prayer before the other turning point (which is his martyrdom) concludes with his acceptance that "I am ready."

BIBLE PASSAGE

"Therefore if any man be in Christ, he is a new creature: old things are passed away; behold, all things are become new." (2 Corinthians 5:17 KJV)

Becket's spiritual transformation shows the radical transformation that can occur after a spiritual awakening.

DISCUSSION QUESTIONS

1. What signs in the beginning of the film show that Becket is capable of spiritual transformation?
2. What do the king's actions show about the nature of power? How have you seen very powerful people act in a similar way?
3. Why does Becket find it so enjoyable to give up what he has for the poor? Have you experienced something similar?
4. How does the film show how political power and spirituality are opposed to one another?
5. Why does Becket let the soldiers into the church at the end of the film? Was it the correct choice? Why or why not?

BEN-HUR

1959

3 hours 32 minutes

CATEGORIES: Bible epic

SUMMARY: Roman authorities arrest the Hebrew Judah Ben-Hur (Charlton Heston) after Judea's new governor is almost accidentally killed. Ben-Hur's childhood friend Messala (Stephen Boyd), now a Roman tribune, condemns him to slavery on a ship. Ben-Hur later returns to Judea seeking revenge, which culminates in a dangerous chariot race and a spiritual awakening when Ben-Hur witnesses the crucifixion of Christ.

Ben-Hur conveys a common theme in the Roman Christian film: the spiritual divergence between Romans and Hebrews or early Christians.

Rome represents not only militarism but a paganism analogous to atheism and nihilism. "It's a strange stubborn faith you keep to believe existence has a purpose," the Roman Messala tells the Hebrew Ben-Hur, who angrily shouts, "Rome is an affront to God!" This duality establishes how, over the course of the film, Judeo-Christian humanity is shown as superior to hard-hearted Roman discipline.[1]

In the first stage of his spiritual journey, Ben-Hur is a Jew obeying Roman authority who proudly retains his heritage and hopes for a redeemer.[2] It also portrays Ben-Hur and the Hebrews as family and community-oriented, while Messala and the occupier Romans are individualistic and ambitious.[3]

"I'm against violence, everyone knows this," Ben-Hur says. But this changes during the next two stages of his spiritual journey. How does one overcome revenge generated by injustice? This question becomes the central dilemma in Ben-Hur's spiritual life.

In the second stage, Ben-Hur is tormented by the imprisonment of his mother and sister and his ongoing hardships as an enslaved person. His firm but somewhat disengaged and complacent faith from the first stage is no longer sufficient to comprehend this suffering. Wealth and status are restored to him after he rescues a Roman commander from a sea wreck. However, these are earthly honors that cannot remedy his spiritual dilemma of losing his faith and wanting revenge.

After returning to Judea at the beginning of the third stage, Ben-Hur acknowledges revenge is problematic but still pursues it. "God forgive me for seeking vengeance, but my path is set," he prays before the chariot race with Messala. However, even winning the race cannot placate him. "It goes on Judah, the race is not over," Messala says to Ben-Hur in his dying words, emphasizing the insatiable quality of revenge.

Although the wise elder figure of Balthazar cautions Ben-Hur about the perils of revenge, Esther also serves as a mentor to him. She tells him about the words of Jesus and warns him, "You seem to be now the very thing you set out to destroy, giving evil for evil." Esther is the embodiment of another convention of the Roman Christian film: a

Christian woman converting a doubting protagonist to belief. These relationships merge spiritual and erotic love.[4]

Esther's words have an effect, but it is ultimately Jesus himself who activates Ben-Hur's transformation at Jesus's crucifixion. Before that, Ben-Hur experiences two critical encounters with Jesus. Jesus gives Ben-Hur water, and Ben-Hur later attempts to give Jesus water. The water represents not only Ben-Hur's physical needs but foreshadows his future spiritual baptism.[5]

The movie also emphasizes Jesus as a figure of atonement. "He has taken the world of our sins onto himself; for this cause he came into the world," Balthasar says. This definition differs from later Bible epic films that emphasize Jesus's teachings rather than theology or miracles.

Although renowned as an epic hero, Ben-Hur is not a savior but is himself saved after a series of reversals and challenges.[6] However, his misfortune and ultimate salvation reflects Christ's own agony and transcendence.[7]

While watching the crucifixion, Ben-Hur hears Jesus say, "Forgive them father, they know not what they do." To this, he responds, "I felt his voice take the sword out of my hand." This pacifist resolution is far different from the redemptive violence associated with some films in the spiritual movie genre. Jesus also becomes the answer to Ben-Hur's desire for a redeemer and shows Ben-Hur is not complete until he becomes a believer in Christ.[8]

BIBLE PASSAGE

"Then said Jesus, 'Father, forgive them; for they know not what they do.'" (Luke 23:24 KJV)

Ben-Hur sees Jesus on the cross saying these words, which finally subdues Ben-Hur's drive for revenge.

DISCUSSION QUESTIONS

1. What does Ben-Hur learn about the nature of revenge? When have you had to spiritually resolve feelings of revenge?

2. How are Messala and Arrius brother and father figures to Ben-Hur? What makes them ultimately unable to reconcile Ben-Hur's spiritual dilemma of revenge?

3. Jesus's face is never shown. What effect did this have on you when watching those scenes?

4. What is lacking in Ben-Hur's faith life in the first part of the film that must be deepened or corrected?

5. How do you interpret the miracle at the end of the film? Why does it happen?

THE BISHOP'S WIFE

1947

1 hour 49 minutes

CATEGORIES: Divine intervention

SUMMARY: Bishop Henry Brougham (David Niven) is so preoccupied with fundraising for a cathedral that the marriage to his wife Julia (Loretta Young) is damaged. He prays for guidance, and help arrives from the angel Dudley (Cary Grant). After some initial conflict, Dudley shows Henry what is truly important in life.

The Bishop's Wife is a variation of what Peter Valenti calls film blanc ("film white"). Instead of showing the gritty dark side of life, as in film noir ("film black"), film blanc displays an ethereal, comical, and altruistic worldview.[1] These fantasy films feature benevolent heavenly figures intervening in human affairs.[2]

Film blanc was initially known for comic portrayals of the afterlife as in *Here Comes Mr. Jordan* (1941), where an overzealous entity claims the body of a prizefighter too soon.[3] However, variations on this formula feature angels coming to earth to assist humans with little or no glimpse of another world.

Those angel-driven films, such as *A Bishop's Wife* and *It's a Wonderful Life* (1946) follow a pattern: A human faces a severe crisis, after which a kindly representative from the world beyond encourages or protects the person in distress. Finally, the divine being helps the human transcend their crisis before returning to the heavenly realm.[4]

The height of film blanc's popularity was during the Second World War. The films confirmed a belief in the supernatural and life beyond death to audiences ravaged by the loss of loved ones in war. A resurgence of film blanc emerged in the 1970s with *Oh God!* (1977) and *Heaven Can Wait* (1978). They continued through the years in secular and spiritual romances featuring angels or ghosts and in comedies including *Bruce Almighty* (2003).

The purpose of the divine intervention spiritual film is conveying a lesson to mortals. In *The Bishop's Wife*, the angel Dudley's intervention provides guidance for how to best live one's life. Like *It's a Wonderful Life* and *Bruce Almighty*, prayer initiates the intercession. Dudley emphasizes that he came to earth because Henry prayed for direction, not to support the grandiose cathedral that Henry is incessantly raising money to build. An important initial message is that praying for guidance will receive a response, while praying for a specific outcome is fruitless.

During his time with the beleaguered Henry, Dudley emphasizes two divine priorities to living life fully.

The first is helping the needy. Dudley distinguishes between the cathedral Henry wants to build and the old neighborhood church Dudley left behind. Dudley shows that true Christianity emanates from a sense of community and helping the less fortunate rather than career ambition and costly buildings.

Dudley's second divine lesson is encouraging people to be more youthful and gregarious. From his schedule (rather, a lack of one!) at Henry's office, Dudley shows that he is no workaholic. The famous scene when Dudley takes Julia ice skating while Henry tends to business matters shows the divine priority for lighthearted youthful leisure. When Dudley directs a choir at Henry's former church, the hymn sung jubilantly proclaims that "Your lord is born this happy day," and Dudley says he came to "disperse the shades of doom and sadness." Even in religious worship, Dudley emphasizes joyfulness.

Unlike some generic screen angels in film blanc, Dudley is familiar with the Bible. He tells Henry and Julia's daughter how David wrote Psalm 23. Earlier, Dudley asks the skeptical Henry, "Do you believe I am what I say I am?" recalling Jesus asking his disciples, "But who do you say that I am?" Dudley says, "we are interested in the lowliest sparrow," a reference to Jesus's words about a sparrow that "not one of them will fall to the ground apart from your Father." Although not a Christ figure, some of Dudley's statements show a connection between his words and some of Jesus's statements.

BIBLE PASSAGE

"A cheerful heart is good medicine, but a crushed spirit dries up the bones." (Proverbs 17:22 NIV)

Dudley shows Henry that God's work must be done cheerfully and that life requires a joyful perspective.

DISCUSSION QUESTIONS:

1. What does the film say about taking one's work too seriously? When was a time in your life where a job weighed you down?
2. Why is youthful behavior and perspective so important? How would you define a youthful outlook, and is it part of your life?
3. When does Dudley believe his mission is over? Why does he feel it's over then?
4. What does Dudley's behavior show about how one should live life? How can you implement this in your life?
5. How is the professor an alter ego to Henry? Why is this man called an atheist more convinced that Dudley is not a mortal man than the pastor Henry?

THE BOOK OF ELI

2010

1 hour 58 minutes

CATEGORIES: Apocalyptic/post-apocalyptic

SUMMARY: Eli (Denzel Washington) is on a journey to the West in a decimated post-apocalyptic America, and he wants to preserve the only surviving copy of the Bible. However, the corrupt businessman Carnegie (Gary Oldman) pursues Eli because he wants the Bible for his own selfish reasons.

The Book of Eli is specifically a post-apocalyptic film, not an apocalyptic film. It takes place in the wreckage after an apocalyptic episode, which appears to be a nuclear war. Rather than building up to a cataclysmic event, the story is about survival after a catastrophe.

The post-apocalyptic film is about starting over again. The hope for restoring a moral society in *The Book of Eli* depends on religion and the preservation of the Bible (along with, as is later shown, important Western cultural artifacts including the works of Shakespeare and Mozart).

Both apocalyptic and postapocalyptic films depict contemporary conditions. Apocalyptic films warn of impending disaster if current situations don't change. They also represent God's judgment and punishment through a correction to a culture unable to correct its errors.[1]

Postapocalyptic films have a different agenda. They are about either surviving after a difficult period or living in the aftermath of a once better time. *The Book of Eli* depicts anxieties about America after the stock market crash of 2008, the ensuing recession, and a decline of opportunity.

The representation shows extreme survivalism, the threat of crime, and the growing power of unethical business, which takes three major forms: Predatory gangs that rob and kill, cannibals (influenced by the zombie movie genre), and the corrupt businessman Carnegie and his underlings.

The Book of Eli is not shaped by science fiction as many apocalyptic/postapocalyptic films are. Rather, it is inspired by Kurosawa's samurai films and Westerns that feature a protagonist restoring order through redemptive violence. Eli uses violence to defend himself but warns of a further justice people will face. "You are going be held to account for the things you've done," Eli tells one criminal.

Because Eli rejects society and doesn't care purely about physical survival, he becomes a metaphysical character.[2] However, Eli is not a Christ or Messianic figure as featured in some apocalyptic and postapocalyptic films. Rather, Eli, the name of the second-to-last Israelite judge succeeded by Samuel before the rule of Kings, is a prophetic figure.[3] He invokes the Bible for power at different points in the film, particularly at moments of danger.[4] He also says he has received divine instruction through an inner voice and believes that he is under God's protection.

Eli (Denzel Washington) in *The Book of Eli* journeys through a dangerous and decimated landscape trying to preserve the Bible. The movie is a post-apocalyptic film, a genre that became increasingly popular as a growing number of Americans felt economic insecurity. Photo courtesy Warner Bros./Everett Collection

Eli is on his own spiritual journey rather than already being spiritually formed. Initially, in his efforts to preserve the last remaining Bible, he repeats a kind of mantra to himself to avoid danger: "Stay on the path, it's not your concern." But after seeing the young woman Solara in trouble, he intervenes. Although reluctant, he takes her on his journey West, which rehumanizes the loner Eli. Regarding the Bible, he later confesses to Solara, "I got so caught up in keeping it safe I forgot to live by what I learned from it."

Through his instructions to her, he establishes a theme in the young adult dystopian apocalyptic or post-apocalyptic film of a young person becoming aware of the fundamental injustice in society.[5] Eli takes this further by making Solara aware of the transcendental by teaching her how to pray and reading the Bible to her.

Consistent with the dualistic representation of religion in many films, Eli represents the true religious figure as an outsider in contrast to the false religious establishment figure of Carnegie. Carnegie calls the Bible a weapon used to manipulate and control, while the sincere religious figure Eli wants to use it to transform, empower, and educate.

BIBLE PASSAGE

"For we walk by faith, not by sight." (2 Corinthians 5:7 NKJV)

Eli recites this to Solara, saying, "It means you know something even if you don't know something." This shows how Eli lives by faith and the transcendental, distinguishing him from the physical survivalism surrounding him.

DISCUSSION QUESTIONS

1. What are the different motivations for using the Bible that Eli and Carnegie have? How do you see that duality in current society?
2. What role does Solara play in Eli's spiritual journey? What role does he play in her spiritual awareness?
3. Backdating the thirty years since the apocalyptic event would make Eli a young adult when it happened. What do you think his life was like to make him the way he was?

4. Has there been a time when you felt you were living in a post-apocalyptic way either for externally imposed or personal reasons? What happened?

5. What is the ending twist about Eli's character? Do you believe it is true? Why or why not?

BRUCE ALMIGHTY

2003

1 hour 41 minutes

CATEGORIES: Divine intervention, redemption story

SUMMARY: TV news reporter Bruce Nolan (Jim Carrey) is passed over for a promotion for news anchor. He cries out against what he feels is God's injustice because of his misfortune and insists God could easily fix his problems. God (Morgan Freeman) turns over his powers to Bruce to see if he can do better.

Although most spiritual movies are serious in tone, the genre is flexible enough to include comedies such as *Groundhog Day* and *Bruce Almighty*. Both movies feature self-centered, career-obsessed TV reporters and are examples of reductio ad absurdum, a comic form emphasizing an absurd event that creates chaos.[1] In *Groundhog Day*, the protagonist lives the same day over and over again, while in *Bruce Almighty*, the protagonist receives God's powers. The absurdity continues until the protagonists attain spiritual breakthroughs.

Bruce Almighty's premise recalls the concluding chapters of the Book of Job, in which God emerges from a whirlwind in response to Job's cries that God has been unfair to him. God's first appearance to Bruce is less tumultuous. It comes in three forms signifying the trinity. The janitor represents Jesus, the electrician the Holy Spirit, and "the boss" in a white suit is God.[2] *Bruce Almighty* goes further than the Book of Job, with God not only speaking but giving Bruce his powers to teach him a lesson.

Bruce's suffering is also distinct from Job's. During what Bruce calls the worst day of his life, he is disappointed he isn't promoted and is later fired from his job. Bruce's problems are negligible compared to Job, who is tormented with painful sores, whose children are killed, and whose business is ruined. However, Bruce's anger reflects something significant about contemporary culture. Prayers and expectations for God are sometimes a disguise for individualistic wish fulfillment.

Bruce's drive for material and career success creates his unhappiness. After his girlfriend Grace asks him if he feels God is picking on him, Bruce replies, "No, he's ignoring me completely." Bruce feels abandoned because God isn't acting as an agent for his desires. Recalling George Bailey in *It's a Wonderful Life*, Bruce is unhappy because he's dissatisfied with his position in life. "I'm not ok with a mediocre job, I'm not ok with a mediocre apartment, I'm not ok with a mediocre life," he laments. Like Bailey, however, Bruce must undergo transformative inner change rather than having his external conditions altered.

And like other redemption stories, there is a three stage of process of the protagonist as first flawed, then conflicted, then finally acquiring a liberated new self. The film is less complex with much less emotional range than *Groundhog Day*. But Bruce, like Phil Connor, proceeds through several faulty phases to navigate the absurdist comic situation. It includes pleasure seeking, revenge, materialism, showing off, and making his life easier in any way possible. This shows the human tendency to fixate on immediate fleeting gratifications rather than considering the ramifications of one's actions.[3]

Redemption stories include conversion scenes that divide the second and third acts. The protagonist leaves behind their old and new identities (the divided self) and forms a more consistent and complete redeemed self. In *Bruce Almighty*, this occurs when, in a rainstorm, Bruce cries out, "I don't want to be God; I want you to decide what's right for me; I surrender to your will." After this capitulation, he is transported to what appears to be a heavenly realm. God probes to find out whether it is a legitimate transformation and confirms that it is because Bruce now values Grace's happiness more than his own.

Ultimately, the movie shows God's supernatural capabilities as limited. God points out that he cannot alter the free will of humans. And because Bruce discovers he cannot make Grace love him, his supernatural godly powers have limited value.[4] The movie also shows the problematic nature of a God who would freely grant prayer requests. Not only does it have a troubling impact on others but, as God points out: "Since when did anyone have a clue about what they want?"

BIBLE PASSAGE

"Will the one who contends with the Almighty correct him? Let him who accuses God answer him!" (Job 40:2 NIV)

Like Job, Bruce Nolan accuses God of inflicting unjust suffering but in the end submits to God.

DISCUSSION QUESTIONS

1. What do you think of the film's use of comedy? What place does comedy have in the spiritual life?
2. Is Bruce justified in being angry at God? Is anger at God sometimes appropriate? Why or why not?
3. How would you describe the character of God in the film? Does it in any way match your own view of God?
4. Why does God single out free will as something he can't change? How much free will do you believe humans have?
5. What is the film's view of prayer? How do you see any of your own prayer life reflected in how the characters pray?

Cast Away

2000

2 hours 23 minutes

CATEGORIES: Redemption story (variation), transcendental style

SUMMARY: Chuck Noland (Tom Hanks) is a time-obsessed, schedule-driven executive at an overnight delivery service company. But he lives by a different sense of time after he's marooned on an uninhabited desert island. He struggles to survive and hopes to return to civilization and his fiancée Kelly (Helen Hunt).

Redemption stories strip away what the Trappist monk and spiritual writer Thomas Merton calls the false self: the ego-based self, as opposed to the spiritual-based authentic identity. The false self is so intricately linked to personality that it often takes a crisis to shock one into confronting the counterfeit self that has been constructed over many years. *Cast Away* uses an extreme crisis of desert island isolation to force the protagonist to overcome his spiritual shortcomings.

Chuck Noland's spiritual trajectory is a variation on the standard three-act redemption story. In the first act of the protagonist's immersion in a flawed state, Noland, like Phil in *Groundhog Day*, is consumed with his career at the expense of deeper human relationships. However, Noland's workaholism is cultural and systemic rather than individualistic.

This can be seen in his girlfriend Kelly's calendar, which is as booked as his, and in the crew of the company airplane flying on Christmas Eve.[1] Noland tells workers, "We live or we die by the clock," and that it is a "sin" to lose track of time. This mania over timeliness suggests he possesses an obsessive desire for control akin to an addiction.[2] He is also a force for globalizing business powers, as he indoctrinates former communist Russian workers with the corporate values of efficiency and timeliness.[3]

Noland's time on a desert island is different from the customary second act in a redemption story between the flawed self and an emerging better self. Noland is lodged in emotional and physical survivalism.

This emerges in his conversations with the volleyball Wilson, who serves as an surface upon which Noland projects his desires and anxieties.[4] His blood on the volleyball, shaped into a face, emphasizes the idea that it is a part of his identity and also indicates pain and suffering. As Noland's time on the island continues, Wilson begins to resemble him. When Noland's hair and beard grow, for example, the volleyball's spiked hair made of leaves adds to Wilson's rugged look.[5] Long takes and ambient sounds put the viewer into a contemplative state consistent with transcendental film style.[6]

The second act ends with Noland leaving the island, which requires him to relinquish control to be rescued. Rather than manmade schedules, he must depend on the natural conditions of seasons, winds, and tides to escape.[7] Wilson's disappearance in the ocean signifies that the identity Noland formed on the island is now gone. With his sail blown away, he casts aside his oars and shows submission. Aiding him are whales—representing providence watching over him—that cool him with bursts of water to wake him to the passing of the barge that rescues him.[8]

The third act, after Noland's return to civilization, culminates in his understanding of two different women that signified hope to him on the island. His fiancée Kelly represents secularism and compromise, and Bettina represents aesthetics and spirituality. Kelly also characterizes civilization, while Bettina's isolation echoes Noland's own.[9]

On the island, Noland only knows Bettina indirectly through the symbolism of wings that she put on her FedEx package, which represents the wings she sculpts. She marks her identity on a corporate product to show she still maintains her identity, unlike Chuck who loses his identity to corporate demands. She lives in remote Texas far away from corporate structures. The wing logo on the box represents Noland's eventual flight and freedom.[10] It also represents spiritual deliverance through art.[11] Noland paints the wings on the makeshift sail he constructs to leave the island as well as on the cave wall.

Refusing to open the box is a symbolic shift away from his drive to know and control and a move toward faith, hope, and providence.[12]

Noland's ending enigmatic smile as he sees another representation of the wings indicates he realizes the enormous part providence played in his life.

BIBLE PASSAGE

"For we live by faith, not by sight." (2 Corinthians 5:7 NIV)

Chuck Noland says his logic was proven wrong and he was living by faith that he would escape the island.

DISCUSSION QUESTIONS

1. How is Chuck Noland initially too career-focused? How does your job affect other relationships or take up too much of your energy?
2. How do you define Noland's relationship with Wilson? Why does he need to have these dialogues?
3. How is God/providence working through Noland's ordeal? When was a difficult time in your own life that you can look back upon and see God working?
4. How have Kelly and Noland both changed after his return?
5. How do you interpret the end of the film? What do you think Noland did?

CHARIOTS OF FIRE

1981

2 hours 5 minutes

CATEGORIES: Difficulty living out faith

SUMMARY: Two athletes competing in the 1924 Olympics have different reasons for wanting to earn gold medals. Eric Liddell (Ian Charleson) believes his running ability is a gift from the Lord and aspires to win to honor God. Harold Abrahams (Ben Cross) wants to win to overcome prejudice he experiences as a Jewish man.

On the surface, Eric Liddell and Harold Abrahams are very different. Liddell is a placid, faith-filled man who frequently speaks in public about his faith. He is distinctive because his religious convictions are so blatantly central to his character.[1] Abrahams is a loner tormented over the prejudice he feels. He takes pride in being Jewish but appears to have no spiritual beliefs or practices. However, both men battle and overcome an elitist secular establishment to succeed on their own terms.[2]

Chariots of Fire is in the category of spiritual films centered on living out faith in a society that can elevate secular priorities over religious belief. In this film, that conflict emerges as Liddell faces both his spiritual principles and the Olympic establishment's demands.

However, the film is also in the sports movie genre. The best films in this genre are never about the mechanics of being an athlete, but about why someone becomes an athlete and what they are trying to overcome within themself. The success of the athlete often corrects a spiritual challenge or a social inequity the athlete experiences.[3]

While Abrahams's story focuses mainly on social inequity, he is also at the beginning of his spiritual journey. This starts by recognizing his increasing dissatisfaction with pursuit of worldly success. Although Abrahams relentlessly desires victory, he feels an accompanying disillusionment with his drive for achievement. "I'm forever in pursuit, and I don't know what it is I'm chasing," he confesses. He also realizes how isolating that chase is. He defines a race as "ten lonely seconds to justify my whole existence."

The narrative of Eric Liddell, the film's other protagonist, is more concerned with the clash between spiritual and worldly values. This comes from pressure about patriotism, which becomes a surrogate religion.

After Liddell refuses to run an Olympic race on the Sabbath, the British Olympic team leaders (and even the Prince of Wales) accuse him of betraying his country. "In my day it was King first, God after," the Master of Caius bluntly says. But the steadfast Liddell says country is subordinate to his religious beliefs. On the day he is to run a race, he preaches on a passage from Isaiah that says, "all nations are as nothing" and suggests that excessive patriotism is a type of vanity.

The clash between the secular priority of winning running races and the demands of his ministry also lead to conflict with his sister Jenny, who thinks he devotes too much time to running. While acknowledging God's true purpose is his ministry, Liddell tries to convince his sister that his ability to run is a gift from God. He also uses running as a metaphor for the faith journey, saying, "It requires concentration of will, energy of soul." But he goes on to suggest that everyone runs their race of faith in their own way, some with more obstacles than others.

Ironically, even though these anti-establishment figures adhere to their principles and motivations, the country ultimately benefits from their efforts because the athletes win.[4] Like the resolution of *Hacksaw Ridge*, both the establishment and the person whose religious beliefs are tested triumph. The difficulty of living out faith in a secular and prejudiced culture is temporarily resolved by an Olympic victory.

BIBLE PASSAGE

"Everyone who competes in the games goes into strict training. They do it to get a crown that will not last, but we do it to get a crown that will last forever." (1 Corinthians 9:25 NIV)

Several times in the New Testament, the faith journey is compared to a race that requires self-discipline and focus on an end goal. This idea is also conveyed by Eric Liddell in *Chariots of Fire*.

DISCUSSION QUESTIONS

1. How are the religious beliefs of Eric Liddell tested? How have your spiritual beliefs been tested by an institution?
2. Can you compare both of the main character's races to a faith journey? In what ways has your own faith journey been like a race?
3. How does Liddell use his fame to express his religious beliefs? How can you do this in your own profession?
4. How does Abrahams handle his feeling that he suffers from prejudice? When was a time in your life when you felt prejudice?
5. Why is Abrahams lonely at times in his pursuit of success? When have you experienced a similar loneliness?

CONTACT

1997

2 hours 30 minutes

CATEGORIES: Search for God

SUMMARY: Astronomer Ellie Arroway (Jodie Foster) devotes her career to searching for extraterrestrial life. After she receives a communication that could be from aliens, the government agrees to send a volunteer into space to find out more information. The religious implications of life in space ignite passionate responses from spiritual leaders, including Christian philosopher Palmer Joss (Matthew McConaughey).

Despite its dated elements—including stilted clips of Bill Clinton and 1990s CNN reporters—*Contact* remains a significant film in the search for god category. Although it's about the search for extraterrestrial life, the moral center of the film is the attempt to reconcile faith and science. It is one of the few films that thoughtfully debates and ultimately finds common ground between religion and science.

In the film, the search for intelligent life in the universe is a simultaneous inquiry into faith. It connects the questioning of God's existence with the question of extraterrestrial life.[1] As the movie unfolds, both searches contain a longing for validation that humans are not alone.

Science and faith are most explicitly represented by the two main characters, with astronomer Ellie Arroway representing science and Palmer Joss representing faith.

Because Arroway is a scientist, she relies on empirical truth. She considers herself a moral person but believes it is impossible to find verifiable data to confirm or deny God's existence. She is agnostic, not atheist. What gives her flexibility in her position is her identity as a seeker. "For as long as I remember, I've been searching for something, some reason why we're here," she says. With her mother dying in childbirth and her

In *Contact*, astronomer Ellie Arroway (Jodie Foster) pursues communication with extraterrestrial life which becomes a symbol of the transcendental. The movie ultimately shows that the verifiable proof that science requires for the supernatural is not always possible. Photo courtesy Warner Bros./Everett Collection

father dying when she was nine, Arroway's longing for her parents is replaced with a longing for meaning.[2]

This quest for meaning and truth is what Christian philosopher and author Joss Palmer finds interesting about her. More than any other character, he represents the possibility of reconciling science and faith. While Joss strongly rejects anti-religious positions, he is also open to the discoveries of modern science.[3] He is not opposed to technology but says he's "against the men who deify it at the expense of human truth."

This makes him different from the other religious characters in the film who are inflexible, ineffectual, or manipulative. The priest who talks to a young Arroway after her father dies offers only platitudes. The leader of the Conservative Coalition is suspicious about aliens who may have no religious beliefs and criticizes science for "intruding into matters of faith."[4] A cult member with a crucifix draped around his neck blames science for the world's problems and tries to sabotage the space project in a mixture of fanaticism and irrationality.[5] Arroway's colleague David Drumlin pronounces religious discourse when it suits his purpose, but in the end appears to have no sincere religious beliefs.[6]

The film culminates with politicians and scientists expressing skepticism about Arroway's experience in space after she offers no scientific proof of her apparent encounter with aliens. Arroway finds herself in the same predicament as religious people who have no proof for their claims but must live by faith and testify about life-changing experiences to an unbelieving world.[7] However, the result of her trip and the subsequent rejection of her account of it gives her a new appreciation of the truth of human experiences that cannot be proven scientifically.[8]

Arroway receives support from Joss, who as a man of faith, accepts her account without requiring scientific verification.[9] He says the two live by a "different covenant," but that their pursuit of truth is the same.

Despite working in the seemingly opposed fields of science and theology, Ellie and Joss show that seeking the truth should unite people, not divide them.[10] The division between religion and science is a false dichotomy because both have insights that complement one another.[11] The movie shows that rigidity in either field is dangerous.

BIBLE PASSAGE

"By faith we understand that the worlds were prepared by the word of God, so that what is seen was made from things that are not visible." (Hebrews 11:3 NRSV)

Contact shows how some experiences in life, including mystical ones, cannot be scientifically explained.

DISCUSSION QUESTIONS

1. How does Arroway's childhood experience of her parents dying shape her spiritual life? How have you had something traumatic from your childhood influence your spiritual outlook?
2. What makes Palmer Joss openminded about science? How do you reconcile science with your spiritual beliefs?

3. How does the film convincingly show science and faith as a false dichotomy? How do you think this dichotomy exists in the current culture?

4. How do you interpret the alien's words to Arroway and the form in which the alien appears?

5. Why is it difficult for politicians and scientists to believe Arroway's account of what happened in space? Have you ever experienced someone not believing a mystical or religious experience you had?

COOL HAND LUKE

1967

2 hours 7 minutes

CATEGORIES: Christ figure

SUMMARY: Arrested for shearing the tops from parking meters, Lucas "Luke" Jackson (Paul Newman) is assigned to two years in a harsh Southern prison road gang. He wins the admiration of other prisoners for being an amusing non-conformist who challenges authority. With each act of rebellion, however, the authorities try harder to break Luke's spirit.

With its egg eating contest and notorious car washing scene, *Cool Hand Luke* may not on the surface seem like a spiritual film. Yet it is a landmark movie for integrating a Christ figure into a contemporary setting.

It was also influential in generating a subgenre of the Christ figure film: the Christ figure in an institution, such as prison or mental hospital. In films like *One Flew Over the Cuckoo's Nest*, *The Shawshank Redemption*, and *The Green Mile*, the institution becomes a metaphor for an oppressive society and the Christ figure a person who comes to liberate others. These films symbolize how people are prisoners of institutions because they limit freedom.[1] The chain gang Luke is sentenced to is a product of both deterministic social forces and social injustice.[2]

At times, Luke falls into what can be called the Christ clown figure.[3] His wise, piercing humor is subversive, which bonds the oppressed prisoners together and angers the authorities. Luke maintains his humor in the direst of circumstances. When he receives a telegram telling him his mother died, he sings the satirical song "Plastic Jesus" as a tribute. Even his final showdown with authorities is full of humor. The beginning and the end of the film are shots of Luke smiling, emphasizing his clown nature.

Luke also feels the burden of being a beacon of hope to the other prisoners.[4] In another significant attribute of the Christ figure, Luke's retreat away from others becomes the equivalent of a Garden of Gethsemane moment. Near the end of the film, Luke enters a church after telling Dragline, "I've done enough world shaking for a while, you can do the rest of it for me." After giving this parting advice to the equivalent of a disciple, Luke alone prays to God. "What you got in mind for me? What do I do now?" Instead of asking for acceptance of God's will, he tries to discern what God's will is. This recalls a moment earlier in the film when Luke shouts to the heavens, "Love me, hate me, kill me, anything, just let me know it!"

Luke experiences a number of mini-resurrections, with one occurring when he emerges from his punishment of time alone in "the box" after his mother dies. Another example is when he comes out of a hole he digs, which is symbolic of a grave, before a final resurrection where he carries on in spirit through others remembering him. The ending shot shows two intersecting roads forming a cross, with a superimposed, torn photograph of Luke that also creates a cross when taped back together. He is a captive who transcends his captivity, at least in spirit, and leads others to the same state.[5]

And what about the famous egg eating scene? It shows how Luke takes on the burdens (sins) of the other prisoners by eating fifty eggs, the exact number of prisoners. Because he is not expected to eat them all, it is the cinematic equivalent of a miracle. Eggs also represent new life, fertility, and resurrection. When Luke is done, he lies in a crucified-like pose surrounded by broken eggshells in the film's most blatant visual symbolism of Christ.

BIBLE PASSAGE

"Father, if you are willing, take this cup from me; yet not my will, but yours be done." (Luke 22:42 NIV)

Luke's bold and honest prayers during the key scenes in the thunderstorm and in the church recall Jesus in the Garden of Gethsemane. Luke earnestly seeks God's will, not his own.

DISCUSSION QUESTIONS

1. Is the road gang an appropriate punishment for Luke's crime? What does this say about the criminal justice system? What parallels can be drawn to the current criminal justice system?
2. What makes Luke a Christ figure? What other Christ figures are there in films?
3. What is Luke's origin and what is his relationship with his mother and father? How does that connect to Luke as Christ figure?
4. Why is Luke's sense of humor such a threat? Where have you seen humor used to challenge authority?
5. A Christ figure trait is a resurrection, where his spirit lives on in others. How is this represented in the film? Are there people in your own life whose spirit carries on in you?

CRIMES AND MISDEMEANORS

1989

1 hour 44 minutes

CATEGORIES: Search for God

SUMMARY: Ophthalmologist Judah Rosenthal (Martin Landau) is having an affair with Dolores (Anjelica Huston), who threatens to tell his wife. Judah arranges for

Dolores to be killed but fears God will punish him. Filmmaker Cliff Stern (Woody Allen) is making a film about TV producer Lester (Alan Alda) but would rather spend his time making a documentary about a philosophy professor.

Crimes and Misdemeanors is a quest into whether there is a divine force that enacts morality and justice. The film shows wicked characters prospering and escaping culpability for crimes, while more noble characters suffer. This seems to show the universe's indifference to good and evil intentions, and that no spiritual entity dispenses or withholds happiness based on actions.[1] However, a closer reading of the film indicates something more complex.

Much of this complexity is embodied in the narrative of Judah, who is having an extramarital affair. The rabbi Ben tells Judah to confess to his wife what happened. He says it represents an opportunity to acquire wisdom, which he defines as "what's real and deep and lasting versus the superficial payoff of the moment." Although they have had discussions about morality over the years, Ben reiterates that life has "a moral structure with real meaning and forgiveness," and that without a belief in a higher power, there is no basis for how to live.

However, Judah rejects the rabbi's advice, which destroys his religious impulses.[2] Instead, he hires his brother Jack to arrange for his mistress's murder. If the rabbi represents the divine, Jack represents the bestial.[3] Judah lacks the courage to confess to his adultery and he murders to preserve a superficial life of status and wealth.[4] For a time, Judah fears God will punish him, but months later, at the end of the film, his fear of retribution appears to have ended.

A deeper reading of the film reveals that, ultimately, Judah is punished because suffering comes from God withdrawing, not God enacting revenge.[5] When Judah is consumed with guilt, he is closer to God. When Judah states that the crisis mysteriously abated, it may be God abandoning him. Judah's lack of remorse is worse than feeling guilty or afraid because it evidences a lack of morality.[6] In the end, suffering comes not in conventional punishment but from being confronted with an empty, meaningless existence.[7]

The film displays a philosophical divide, with the rabbis Ben and Sol espousing a spiritual perspective and the other major characters as existentialists. This mirrors the divide between Jewish secular intellectualism and traditional Jewish theology.[8]

Although the existentialists don't believe in a universal meaning of life, they fill that lack of overall purpose in different ways. Judah, Jack, and Lester live by the philosophy expressed by Judah's Aunt May, who says that "might is right," and that even committing a crime is permissible if the criminal isn't bothered by it. When the world is devoid of God, all acts are permissible—even murder.[9] This nihilistic worldview leads to an embrace of hedonism, where one is justified in doing whatever one wishes.[10] This value system replaces traditional morality and religion with individual pleasure.[11]

However, a more moral existentialism is expressed by the philosopher Levy, whom Cliff is making a documentary about. Levy stresses that, in the absence of a retributive God, human beings fill the moral vacuum and do good even though they might suffer.[12] The idea of a morally empty universe is too much for human beings to take, so they fill it by making choices motivated by an individualized sense of right and wrong.[13] "We define ourselves by the choices we have made, we are in fact the sum total of our choices," Levy says.

In contrast, the two rabbis embody belief in a higher power. "If necessary, I will always choose God over truth," says Sol, showing an unconditional faith against rationality, which underpins the secular world's definition of truth.[14] Ultimately, Ben's blindness is symbolic of inner spiritual insight.[15] However, the film noticeably avoids discussion of retributive justice in an afterlife. It is a film that focuses on morality in this life.

BIBLE PASSAGE

"Those who are evil will be destroyed, but those who hope in the Lord will inherit the land." (Psalm 37:9 NIV)

In this and similar passages, the Bible shows justice as an attribute of God, an idea this film explores.

DISCUSSION QUESTIONS

1. Why don't the characters get what they deserve? How do you explain the wicked prospering and the righteous suffering in the film and in life?

2. How do the characters connect God with morality? How much do you define God with morality?

3. How do Judah and Lester have good qualities? How do Cliff and the professor show shortcomings?

4. How are the narratives of Judah and Cliff the same? How are they different?

5. How do you interpret the ending conversation between Judah and Cliff?

CRY, THE BELOVED COUNTRY

1995

1 hour 46 minutes

CATEGORIES: Religious figure (Episcopal priest)

SUMMARY: Anglican priest Stephen Kumalo (James Earl Jones) travels from his small South African village to the crime-ridden city of Johannesburg. With the help of young priest Theophilus Msimangu (Vusi Kunene), Kumalo searches for missing family members. He locates his son Absalom (Eric Miyeni), who is in prison after being charged with killing the son of wealthy landowner James Jarvis (Richard Harris).

Stephen Kumalo is vulnerable, overwhelmed, and emotionally raw after he leaves his small hometown and his friendly churchgoers for the metropolis of Johannesburg. However, his trip to find estranged family members leads to his spiritual growth. Like a pilgrimage, it is a transformative journey of spiritual discovery and understanding.[1]

The brokenness of the city serves as a striking contrast to the peaceful country life of Kumalo's hometown.[2] The crime and brutality in Johannesburg also illustrate a breakdown in traditional values that Kumalo struggles to understand and overcome.[3] Kumalo's quest serves an important purpose because it forces him into a greater understanding of himself and the overall culture.[4] Because of the remoteness of his small town, he never fully confronted the larger problems of society and did not learn how to deal with them.[5]

One cause of some of these problems is the racism of segregationist apartheid, which forms a persistent backdrop to the story.[6] However, while the film shows the brutality of segregation, identifying the root cause and its remedy require a spiritual perspective more than a political one.

The limitation of political solutions is illustrated by Kumalo's brother John, a charismatic politician who speaks eloquently and forcefully about justice. However, his disdain of the church and his self-centeredness show that something more is needed than political activism and speeches. "How can he have truth on his side and not God?" Kumalo asks. Later, a judge declares the law cannot show mercy or assess if the system of racial segregation contributes to crime. The failure of secular ideology and institutions leads to a central tension in the film: how does a spiritual person live in a world filled with oppression?[7]

While not having enough Christlike traits to make him a Christ figure, Kumalo at times undergoes martyr-like affliction. He endures pain and suffering like King David, who also lost his rebellious son Absalom (the name of Kumalo's son), and Kumalo shares the same first name with Stephen, the original Christian martyr.[8]

To overcome the widespread suffering they see, Kumalo and others use prayer, endurance, and acts of altruism. When Kumalo calls the young priest Theophilus a kind person, he disagrees. "I'm not kind, I'm a sinful and selfish man, but God put his hands on me." This quote captures well how the film adheres to the Christian idea of sin redeemed through spiritual transformation.

Forgiveness also becomes a crucial means to transcend the effects of sin. Kumalo both asks for forgiveness and grants it. Jarvis shows forgiveness toward the father of his son's killer. Like Kumalo, he too goes on a journey of understanding about his son.[9] This brings the two together in a mutual recognition of each other's pain and sorrow. The film garners much of its emotional force from the struggle of the two fathers to understand and reconcile during their twilight years.[10]

By the end of the film, the solution to transcending pain is not only forgiveness but enacting faith through religious commitment. Jarvis donates money for a new church as an act of redemption and to honor his son who fought against racism. Kumalo climbs to the top of a mountain to pray, showing a powerful desire to connect with the divine. His ascent of the mountain at dawn shows the promise of resurrection and a new life.[11]

However, part of his spiritual realization is that in the life of faith, suffering must be accepted as a mystery. "The purpose of our lives, the end of all our struggle is beyond all human wisdom," Kumalo says.

BIBLE PASSAGE

"Above all, love each other deeply, because love covers over a multitude of sins." (1 Peter 4:8 NIV)

The major characters in the film overcome sin and regret through acts of love, kindness, and forgiveness.

DISCUSSION QUESTIONS

1. In what ways is Kumalo vulnerable and in what ways is he strong?
2. How are city life and rural life spiritually contrasted? When have you experienced a contrast in cultures in your life?
3. What makes James Jarvis capable of forgiveness? Do you believe you could forgive under such circumstances?
4. Does the movie suggest that oppressive social conditions create crime and sin? Do you feel that's true?
5. What does the ending scene indicate about Kumalo's spiritual outlook and beliefs?

DEAD MAN WALKING

1995

2 hours 2 minutes

CATEGORIES: Clergy figure, redemption story

SUMMARY: Death row prisoner Matthew Poncelet (Sean Penn) contacts the nun Helen Prejean (Susan Sarandon) to get help attaining a reprieve for his death sentence. Prejean assists Poncelet despite public opposition and skepticism from her family and other clergy.

Although known as a film about the death penalty, the significance of *Dead Man Walking* in the spiritual movie genre derives from its presentation of two compelling spiritual narratives.

Sister Helen Prejean's journey is a nun's search to find some element of humanity and fragment of Christ within the soul of a convicted killer.[1] The journey for death row inmate Poncelet is whether salvation is possible for those who commit the most heinous acts. Is anyone capable of redemption? If so, what does it take to achieve redemption?

It is also a landmark film for its portrayal of a nun. Films such as *Black Narcissus* (1947), *Heaven Knows, Mr. Allison* (1957), and *A Nun's Story* (1959) express sexual tension between a nun and what can be called ungodly men.[2] Other films, like *The Bells of St. Mary's* (1945) and *Doubt* (2008), show an ecclesiastic clash with male clergy figures. *Dead Man Walking* focuses on Prejean's work rather than on repressed sexual feelings or conflicts with male clergy.

The intimacy that develops between the nun and the central male figure, the death row convict, is not based on personal attraction or any kind of affinity.[3] Instead, Prejean must overcome aversion to him.[4] Their eventual bond becomes emblematic of the love between God and undeserving humanity.[5] Prejean's love for Poncelet is radically Christian, unconditional, and different from any previous feeling he had ever experienced.[6]

Prejean shows her love through self-discipline, courage, and active listening. In a prison, she submerges herself into the vulgar world of

74

Helen Prejean (Susan Sarandon) in *Dead Man Walking* is both heroic clergy figure and a Christ figure. She tries to find humanity in a murderer and make him repent before the culmination of his death sentence. Photo courtesy Gramercy Pictures/Everett Collection

Poncelet, his family, and death row.[7] This movement downward demands that she leave behind privileges and power to enter the human experience and bring salvation to it in a manner reflective of the Christian idea of kenosis.[8] This hands-on faith and the willingness to persevere distinguishes Prejean from the jaded Father Farley, who regards his prison chaplaincy as a dead-end job.[9]

A critical part of the film deals with how Prejean's efforts to shift Poncelet's pursuit of a false sense of redemption toward a real one. "I know Jesus died on the cross, and I know he's going to take care of me when I appear before God on Judgment Day," Poncelet says, apparently believing all will be forgiven in the afterlife no matter what. However, Prejean tells him, "Redemption isn't some kind of free admission ticket you get because Jesus paid the price; you got to participate in your own redemption. You've got some work to do."

This is a key concept in the third act of the spiritual film redemption story, which requires an active transformation to a new self. For Poncelet, this manifests in his confession, recognition of divine love, and asking for forgiveness.[10] He acknowledges the pain he caused others rather than fearing his own execution. His confession is the moment Prejean worked toward throughout the entire movie. He drops pretenses and alibis, admits he committed murder, and takes responsibility for it before God.[11] Prejean struggled to push Poncelet toward the truth because she believes his self-liberation is necessary for his salvation.[12] In the end, divine justice is achieved not by punishing the physical body through the death penalty but by saving the soul.[13]

Dead Man Walking is also about the enormous consequences of sin. In some ways, it is an Old Testament-like exploration of violence and its corruption of both the self and society. Poncelet is never romanticized. Flashbacks of the murder emphasize the brutal violence of his crime.[14]

The spiritual solution is the struggle for forgiveness. This is demonstrated during the ending scene with the murdered son's father and Prejean praying in church. Forgiveness, like redemption, requires effort. "It's not faith," Prejean says. "I wish it were that easy; it's work."

BIBLE PASSAGE

"Then you will know the truth, and the truth will set you free." (John 8:32 NIV)

Prejean emphasizes this passage to Poncelet, illustrating how salvation occurs after admitting the reality of one's sins.

DISCUSSION QUESTIONS

1. What is the film's view on whether redemption is possible for anyone? What's your opinion?
2. Do you think the film presents believable multiple points of view about the death penalty? Why or why not?
3. How is Sister Helen Prejean an effective listener? Why is listening such an important spiritual quality?
4. How does the film's director show the growing closeness between Prejean and Poncelet through both dialogue and how the film is shot?

5. How does the film show how difficult forgiveness is? Have you had a hard time forgiving or are you in the process of trying to forgive?

DERSU UZALA

1975 (Russia)

2 hours 22 minutes

CATEGORIES: Retaining Indigenous community and culture

SUMMARY: In 1902, Russian army captain Vladimir Arsenyev (Yuriy Solomin) leads a group of soldiers into the Siberian wilderness for a land surveying expedition. The captain befriends Dersu Uzala (Maksim Munzuk), a Goldi native who lives off the land and guides the men on their mission. Five years later, Arsenyev returns to Siberia on another survey and is reunited with Uzala.

This movie is a variation on the retaining Indigenous community and culture category because the hunter Dersu Uzala lives alone in the Siberian wilderness without a tribe. Subsequently, the film does not contain the Indigenous religion theme of honoring ancestral tribal tradition. However, *Dersu Uzala* expresses a primary element of the category, which is the connection between Indigenous spirituality and the natural world. Also consistent with this category are the film's presentations of modernism, technology, and the economic system as threatening to Indigenous spirituality.

Uzala's spirituality is based on animism, the idea that spirit dwells in all things, and he refers to forces in nature as "people." "Look around, all is people," Dersu says. "Water is alive." Uzala calls fire, water, and wind "three mighty people" and refers to the sun as the most important being. By being aware of the power of nature, Uzala knows that he is an insignificant part of it.[1] This is emphasized in Akira Kurosawa's direction, who only sparingly uses close-ups in order to show the characters in relation to nature as the story unfolds to the cycles of the natural world.[2] This makes the Siberian landscape a character itself.[3]

The film, however, does vary from some retaining Indigenous community and culture films by depicting nature as a merciless, rather than benevolent, force. When the captain and Uzala are trapped on a frozen lake as the sun sets and the temperature drops, the captain's compass and gunshot signals cannot save them from possible death. Only through Uzala's instruction to quickly cut reeds and build a hut do they survive a night on the frozen tundra.[4] Later on, Uzala is in anguish because he shoots a wild tiger—a creature he sees as the spiritual center of the universe—which he believes he's angered.[5]

Uzala's pursuit of harmony with nature helps his relations with the men who rely on him for guidance and insight about the natural world.[6] His relation to nature is also highly rational and based on practical knowledge and empirical observation.[7] Dersu can logically infer information from tracks, sounds, and weather changes.

The film, shot in Siberia with a non-Japanese cast, differs from the samurai films Kurosawa is best known for. Like a samurai, however, Dersu is extremely competent.[8]

"He had acquired knowledge and wisdom during his long life in the taiga," the captain observes about Uzala. "And he also had a beautiful spirit." Part of Uzala's wisdom comes from his clear sense of good and evil and his practice of generosity and empathy. He disdains immoral behavior by humans and is especially outraged at the waste of resources. Both Uzala and the captain distance themselves from the somewhat childish behavior of the soldiers. They are both looking for a more meaningful spiritual connection with someone. During their initial parting, the captain says, "May God watch over you," illustrating that both believe in a spiritual force.

The friendship between Uzala and the captain is the emotional center of the film. When the two are reunited after a five-year separation, the captain seems to gain something essential to his vitality, and Uzala appears to be no longer as fulfilled by his solitary life in the wilderness.[9]

The film avoids the cliché of having an outsider integrate into the wilderness or adopt the Indigenous religion. The Indigenous character also does not successfully integrate into modern culture. In the end, Uzala symbolizes the good that modern technology eliminates.[10] The film concludes with a farewell not just to Uzala, but to his natural habitat, which is vanishing under the violence of development.[11]

SPIRITUAL TERM

Animism—A belief among some Indigenous people that spirit dwells in objects in nature itself.

DISCUSSION QUESTIONS

1. Why do Uzala and the Captain become such good friends? Describe a close friendship you've had with someone from a different background or culture.
2. How is friendship an important part of this story? What other films portray friendship in such a convincing way?
3. Why are Uzala and the Captain unsuited for each other's environment? What is an environment you have found it difficult or would find it difficult to live in?
4. Why does Uzala live alone? When have you had a period of living in solitude?
5. Why does Uzala shoot the wild tiger, and why does he fear retribution because of it?

THE DEVIL WEARS PRADA

1 hour 49 minutes

2006

CATEGORIES: Hero's journey

SUMMARY: Andy Sachs (Anne Hathaway) is a recent college graduate who reluctantly accepts an entry level job at a glamorous fashion magazine. Determined to gain the experience necessary to eventually land a job as a news reporter, she vows to stay despite her demanding and powerful boss, editor Miranda Priestly (Meryl Streep). As Andy integrates more into the enticing fashion world, she becomes increasingly ostracized from her friends, boyfriend, career goals, and moral center.

The Devil Wears Prada recalls the journey Christian makes through Vanity Fair in *The Pilgrim's Progress* and the story of *Faust*, who gave away his soul for worldly gain. The movie primarily follows the hero's journey formula, but it does not take place in a dream realm such as *The Wizard of Oz*, the fantastic voyage of *Life of Pi*, or the mixture of the real world and magical events as in the *Harry Potter* series.

Instead, like *Wall Street*, the story is entrenched in the reality of the center of commerce in New York City. Also like *Wall Street*, the film shows how the commercial realm is both alluring and detrimental. And keeping with the hero's journey plot, the main characters are a mentor/guide (Nigel), a tempter (Christian), and a villain (Miranda Priestly, whose last name indicates her status in the field of fashion and American commercial culture).

Initially, Andy is not morally flawed but simply inexperienced. This leaves her vulnerable to the temptations and pitfalls of the superficiality of the fashion business, the demands of a job that damages her personal life, and the idea that she can compromise her values for a limited time. The somewhat naive Andy is particularly susceptible to being morally reshaped by the charismatic and powerful leader, world-renowned fashion editor Miranda Priestly, just as Bud Fox is susceptible to the high-power financial tycoon Gordon Gekko in *Wall Street*.

Joseph Campbell's spiritual narrative of a Hero's Journey can take place in fantasy realms or in contemporary life. In *The Devil Wears Prada*, Andy Sachs (Anne Hathaway) the Hero's Journey occurs after she takes a job working for the narcissistic fashion magazine editor Miranda Priestly (Meryl Streep). Photo courtesy 20th Century Fox/Everett Collection

Andy's downfall is caused by her exhausting work and her misguided attempt to use the position as a stepping stone to a job with more integrity. In some ways, the film is a cautionary tale about the difference between a calling or vocation and a job that doesn't align with one's values to merely earn a paycheck.

As much as her time at the fashion magazine *Runway* damages Andy, it equips her with crucial self-knowledge. She becomes a wiser person for confronting her tendency to compromise her values and true identity. She suffers a loss of identity by cultivating a fashionable self-image, being surrounded by influential people, and sacrificing her personal life for her work life.

Andy justifies what she must do to survive in her job by saying, "I didn't have a choice." But she realizes she can transcend that survivalist ideology after Miranda makes the Nietzschean observation that Andy can "see beyond what people want and need and you can choose for yourself." After Miranda adds that Andy reminds her of herself, Andy realizes she is in peril of losing her true identity even further. She then quits her job, which becomes the crucial step in the return home stage of the hero's journey.

Part of the film's enduring appeal has less to do with the fashion world it portrays than its depiction of a demanding workplace. Workaholism and forfeiting personal life for career remain spiritual dilemmas in contemporary culture. *Prada* is one of the few movies that portrays how work can become a type of idol and critiques the danger of making workplace identity a primary source of identity.

Not only does work hijack the characters' personal lives, but they don't seem to enjoy themselves. They feel a sense of duty in their high-profile roles, relish people envying them, and demarcate those in their insulated world from those who aren't in it. But because of the lack of authentic interpersonal relationships in the workplace, they appear ultimately unfulfilled. They are guided by a sense of importance they attach to their jobs rather than positive human connections.

BIBLE PASSAGE

"What good will it be for someone to gain the whole world, yet forfeit their soul? Or what can anyone give in exchange for their soul?" (Matthew 16:26 NIV)

These questions Jesus asks have ramifications both in the workplace and in *The Devil Wears Prada*.

DISCUSSION QUESTIONS

1. What is the work-life balance of the characters at *Runway* magazine? Do you have a good balance of the two in your life?
2. How does Andy abandon her values during the course of the film? When was a time your values were threatened by a job?
3. Why is career identity so important to the characters? How much of your identity is shaped by your job?
4. Andy feels she can work for a year at *Runway* magazine and then go on to the career she wants. Why is this a misguided belief?
5. Part of the hero's journey is a return home with acquired knowledge. What do you think Andy learned?

DIARY OF A COUNTRY PRIEST

1951 (France)

1 hour 55 minutes

CATEGORIES: Religious figure, Christ figure, transcendental style

SUMMARY: A frail unnamed young priest (Claude Laydu) is assigned to a parish in a small French village. He tries to connect with his parishioners and residents but is mostly met with disdain. On a meager diet and sometimes in physical pain, the ascetic priest struggles to strengthen his faith.

Along with being perhaps the most realized version of French director Robert Bresson's influential use of transcendental film style, the gentle, anguished protagonist makes *Diary of a Country Priest* a significant film in the spiritual movie genre.

The central character is an ill country priest who, in a communion-like diet, eats only bread and wine. The film sets up a pattern for spiritual progression also used in Bresson's 1966 film *Au Hasard Balthazar*: a character going through a variation on the Stations of the Cross.[1] A movement through a world of sin leads to a sacrificial crucifixion. The priest's spiritual life intensifies as his physical body experiences hardship.[2] However, as his suffering enlarges his spiritual perception, his awareness of grace increases.[3]

Like many Bresson films, the Christ figure becomes a suffering servant.[4] The priest's illness develops into a type of stigmata.[5] Many of Bresson's films, such as *A Man Escaped* (1956) and *Pickpocket* (1959), emphasize incarceration. In *Diary of a Country Priest*, confinement takes the form of the priest's imprisonment within himself.[6] He suffers three levels of imprisoning alienation: a sense of being a prisoner in a body slowly destroying him; being isolated from the people he is supposed to minister to; and a sacred solitude in his struggle with evil and sinfulness in himself and others.[7]

The diary he reads from reinforces this sense of inner struggle, with the doubling of voice and image intensifying the priest's words.[8] The voiceover narration highlights how his interior world and exterior reality infringe on each other.[9]

The priest's agony alienates the community that he appears unable to significantly influence.[10] Similar to Balthazar in *Au Hasard Balthazar*, the characters the priest encounters represent different spiritual conditions or manifestations of specific sins. Through the priest's interactions with these characters, the film shows how the most genuine moments are spiritual and altruistic.[11] Through these encounters, the priest is energized into compassion and action.[12]

However, at times, the priest does play a small role in helping some characters achieve spiritual breakthroughs. The Countess initially exhibits the sin of pride through a deep mourning for her son. She will not accept what happened and shuts everyone else out.[13] The priest forces her to stop her excessive mourning by emphasizing the concept of grace, the source of true social connection.[14]

The film's transcendental style, manifested in its use of long takes and ambient audio, invokes a contemplative state. However, the film resists conventional drama and emotion through Bresson's approach to acting, camerawork, and narrative.

Bresson chose actors not for their ability but for their appearance—often specifically for austerity in facial expressions, a monotone voice, and lack of artifice.[15] Because emotions are not apparent, the viewer must reflect to search for the characters' motivations.[16] Bresson thwarts the expectation for psychological explanations for actions by emphasizing instead a somewhat mysterious interior spirituality.[17]

The viewer also cannot usually look to camera compositions for clues. Bresson avoids the self-serving beautiful image that draws attention to itself and away from inner drama.[18] However, in the concluding shot of each of his films, Bresson creates an image of stasis—a long lingering final image that makes a spiritual statement—which in *Diary of a Country Priest* is a shadow of a cross.[19]

The film's narrative also opposes the contrived, dramatic events of conventional films.[20] This eliminates the sense of suspense found in many films.[21] The real drama is interior conflict: the fight within oneself.

BIBLE PASSAGE

"But he said to me, 'My grace is sufficient for you, for my power is made perfect in weakness.' Therefore I will boast all the more gladly about my weaknesses, so that Christ's power may rest on me." (2 Corinthians 12:9 NIV)

The famous final words of the film, "all is grace" shows how the priest views grace as the ultimate spiritual state.

DISCUSSION QUESTIONS

1. How would you describe the priest? How does he compare to other screen portrayals of priests?
2. How would you categorize the film's style and pacing? Did you find it effective? Why or why not?
3. What impact does the priest have on the other characters? How does he make a difference?
4. The Countess's daughter Chantal declares she wants to try everything and indulge in sin. What is the priest's reaction, and why does he say what he does?
5. How does the priest's narrative become a version of the Stations of the Cross and his death a crucifixion?

ENLIGHTENMENT GUARANTEED

1999 (Germany)

1 hour 49 minutes

CATEGORIES: Westerner seeking Eastern wisdom

SUMMARY: Gustav (Gustav-Peter Wöhler) is preparing for a retreat to a Zen Buddhist monastery in Japan. After his wife abruptly leaves him, Gustav's brother Uwe (Uwe Ochsenknecht) convinces Gustav to bring him along. After a disorienting experience in the frenetic streets of Tokyo, they arrive at the monastery hoping to find direction, insight, and peace.

Enlightenment Guaranteed does not follow most of the clichés of the Westerner seeking Eastern wisdom film. It is not centered on an idealized spiritual leader as in *Seven Years in Tibet* (1997) and *Kundun* (1997). It does not revolve around reincarnation like *Little Buddha* (1993). And it does not focus on the monastic life as in *Spring, Summer, Winter, Fall and . . . Spring* (2003). Instead, this quirky, low-budget semi-comedy shows drifting Western characters on a pilgrimage to an Eastern monastery.

It also breaks from the trope common in Eastern religion films of a wise monk imparting wisdom to a Westerner. In a few brief scenes, both of the main characters receive private audiences with a monk to discuss their spiritual challenges. However, the film is not centered on a relationship between a seeking Westerner and a charismatic Eastern monk. Consistent with the trope in Westerner seeking Eastern wisdom films, though, it does criticize an emptiness in the secular Western world that leads to an idealization of Eastern spirituality as a possible corrective force.

The first part of the film sketches the limitations of modern Western life. Uwe has the flaw of escapism. He neglects family responsibilities to be left alone. He is also a rationalist who likes to measure household objects. As a kitchen counter salesman, he describes the ideal kitchen as a place to do "aerobics for the soul." Gustav practices a superficial version of spirituality by dabbling in Feng Shui and astrology.

However, Gustav explores Buddhism and meditation, indicating that he is searching for something more substantial.

Set in Tokyo, the second part of the film shows the two main characters starting to lose their Western-shaped identities. After a night in an overpriced restaurant, they cannot find their way back to their hotel. This leaves them disoriented, out of money, and temporarily homeless. They lose what Westerners associate with their security and identity—including the power of money and individual will. As a result, Gustav and Uwe must abandon their individualistic expectations, but their surrender furthers their spiritual progress. Their loss of a feeling of control leads to spiritual knowledge.

The final section of the film defies the convention in Westerner seeking Eastern wisdom films of a Buddhist monastery being a utopian setting. It is not a blissful, painless retreat. The two must wake up at four o'clock in the morning to take a cold shower and perform manual labor by cleaning the monastery. Unlike many Eastern religion–inspired films, *Enlightenment Guaranteed* places more emphasis on spiritual disciplines than teachings. Through these disciplines, the characters experience epiphanies about themselves. The way they perform manual labor reveals character traits they must modify. "It's like I'm trying to move a mountain," Gustav says, regarding his spiritual improvement. "But every day something new becomes clear, and I feel freer."

In this section of the film, prolonged shots of nature surrounding the monastery evoke a sense of peace, along with the utilization of transcendental style filmic elements like ambient sounds. This technique recalls the transcendentalism of the Japanese director Ozu, who made quiet meditative films. The viewer is placed into a contemplative state by shots of nature and household objects. These transcendental style techniques help separate the monastery segment in tone and feeling from the other two parts of the film.

Like *The Apostle* (1997), the film effectively juxtaposes non-professional actors with professional actors, as well as utilizing real locations rather than studio sets. This often gives the movie a more authentic documentary-like style. An additional layer to this realistic approach is the self-reflective monologues the two main characters record to a video camera at critical junctures.

SPIRITUAL TERM

Four Noble Truths—In the first formal discourse after his spiritual awakening, the Buddha revealed key discoveries he called the Four Noble Truths.[1] The First Noble Truth is that life as typically lived is suffering, which Uwe reads in Gustav's book on Buddhism. The other noble truths are that desire is the cause of suffering, that the cure for suffering is overcoming desire, and that practices that promote intentional living overcome ignorance and suffering.[2]

DISCUSSION QUESTIONS:

1. What spiritual qualities do the two men lack at the beginning of the film? What are your most pressing spiritual challenges?
2. What happens to the two brothers in Tokyo that changes them spiritually?
3. What spiritual transformations do the two characters undergo at the monastery? Have you ever been on a spiritual retreat? Or would you like to go on one? Where would you go? Why?
4. How is their stay in the monastery different from what one might expect?
5. What do you make of the ending scene? Where does this leave them on their spiritual journeys?

ENTERTAINING ANGELS: THE DOROTHY DAY STORY

1996

1 hour 50 minutes

CATEGORIES: Religious figure, redemption story

SUMMARY: Dorothy Day (Moira Kelly) works as a journalist writing stories about social injustice during the First World War in New York City. After befriending a nun, Day becomes a Catholic—subsequently ending her relationship with her atheist boyfriend. Under the guidance of French philosopher Peter Maurin (Martin Sheen), she begins a faith-based movement to help the needy.

Social activist Dorothy Day deserves a more comprehensive, sweeping epic film than *Entertaining Angels*. But even with its shortcomings, the movie is an effective portrayal of an important spiritual figure who emphasized the connection between Christianity and helping the needy.

Most of the film treats Day's life beginning at age twenty in 1917 through the 1930s. The film has been justifiably criticized for being limited to this time period, even though Day was active until her death in 1980. The movie has also been disparaged for highlighting the morality of Day's sexuality early in life at the expense of Catholic social teachings.[1]

For whatever reason, the filmmakers chose to feature Day's spiritual awakening during this period of her life. This places *Entertaining Angels* in the spiritual movie categories of search for god and redemption story. The film briefly covers her pacifism, battles with institutions, and accusations that she was a communist. But this isn't in the difficulty living out faith category about a woman clashing with civil and religious authorities. The film does feature some of the tension with power structures characteristic of that subgenre, but it is more of a universal story of someone searching for purpose and meaning.

Day's search for god contains a different definition of God than other films in the category, like the God connected to science in *Contact* or morality in *Crimes and Misdemeanors*. Day associates God with providing direction to help her alleviate injustice. As she commits to the Catholic faith, she discovers both direction and a moral compass, which she determines are missing from her circle of literary friends and colleagues, who have a heightened sense of intellectualism, politics, and aesthetics, but disdain the spiritual worldview.

The movie begins in Greenwich Village, where Day—in her pre-redeemed state—leads what can be called a bohemian lifestyle. However, she is aware of a yearning for deeper meaning that separates her from other characters in redemption stories not conscious of their inadequacies. "I'm restless, I have something to give but I don't know what it is, or who I'm supposed to give it to," she confesses to the writer Eugene O'Neill.

The shift into the second act of the redemption story of conflict between an old and new self occurs after Day meets a nun in Staten Island who feeds the poor. After committing to Catholicism, she struggles externally with her atheist boyfriend, who cannot accept her as a practicing Catholic. She and her daughter's baptism against his wishes symbolizes rebirth and a new way of living.

The third act, which eventually leads to full redemption, begins after Day prays for direction from God. The answer for guidance comes soon after with the appearance of the eccentric spiritual mentor Peter Maurin. However, she doesn't attain true spiritual understanding until her faith and mission are tested by revolts, crimes, and tensions in her houses of hospitality that aid the poor. Although not a Christ figure, she experiences a Garden of Gethsemane moment during a point of despair and shouts to God in an empty church, yelling, "Where are you? Why don't you answer me?"

She obtains a deeper sense of peace and mission after she realizes she feels love and senses the divine within even the most troubled people. She also recognizes that she may not fundamentally change the existing social structures that create or permit suffering. "I don't think that God will judge us on how successful we are at changing the world," Day says. "I do think he will judge us on how faithful we are in serving His poor."

BIBLE PASSAGE

"If a brother or sister is poorly clothed and lacking in daily food, and one of you says to them, 'Go in peace, be warmed and filled,' without giving them the things needed for the body, what good is that?" (James 2:15–16 ESV)

To truly find spiritual meaning, Day must help others with their basic needs and not just write newspaper articles about injustice.

DISCUSSION QUESTIONS

1. What do you make of the bohemian existence that Dorothy Day lives at the beginning of the film? What is a modern equivalent to this lifestyle?
2. Why does Day initially reject Christianity? What turns her around?
3. How does Day meet resistance when she becomes interested in Christianity? Has that ever happened to you?
4. Although Day performs what many believe is a noble act by helping the poor, what are some of her shortcomings?
5. Day says knowing the poor is where she meets God. Where do you most find God?

FRANKENSTEIN

1931

1 hour 10 minutes

CATEGORIES: Cautionary tale

SUMMARY: Obsessed with discovering the secret to creating life, scientist Henry Frankenstein (Colin Clive) assembles parts of dead bodies and succeeds in constructing a living creature. The monster he makes (Boris Karloff) becomes an outcast because of his horrific appearance. The misfit creature retaliates against those who reject and mistreat him.

This cautionary tale depicts a human consumed with attaining god-like knowledge, with clear references to the creation story and the Fall in the Book of Genesis.

Scientist Henry Frankenstein brings a creature to life through the primal source of lightning, recalling the first creation in the Book of Genesis: light.[1] However, the most striking parallel to the Book of Genesis is that Henry Frankenstein, like Adam and Eve, attempts to become more godlike through achieving knowledge.

After excitedly bringing the creature to life, Frankenstein declares, "Now I know what it feels like to be God!" This is a reference to the serpent's promise to Eve that if she eats fruit from the Tree of Knowledge, "you will be like God, knowing good and evil." In both instances, a desire for knowledge and power overshadows morality and submission to the divine, resulting in disastrous consequences.[2]

The cautionary voice comes from Frankenstein's college instructor Professor Waldman, who warns, "Only evil can come of it." The movie highlights the hubris of Frankenstein creating the monster, which in turn makes the monster a victim, the tragic outcome of Frankenstein's quest to know the ways of the divine.

Henry Frankenstein is akin to a neglectful parent. The monster is not educated about the world, which leads to catastrophe when he throws a young girl into the water thinking she can float like a flower. And like an infant, the monster mirrors how he is treated. When treated with violence, he responds likewise.

The monster is not the devious articulate figure with gentleman-like eloquence in Mary Shelley's 1818 novel. The monster, played by Boris Karloff, does not speak and is in some ways more sympathetic. He is not calculating, vengeful, or misleadingly manipulative through speech. Instead, he is like a vulnerable child trying to fit in to a hostile world. He seems almost childlike in his desire for companionship.[3]

However, his childlike physical movements do not elicit sympathy or pity but instead generate terror and anxiety.[4] This concludes with an extended sequence at the end of the film with a lynch mob of angry villagers pursuing him with barking dogs and fiery torches.[5]

The screen adaptation of Mary's Shelley's *Frankenstein* starring Boris Karloff as the monster, is a notable example of the Old Testament-inspired cautionary tale. Scientist Victor Frankenstein creates the monster in an arrogant and vain attempt to play God. Photo courtesy Universal/Everett Collection

The sequel, *Bride of Frankenstein* (1934), carries the lynching motif further by having the monster strung up on a tree with an angry cluster of men surrounding him.[6] Both films reinforce the monster's alienation from the world by positioning him among dark, nightmarish Gothic architecture and shrouding him in cinematography influenced by German expressionist films such as *The Cabinet of Dr. Caligari* (1920) and *Nosferatu* (1922).[7]

In the horror movie genre, monsters represent what the culture fears. In *Frankenstein*, released during the Great Depression, the monster signifies rebellion of the underclass. His dead body parts are like a patchwork of the forgotten. He represents tough times and an "everyman-for-himself" mentality as well as potential destruction.[8] He is a tragic figure who is the victim of his base instincts, which emerge from his societal rejection.[9]

Frankenstein's sin of grasping for godlike knowledge doesn't only lead to his own fall from grace. He both damages his creation and gen-

93

erates societal chaos. In the movie's variation on The Fall, society itself becomes neglectful to the needy, represented by the monster.

Society is also portrayed as chaotic and capable of slipping into a dangerous vigilantism when threatened. The last part of the film attempts to restore societal harmony by re-establishing the legacy of the aristocratic Frankenstein family.[10] Despite this respite, the film's conclusion remains that a scientist's folly of trying to achieve godlike knowledge has unraveled the social order.

BIBLE PASSAGE

"For God knows that when you eat from it your eyes will be opened, and you will be like God, knowing good and evil." (Genesis 3:5 NIV)

This desire to be like God is at the center of Henry Frankenstein's motivation to create the monster.

DISCUSSION QUESTIONS

1. How does the film show that Frankenstein wants to become godlike? Are there figures or specific ideas in contemporary society that show a desire to become godlike? What are they?
2. What is the importance of friendship in the film?
3. Movie monsters express traits of what society fears. What are the deepest fears in contemporary culture? Have they changed?
4. How does the monster's narrative mirror Frankenstein's story? How are he and the monster similar?
5. Why is the monster viewed with such fear and derision? Who do you feel in society is regarded this way? Why?

THE FUGITIVE

1947

1 hour 44 minutes

CATEGORIES: Christ figure, religious figure

SUMMARY: An unnamed man (Henry Fonda) is possibly the last surviving priest in a country that has outlawed religious worship. He arrives at a small village with appreciative and dedicated peasant Christians, but the priest is soon pursued by police who want to execute him.

Like *Rome, Open City* (1945), *Romero* (1989), and Alfred Hitchcock's *I Confess* (1953), John Ford's *The Fugitive* utilizes a priest as a Christ figure. However, the priest in this film is markedly different from its counterparts.

He appears to be aimlessly drifting, more like a wanderer than a self-assured spiritual leader. While he shows courage at times, it is almost always accompanied by a subtext of confusion, as if he were looking for redemption and didn't know how to achieve it. This discomfort, however, defines the character and makes him palatable.[1]

Based on Graham Greene's novel *The Power and the Glory*, the movie excludes the priest's tainted past, which makes him a largely silent character with no background.[2] But being silent does not mean he is blank or vacuous; rather, he generally appears overwhelmed and unsure. He shows a weariness that comes with the obligation of being a chosen one, which in this case is the final priest the government is hunting down.[3]

The movie relies on images rather than dialogue to reflect the priest's inner turmoil. This includes the use of shadows and light and his position in the frame, which sometimes places him in a subordinate position. Only toward the end of the film does the priest verbalize his feelings of inadequacy. "It wasn't courage, it was only pride," he says about remaining the solitary priest under dangerous conditions. The priest's sins include pride, moral arrogance, and separation from the world.[4] He is a missionary in a morally privileged position who is tortured over his shortcomings.[5]

It is only with impending death that the priest appears more at peace. Does he feel he's achieved redemption? Is it because his searching and questioning will soon end? The turning point is likely when Maria Dolores hands him a small cross through prison bars, which seems to make the priest realize that he is irrevocably connected to Jesus through his suffering.

"I want to live my death," he says, refusing brandy to ease his mind before his execution. The priest's acceptance of his martyrdom is a critical moment typical of Ford films, in which characters often define themselves in a moment of a crisis. These critical junctures bring them face-to-face with something larger than themselves and makes them exceptional people.[6]

Another characteristic in the Christ figure film are representations of other characters from the gospels. In some ways, *The Fugitive* is an allegory of a Passion Play.[7] The fallen woman Maria Dolores is a Mary Magdalene-type character. The relentless lieutenant who chases him recalls Pontius Pilate. The traitor who provides information for the police to arrest him is a Judas Iscariot figure. El Gringo, who defends him in dangerous situations, is the equivalent of the penitent thief on the cross.

Also consistent with Christ-figure films is a political structure that oppresses and ultimately kills the Christ-like character. In *The Fugitive*, the oppressive governing force is a totalitarian regime reminiscent of both fascism and communism.

In the Ford canon, *The Fugitive* is distinctive for conveying a great sense of evil, a searching quality in its protagonist, and, ultimately, hope only in God.[8] The film also illustrates how moments of humanity can break through the bleakness of life.[9]

The Fugitive is also consistent with themes Ford explores in many of his films, including *The Grapes of Wrath*, *The Searchers*, and *Three Godfathers*. They often tell the stories of characters who sacrifice for the survival of a group—whether it is a family, a community, the cavalry, or a nation.[10] Ford also consistently shows an affection for the poor, the dispossessed, and the humble.[11] His movies often feature an isolated community facing physical and spiritual dangers, which is shown in *The Fugitive* through the lives of the peasants.[12]

BIBLE PASSAGE

"To this you were called, because Christ suffered for you, leaving you an example, that you should follow in his steps." (1 Peter 2:21 NIV)

The movie suggests that a Christ-like imitation of self-sacrifice and suffering devoid of ego leads to redemption.

DISCUSSION QUESTIONS

1. How would you characterize the priest's spiritual journey?
2. In the film, a totalitarian regime brutally suppresses religion. What is a contemporary parallel?
3. Why do Maria and El Gringo help the priest? Why are the lieutenant and the police informer so willing to work against the priest?
4. Do the lieutenant and police informer feel remorse or regret? Why or why not?
5. How does the film portray the resurrection motif that is an important component of the Christ figure film?

GANDHI

1982

3 hours 11 minutes

CATEGORIES: Religious figure, Westerner seeking Eastern wisdom

SUMMARY: The Indian lawyer Mohandas Gandhi (Ben Kingsley) is removed from a train in segregated South Africa for sitting in a whites-only section. Gandhi then starts a nonviolent movement to end discrimination. He later uses the same tactics to lead India in a campaign for independence from Great Britain, earning him the name Mahatma, meaning "great soul."

Aside from Spike Lee's *Malcolm X*, *Gandhi* is an epic film about a political and spiritual leader that hasn't been duplicated in scope since. In scale, both films recall the Bible-based epics of the 1950s. They follow their protagonists over many years in the battle between their spiritual beliefs and a despotic culture. This mirrors the clash in epic Bible-era films between early Christians and Roman authorities.

Malcolm X's spiritual development occurs in prison through self-education and mentoring from a Black Muslim. Gandhi's true awakening occurs when he takes a pilgrimage across poor, rural areas to "find the real India," as a mentor figure tells him. His spiritual epiphany commands him to identify with the peasants and live as they do in a modest, simple way. This manifests in humility and a work ethic that possesses the Westerner seeking Eastern wisdom film's trope of a guru-like character possessing a spiritual purity free of the corrupting forces of Western industrialization.[1]

However, the film is not a spiritual autobiography. Rather, it is the story of how a determined and shrewd person with a fervent, non-violent ideology ultimately topples British rule. Gandhi's spiritual beliefs largely emerge in conversations or in speeches rather than spiritual practices. After the opening scene, Gandhi's history begins with his activism, which is what defines him more than spiritual self-discipline.[2]

The dominant spiritual belief Gandhi espouses is resisting evil through what he calls "peaceful, nonviolent noncooperation." He believes this will raise the consciousness of both the public as well as of institutional oppressors more effectively than violence or revenge.

"Do you fight to change things or do you fight to punish?" he asks, adding, "I've found we're all such sinners we should leave punishment to God." He directly connects religion to nonviolent resistance. In South Africa, he encourages an audience to vow to God that they won't comply with an unjust law. For Gandhi, spirituality is linked to resistance rather than acquiescence to sinful institutional power.

Gandhi also emphasizes the connection between religions. He tells a reporter that he remembers being younger and hearing someone read back and forth between the Hindu *Bhagavad Gita* and the Muslim *Koran*, as if to say both texts were part of worshipping God. His biggest spiritual trial is not resisting the British but when Hindus and Muslims clash, which challenges his strong belief that people of different faiths can unite.

The movie stops short of making Gandhi a Christ figure, although he takes on the messianic characteristic of representing the oppressed. This occurs when he makes salt in defiance of the country's salt laws—an act akin to a supernatural miracle. It recalls Christ turning water into wine, Moses leading the Israelites to freedom, and the Hindu god Rama marching.[3]

In keeping with the generalizations of the Eastern religion–influenced film, Gandhi is sometimes oversimplified as a variation of an Eastern guru figure that flawed, materialistic, and ambitious Westerners idealize. This is particularly shown through Gandhi's relationship with two Western professionals: the *New York Times* journalist Vince Walker and photographer Margaret Bourke-White.

They are so enamored with Gandhi that they give up their professional distance and consider him someone to learn from. This adulation of Gandhi also occurs in a news story that asserts Ghandi "made humility and simple truth more powerful than empires" and describes him as "the spokesman for the conscience of all mankind."

BIBLE PASSAGE

"I tell you, do not resist an evil person. If anyone slaps you on the right cheek, turn to them the other cheek also." (Matthew 5:39 NIV)

Gandhi tells a Christian pastor that following this idea means one must have courage to not strike back or be turned aside. When that happens, "Something in human nature makes his hatred for you decrease and his respect for you increase," he says.

DISCUSSION QUESTIONS

1. Why was Gandhi's nonviolent resistance so effective?
2. How could nonviolent resistance happen in contemporary society? Do you feel this idea is spiritually based? Why or why not?
3. What does Gandhi see on his initial trip through India that changes him? Have you been on a similar pilgrimage or would you like to go on one? Where?

4. What gives Gandhi courage to lead his campaign? On a smaller scale, when have you had to lead a fight against injustice? If you haven't, would you like to?

5. Despite all the demands on him, how does Gandhi live a simple life? What are ways you can live a simpler life?

GLADIATOR

2000

2 hours 35 minutes

CATEGORIES: RELIGIOUS/BIBLE EPIC (VARIATION)

SUMMARY: The aging emperor Marcus Aurelius (Richard Harris) wants the war hero Maximus (Russell Crowe) to succeed him as ruler of Rome. However, Aurelius's son Commodus (Joaquin Phoenix) murders the emperor to usurp the throne. Maximus's family is killed and he is sold into slavery and forced to be a gladiator.

Gladiator does not depict a clash between pagan Roman authorities and Christian believers set during the time of Christ or directly afterward, as many historical Roman films do. Instead, it takes place beginning in 180 CE at the end of Stoic philosopher king Marcus Aurelius's reign.

Stoicism emphasizes logic, virtue, and self-control embodied in the film's heroic general and gladiator Maximus. He tells both his troops and gladiators to live by the code "strength and honor."

However, Maximus goes beyond stoicism to a belief in the transcendental. "What we do in life echoes in eternity," he says. He believes in an afterlife determined by how one has lived, separating him from stoics who do not believe in an afterlife. Maximus believes he will enter Elysium, where the righteous go after death.[1] This contrasts with Marcus Aurelius, who says that when a man sees his end he wants to know there was some purpose to his life." Aurelius fixates on his legacy on earth, while Maximus focuses on the afterlife. Maximus's emphasis on the afterlife is the foundation of the film in much the same way The Force is the center of the *Star Wars* movies. Because of the emphasis on the afterlife, prayer, and justice, the film's spirituality transcends Roman creeds and makes it relevant to viewers of contemporary faiths.

Although the film is set in ancient times, it expresses contemporary societal spiritual problems. One of these problems is a longing for something more meaningful than one's work. Maximus is an acclaimed and effective military general, but he finds deeper meaning in his family. Whether it's his duty as a general or a gladiator's survivalism, these are limited or unsatisfactory identities. The desire Maximus feels for home shows a contemporary cultural yearning for a modest life removed from workplace demands.

For Maximus, family life is salvation. The figurines he carries of his wife and child make for a family shrine wherever he goes, and his ultimate goal is the otherworldly restoration of his family.[2] He has a longing for home and family that is more important to him than power.[3] His prayer to the figurines also shows that his spirituality is private, connected to family, and not linked to the worship of Roman deities.[4] This reflects contemporary trends that eschew institutional religion in favor of a more personalized spirituality.[5]

The film's fights to the death in arenas reflect another contemporary anxiety: increasingly violent and escapist entertainment. Rather than war or slavery, the entertainment business is the most oppressive force (aside from the emperor) in *Gladiator*. Maximus's mocking shout, "Are you not entertained?" during one performance shows a defiance that the oblivious arena audience doesn't comprehend.

The movie also juxtaposes two versions of masculinity, reflecting another current cultural anxiety about the loss of heroic masculine values. Commodus is effeminate, morally corrupt, vain, overly emotional, and vicious.[6] He has an incestuous desire for his sister and has questionable intentions toward his nephew.[7] Maximus is a disciplined warrior aligned with those who will restore Rome from an Empire to a Republic.[8] He reveres a more traditional sense of family.

After a devastating reversal of fortune in *Gladiator*, Maximus (Russell Crowe) descends into a brutal life killing others in ancient Rome. However, Maximus ultimately adheres to a spirituality centered on a firm belief in the afterlife. Photo courtesy DreamWorks/Everett Collection

From the beginning of the film, shots of Maximus's hand touching wheat and rubbing dirt into his hand before he fights cast him as a man of the earth.[9] This is juxtaposed with the urban lifestyle of Commodus. To overthrow the inferior masculine figure and restore moral order, Maximus executes redemptive violence against Commodus.

Although Maximus is portrayed as heroic, he still needs to undergo spiritual crisis to grow. "Imagine where you will be and it will be so," he optimistically states at the beginning of the film, believing he will reunite with his family in a few weeks. Instead, he descends into a brutal underworld of arena entertainment that alters him. "That man is gone," he says when reminded of his past nobler self. But after a spiritual realization, Maximus shifts to a plan for widespread justice beyond revenge.

BIBLE PASSAGE

"For this world is not our permanent home; we are looking forward to a home yet to come." (Hebrews 13:14 NLT)

Maximus's ultimate goal is to be with his family in eternity, making *Gladiator* a rare film focused on the afterlife.

DISCUSSION QUESTIONS

1. What is the film's view of the afterlife? How does it match your view?
2. How is Roman society depicted? Are there parallels to contemporary society?
3. What are the connections between Maximus's spiritual beliefs and other religions, particularly Christianity?
4. What are some of the spiritual differences between Maximus and Commodus?
5. What does the Juba's gesture at the end of the film symbolize?

THE GOSPEL ACCORDING TO ST. MATTHEW

1964

2 hours 17 minutes

CATEGORIES: Bible epic (Gospel film)

SUMMARY: Mary and Joseph flee with the infant Jesus from Bethlehem to Egypt after King Herod orders the killing of newborn male children. As an adult in Judea years later, Jesus heals, teaches, and performs miracles. After his disciple Judas Iscariot betrays him to authorities, Jesus is arrested, tried, and crucified.

For decades, the standard for gospel movies was *King of Kings* (1927), reissued in the sound era with synchronized sound effects and music. Filmmakers could not out-DeMille director Cecil B. DeMille, who combined spectacle, dramatically composed scenes, and a reverential portrayal of Jesus. Nicholas Ray tried in *King of Kings* (1961), as did George Stevens in *The Greatest Story Ever Told* (1965), but these gospel-based films could not significantly expand on DeMille's presentation of the gospel.

So how could the gospel movie genre go forward? In a direction that was the opposite of DeMille's epic style—a direction that came not from Hollywood, but from a neorealist Italian filmmaker.

Director Pier Pasolini avoids gospel film conventions. Although there are some rearranging and omissions, Pasolini does not insert non-Biblical dialogue or scenes. Adding subplots, expanding characters, and injecting romance and sex was a convention in Bible epics to make the stories historical dramas that appealed to the non-religious. Pasolini's gospel film is not a historical reconstruction or an intellectual interpretation but is based on the gospel itself.[1]

Consistent with many neorealist films, the actors are non-professionals. And rather than the somewhat passive Jesus of the epic gospel film, Pasolini's screen Jesus is young, angry, and energetic. *The Gospel According to St. Matthew* presents Jesus as much more emotionally expressive than films that preceded it.[2] Although his anger makes him somewhat detached and distant, it brings a vitality to Jesus.[3]

Pasolini shot *St. Matthew* in impoverished Southern Italy, severing the gospel film from big budget Hollywood sets and locations. The innovative use of music—everything from Odetta's "Sometimes I Feel Like a Motherless Child" to Bach and Mozart—breaks from the dramatic orchestral music associated with gospel epics. This expanded the use of music in gospel films and led the way for films such as *Jesus Christ Superstar* (1973).

The Gospel According to St. Matthew also changes the practice in gospel movies of merging the gospels together in a process known as "harmonizing." Almost like a greatest hits of the gospels, most gospel films pull from each of the four gospels. Pasolini discards this tactic by adhering solely to Matthew's gospel. He considered Matthew the most revolutionary of the four, regarding Mark as too crude, John too mystical, and Luke too sentimental.[4]

The result of adhering to the narrative of one gospel is a pastiche of episodes, not a cinematic biography.[5] This is strengthened by the film's neorealist film style, which at times becomes approaches a documentary mode. For instance, Pasolini used shots of peasants to avoid centering the film's imagery around the figure of Jesus. Pasolini shows portraits of faces, whether alone or in groups, and moves the camera over the group to record their actions.[6] This has the effect of connecting the peasants to Jesus, which puts Jesus squarely in the midst of his fellow strugglers.[7]

Jesus is often shot head on.[8] This visually symbolizes the power and decisiveness of an intense and rugged Jesus with so much energy he doesn't seem to need a home or even a resting place.[9] He rarely speaks but shouts.[10] With so much to say, he is portrayed primarily as a teacher.[11] At the time of the film's release, Jesus was becoming an icon of 1960s counterculture, and the righteous anger it infuses him with appealed to a culture becoming more radicalized.[12]

However, this is not just a film for the religious left. It appeals to conservatives by using solely Biblical material. The appeal to both the religious left and religious right is likely why it remains the most critically praised gospel film to date.

BIBLE PASSAGE

"Do not suppose that I have come to bring peace to the earth? I did not come to bring peace, but a sword." (Matthew 10:34 NIV)

This passage embodies the angry and somewhat revolutionary tone this screen Jesus possesses.

DISCUSSION QUESTION:

1. What do you think of non-professional actors playing major roles? Does it match in some way how you imagine the Biblical figures? Why or why not?
2. One of the film's techniques is using shots of the peasants to avoid centering the entire film on Jesus. What effect did this have on you while watching the film?
3. How does the movie show that Jesus lived and ministered in the real world? How is that different from other media presentations of Jesus?

4. What did you think of the anger Jesus expresses? How can anger be spiritually appropriate?
5. What influence do you think this movie had on other screen presentations of Jesus or how Jesus is viewed in popular culture?

GRAN TORINO

2008

1 hour 56 minutes

CATEGORIES: Christ figure, redemption story

SUMMARY: Korean War veteran Walt Kowalski (Clint Eastwood) is estranged from his family and community. He is initially antagonistic toward his new Hmong neighbors, including Thao (Bee Ving) and Sue (Ahney Her). But after he gets to know them better, he grows increasingly concerned about their future.

Director Clint Eastwood frequently depicts characters searching for salvation in a post–American Dream culture. The aging Walt Kowalski is one of his most realized visions of that struggle.

Like other movies in the spiritual movie's redemption genre, the protagonist proceeds through three stages: flawed pre-redemption state, battle between old self and emerging new self, and redemption after the formation of a new self.

In his pre-redemption condition, Kowalski is alienated from American institutions and community structures that are intended to provide a sense of meaning, purpose, and identity. One of those primary structures is family. Instead of his two sons and their families viewing him as someone with knowledge, they see him as a problem and someone to get something from, including his prized 1972 Gran Torino.[1]

Kowalski feels ostracized from his community as houses become more dilapidated and crime more pervasive. Because he is retired, he has no workplace identity. And the church doesn't provide consolation because a young priest cannot connect with him. The film portrays issues that accompany aging, such as widowhood, isolation, failing health, and the meaning of work and retirement.[2] It defies stereotypes of the old as grandparents enjoying a worry-free retirement or as physically helpless victims.[3]

Kowalski exhibits a loner lifestyle and uses sarcastic, cynical humor to distance himself from others, just as pre-redemption characters do in *Groundhog Day* and *About a Boy*. Kowalski distances himself from others by uttering ethnic and racist slurs. Similar to other redemption stories, though, Kowalski is filled with a sense of self-loathing, confessing at one point, "I'm not a good man."

The film is more complex than many redemption stories because Kowalski is not the sole cause of his unredeemed state. He is a victim of a failing culture. Some of his Christ-figure quality comes from the suffering inflicted on him by war, marginalization because of his age, and a consumerist culture. Kowalski's appreciation of old cars, home ownership and upkeep, and fixing things is an anti-consumerist message fitting with a gospel call to stewardship.[4] In many ways, the Gran Torino is a metaphorical representation of his character, signifying a different time and generation.[5]

In the middle phase of his redemption story, he discovers his spiritual nature by forming a surrogate family. He helps Thao become a man by giving him confidence through the work he performs for Kowalski.[6] Kowalski overcomes his racist stereotypes by enjoying Asian food and culture, which opens him up to sentiments associated with family, including genuine feelings, authentic relationships, and mutual giving.[7] Seeing the Hmong man's commitment to family honor and tradition changes Kowalski's perceptions of him, and Kowalski sees that family is less about blood relations and more about relationships.[8]

All redemption stories have a turning point, which, in *Gran Torino*, is simultaneously the moment when the protagonist's Christlike traits clearly emerge. After a drive-by shooting and a rape, Kowalski punches his glassed kitchen cabinets in frustration and agony. The blood dripping from his wounded hands resembles the stigmata and indicates his desire not for violence but self-sacrifice.[9] The Christ-figure pattern of the Garden of Gethsemane moment then comes as Kowalski sits alone in the dark of his house planning his redemption.

His redemption involves a willing sacrifice and a free decision. He is aware of the consequences and prepares for them by taking care of his affairs, making a confession to a priest, and partaking in a few small pleasures.[10] The movie subverts the expectation that Kowalski will enact redemptive violence to remove the threat of evil. Instead of vengeance or retaliation, he performs a self-sacrifice so no further blood will be shed.[11] His declaration, "I finish things; that's what I do," recalls Christ saying, "It is finished" (John 19:30) before he dies on the cross.

BIBLE PASSAGE

"For whoever does the will of my Father in heaven is my brother and sister and mother." (Matthew 12:50 NIV)

Forming a surrogate family rather than a biological family is something Kowalski does with his neighbors.

DISCUSSION QUESTIONS

1. Why is Kowalski so alienated from his culture and community? When have you ever felt that way?
2. Why does Kowalski hold racist prejudices against his Hmong neighbors and others? How does he overcome them?
3. Why does Kowalski feel the priest is so inadequate? Is this his shortcoming or the priest's? Why?
4. How does the mentoring relationship in the movie change both the mentor and the person being mentored?
5. How does this film follow the death and resurrection motif in the Christ figure film?

GRAND CANYON

1991

2 hours 14 minutes

CATEGORIES: Search for God

SUMMARY: The lives of six people in Los Angeles intertwine as they attempt to overcome social, economic, and racial divides. At the center of the film is a friendship that develops between immigration lawyer Mack (Kevin Kline) and tow truck driver Simon (Danny Glover) after Simon rescues Mack from an assault and robbery. In a city overrun with violence and inequality, the characters search for spiritual and moral meaning.

Grand Canyon is an example of the multiple-character movie that accelerated in the decades after the film's release. These unconventional narratives are the product of a fragmenting postmodernist condition that revolts against master narratives and reflects the increasing popularity of short form media on the Internet.[1] Instead of featuring one main protagonist, *Grand Canyon* uses an ensemble plot featuring multiple protagonists within one geographical area.[2]

Some multiple-character films are spiritual films because they show how seemingly unrelated lives are connected by providence disguised as chance. In other words, God may be at work within what some call coincidence. Within these magical coincidences, lives are mysteriously shaped.[3] *Grand Canyon* engages with these themes and thus falls within the Search for God category of spiritual films. The characters search for God and meaning through reflecting on and exploring those connections and coincidences.

The influence of film noir on *Grand Canyon* is also apparent in the proliferation of urban danger and violence in its depiction of Los Angeles. In traditional film noir, the private detective is a rugged seeker of truth in a world of corruption, wealth, and power.[4] *Grand Canyon*, on the other hand, reflects neo noir and Robert Altman's Los Angeles ensemble films that explore corruption and chaos beneath the sunny California façade.[5] This chaos comes from social, economic, and cultural disorder resulting from class divisions and racial prejudice.[6] Director Lawrence Kasdan conveys a sense of alienation through the Los Angeles highways and city streets. The characters spend much of their time in the protective shell of a car, blocking them from contact with others.[7]

Although *Grand Canyon* depicts the collapse of civic life in America, it is also about a few people who refuse to accept moral and spiritual decay as the norm.[8] The movie shows that the primary way to defeat alienation and injustice is by making connections through altruistic acts, which facilitates the emergence of meaning and spirituality.

Mack's wife Claire believes her discovery of an abandoned baby might be a possible miracle. Mack also believes the supernatural may be contained in these coincidences. When Mack recalls being saved from being hit by a bus by a mysterious woman, he wonders if she was an angelic or supernatural being.

Claire and Mack are transformed because of these experiences. However, the movie producer Davis (Steve Martin) does not ultimately change even after undergoing what he calls a "religious experience." While recovering from being shot by a thief, Davis pledges to stop making violent films and instead produce films about the "life force, the creation of life, the very instinct for living." In the end, he dismisses that as irrational, seemingly believing violence cannot be overcome through spirituality. In the last shot the viewer sees of him, he is engulfed in the darkness beyond a huge door leading to a soundstage, retreating into the illusory realm of filmmaking.

For other characters, the cavernous Grand Canyon becomes a symbol for spiritual meaning. Simon believes it is a sublime place of transcendence that instills how insignificant human problems are when one becomes aware of time and space.[9] The ending shot of the film, like the final shot of Jean Renoir's *The River* (1951), shows the canyon as a metaphor for something timeless and eternal beyond human struggles.

BIBLE PASSAGE

"Why, you do not even know what will happen tomorrow. What is your life? You are a mist that appears for a little while and then vanishes." (James 4:14 NIV)

The imagery of the massive and ancient Grand Canyon makes the characters aware of time and their place in the world.

DISCUSSION QUESTIONS

1. What social problems are depicted in Los Angeles? If you were making a movie about the city or place where you live, what would be the social problems most important to depict?
2. What other movies contain multiple plotlines that intersect? How is this an effective way to convey spiritual themes?
3. Do you believe the ways the characters meet are coincidences or acts of providence? Have there been any examples in your life of coincidences containing an underlying spiritual meaning?
4. Why do the characters say violence is so prevalent? How do you cope with the prevalence of violence in the culture?
5. How do the five main characters (Simon, Mack, Claire, Davis, and Dee) spiritually transform or remain the same?

GROUNDHOG DAY

1993

1 hour 41 minutes

CATEGORIES: Redemption story

SUMMARY: Weather forecaster Phil Connor (Bill Murray) covers Groundhog Day festivities in a small Pennsylvania town. He loathes the assignment and rushes to leave as soon as possible. But after being snowed in and forced to stay, he awakens each day to discover that he is reliving Groundhog Day again.

Because there is no explanation for Phil repeatedly re-experiencing the same day, *Groundhog Day* has generated several theological interpretations.

Some view it as a Westerner seeking Eastern wisdom film. Although reincarnated in the same body and not different ones, Phil is trapped in a cycle of rebirth. Only by performing altruistic deeds and accumulating enough good karma can he escape endless rebirth and move on to a higher plane (represented by a new day). A Catholic interpretation is that Phil is stuck in purgatory, where he must be purified. A Jewish interpretation is that Phil performs mitzvahs (good deeds) to improve life in this world.[1]

Within the spiritual movie genre, *Groundhog Day* is most convincingly a redemption story. That genre aligns with the Christian theology of progressing from a sinful flawed state to redemption.

Phil's initial flaws stem from his self-centered nature. He is cynical, hedonistic, career-obsessed and a loner not interested in other people. Initially, Phil lives in a condition of malaise.[2] He is bored and restless, which manifests in him maintaining a sarcastic distance from the world.

After Phil starts reliving the same day, he proceeds through five states before the beginning of his redemption: confusion/disorientation; anger; a false sense of freedom because of a perceived lack of consequences; manipulation to attain pleasure (his attempts to seduce Rita); depression; and suicide.

Like many other protagonists in the spiritual redemption story, a significant change occurs after the lowest point. After Phil's series of suicides, he tells Rita the truth about what he is experiencing and ceases trying to manipulate her. She responds favorably to his sincerity. Then she makes an important observation about reliving the same day. "Maybe it's not a curse, it just depends on how you look at it," she says. This suggestion is a catalyst for Phil's transformation.

Phil's redemption then unfolds with three major actions: performing good deeds; becoming a creative/aesthetic individual; redefining his relationships with others, particularly Rita.

The good deeds range from saving lives to bringing coffee for his co-workers. Phil develops a sense of creativity to counteract the ambi-

Television weather forecaster Phil Connors (Bill Murray) In *Groundhog Day* painfully and gradually redeems himself. Because it isn't specified what causes the film's loop of repeating days, the film often leads to both Eastern and Western religious interpretations. Photo courtesy Columbia Pictures/Everett Collection

tion associated with his career identity. He learns how to play the piano, reads literature, and makes ice sculptures. He helps other people and changes his relationship with Rita.

With Rita, Phil shifts from eros love—seductive love driven by the desire to achieve pleasure by controlling others—to agape love, genuinely caring love.[3] He stops being driven by self-love, gives up using people to his personal advantage, and becomes a benefit to others.[4] By the end of the film, he says to Rita, "Is there anything I can do for you today?" This sums up what his spiritual progress.

Phil's transformation occurs in a small town, a terrain with a spiritual mythology in American film. The calm façade of small-town life often conceals an invisible presence or God.[5] People live humble lives, which alters the hedonism and ego of outsider protagonists like Phil Connor.

Like George Bailey in *It's a Wonderful Life*, Phil initially views small-town life as limiting but later realizes its deeper meaning and purpose. Part of his redemption derives from improving the lives of the residents he once disdained as "hicks." As a result, he is no longer a hostage of the town but a creator of it.[6]

BIBLE PASSAGE

"Yet when I surveyed all that my hands had done and what I had toiled to achieve, everything was meaningless, a chasing after the wind; nothing was gained under the sun." (Ecclesiastes 2:11 NIV)

Like the writer of Ecclesiastes, Phil Connor pursues pleasure, money, and wisdom to manipulate others, but remains dissatisfied. He must exhaust himself by chasing these worldly pursuits before he can redeem himself.

DISCUSSION QUESTIONS

1. "You'll never love anyone but yourself," Rita tells Phil. "I don't even like myself," Phil replies. What does Phil's statement say about the pursuit of pleasure?
2. What is Rita's role in Phil's redemption?
3. How is the freedom from consequences actually not freedom?
4. Why is pleasure ultimately ungratifying? When was a time you've experienced this insight?
5. What is a parallel between your life and the repetition of Groundhog Day in the movie? How are we all in some ways living a Groundhog Day kind of life?

HACKSAW RIDGE

2016

2 hours 19 minutes

CATEGORIES: Difficulty living out faith

SUMMARY: Seventh-Day Adventist Desmond Doss (Andrew Garfield) signs up to serve in the Second World War as a combat medic. However, once enlisted, he refuses to fire a rifle because of his religious beliefs. After a failed attempt to court-martial him, he rescues many soldiers during intense warfare at Hacksaw Ridge in Japan.

Generally, movies venerate nonviolence and pacifism but ultimately show these strategies as unrealistic. This reflects shows the prevalent cultural perception that pacifism is a noble but impossible ideal.[1]

This duality is present in films featuring non-violent Christian denominations such as the Amish or Quakers. Their pacifism is represented as a virtuous spiritual model. When war or violent confrontations arise, though, nonviolence is portrayed as an unreasonable response.

A notable example of this is the 1941 film *Sergeant York*. The pacifist Alvin York, played by Gary Cooper, objects to shooting his gun after being drafted to serve in the First World War. After reading a United States history book a military officer gives him, York picks up his rifle and shows no hesitation in shooting the enemy. The message? Violence in the name of nationalism is more important than religious conviction.

Hacksaw Ridge is groundbreaking for transcending such clichés about the impracticality of pacifism and the subordination of religious conviction to nationalism. The movie integrates acceptance of pacifism into the last place it might be expected: the military during wartime.

Most of the film is about the clash between the military and Doss's pacifism. Less time is devoted to his spiritual formation, which is shown to be largely shaped by family dynamics rather than his religious convictions as a Seventh-day Adventist. He is impacted by his pacifist mother and a father damaged by his service in the First World War.

However, the main influence on Doss's commitment to non-violence is a realization about his own potential for violence. While defending his mother against an attack from his father, he points a gun at him. Although he does not shoot, he is disturbed that he killed him "in my heart," as he later tells another soldier.

The movie avoids lengthy philosophical or spiritual discussions about Doss's pacifism. Doss is not an evangelist about it. He calls himself a conscientious cooperator, not a conscientious objector. The film thus gains commercial appeal by employing a prominent trope in secular American popular culture: holding to one's convictions no matter what the opposition. "I don't know how I'm going to live with myself if I

In *Hacksaw Ridge*, Desmond Doss (Andrew Garfield) shows the difficulty of living out faith in an antagonistic secular culture. But his religious-based pacifism ultimately earns him respect. Photo courtesy Lionsgate/Everett Collection

don't stay true to what I believe," he says at a key point. The line could appear in many non-spiritual movies about following one's principles.

Nonetheless, *Hacksaw Ridge* is an important entry in the "difficulty living out one's faith" category of spiritual movies. It shows how the cost of faith can be rejection, isolation, and even physical attacks. It is also innovative for bringing up the harmful stereotypes about pacifism, which Doss effectively counteracts. When Doss mentions the commandment to not kill, he is told that it only refers to murder and that killing does not have the same meaning in war. The Second World War is even reframed as a kind of Holy War. "This is Satan himself we're fighting," an army officer says. The other soldiers dismiss Doss and pacifists more generally as cowardly, overly cerebral, unpatriotic, and uncaring.

Doss overcomes these misperceptions during the extensive battle sequences. The soldiers expand their definition of courage and strength to see it can come through nonviolent actions too, and they grow to respect his spirituality. "Most of these men don't believe the same way you do, but they believe so much in how much you believe," his captain tells him.

BIBLE PASSAGE

"Greater love has no one than this: to lay down one's life for one's friends." (John 15:13 NIV)

The soldiers in combat discover that Desmond Doss is willing to risk his life as much as those who carry weapons.

DISCUSSION QUESTIONS

1. What in Doss's background informs his views on nonviolence? What in your background shaped your views on violence?
2. What do you think makes Doss able to stand up for his beliefs despite being ridiculed and harassed about them?
3. How does Doss ultimately win over those who were once opposed to him? What has been a time in your life when you've had to win over people dismissive of your beliefs?
4. What does the ending of the film symbolize in religious imagery? Why do you think the film ends that way?
5. What role do you think pacifism and nonviolence have in the church or in society? Is it just an ideal or can it be lived out? Why?

HARRY POTTER

Series of eight films 2001–2011

CATEGORIES: Hero's journey, Christ figure

SUMMARY: The orphan Harry Potter (Daniel Radcliffe) leaves his oppressive relatives to attend Hogwarts School for Witchcraft and Wizardry. Harry makes two important friends, Ron Weasley (Rupert Grint) and Hermione Granger (Emma Watson), and acquires several influential mentors—including the school's headmaster Albus Dumbledore (Richard Harris/Michael Gambon)—who help Harry in an ongoing battle against evil forces commanded by the sinister Voldemort.

The *Harry Potter* series can be approached in two ways. One is to view *Harry Potter and The Sorcerer's Stone* as a standalone film demonstrating the hero's journey with Harry Potter as a Christ figure. The other is to examine the entire series, where the Christ figure theme deepens and culminates in *Harry Potter and the Deathly Hallows Part 2* with a Passion, death, and resurrection.

Initially, the books and movies were controversial in some Christian circles because of their use of magic, which some claimed promoted witchcraft. But, as John Granger clarifies, the magic is consistent with magic in English fantasy literature, which is incantational, showing a transcendental reality beyond the physical world,[1] as opposed to invocational magic, which calls on demonic principalities for personal power and advantage.[2]

The other significant objection to the stories was that the magic did not occur entirely in another realm, as in C.S. Lewis's *Narnia* books or Tolkien's *Lord of the Rings*.[3] However, the mixture of realism and the supernatural is perhaps why the series was so successful. The movies are both romance and realism, both coming-of-age stories and Gothic-like supernatural stories.

This combination makes the Harry Potter films an example of magic realism, a hybrid of the real and the fantastic.[4] Magic realism disrupts the conventional world of cause and effect and allows characters, for example, to abruptly jump from one location to another using Platform Nine and Three Quarters, the portal to the Hogwarts Express.[5] Most of the films take place at Hogwarts School of Witchcraft and Wizardry, a transitional space situated between childhood and adulthood, between earthbound and magical worlds.[6]

Like Neo in *The Matrix* and Katniss in *The Hunger Games*, Harry is designated as a messianic figure and is called The Chosen One. He is a Christ figure whose most significant trait is ultimately a readiness for self-sacrifice. And like Katniss in *The Hunger Games*, other characters sacrifice themselves for the Christ figure. Both films series emphasize self-sacrifice as the highest form of love. In the Harry Potter films, his mother protects him from death and several others also give

The *Harry Potter* film series utilizes the Hero's Journey and at times portrays Potter (Daniel Radcliffe) as a Christ figure. The movies feature an epic battle between good and evil that emphasizes the spiritual qualities of friendship. Photo courtesy Warner Bros./Everett Collection

their lives for him. Harry and his friends Ron and Hermione all sacrifice in small and large ways for each other. Self-sacrifice is not just a noble thing to do but the Christian thing to do because it reflects the selfless love of God.[7]

This ethics of self-sacrifice is at its most powerful when battling Voldemort, the primary force of evil in the films, and it accelerates after Voldemort's dramatic resurgence at the end of the fourth film, *Harry Potter and the Goblet of Fire*. Voldemort's evil propels the final four films, separating the film series into two halves.

Voldemort begins in *Sorcerer's Stone* as a Nietzsche-like figure, saying, "There is no good and evil; there is only power and those too weak to seek it." But he develops into a more disturbing movie villain because he exhibits a profoundly disturbing evil that can transform and possess others. This concludes in the discovery in later films of Horcruxes—objects where Voldemort conceals parts of his soul. By displacing his life force into these magical objects, Voldemort mutilates his spiritual self and commits both self-violence and violence toward others.[8]

The series consistently demonstrates how friendship combats evil. Friendship also replaces romance, the conventional primary focus in young adult novels and movies. Even the absence of friendship can be a sign of evil. "You'll never know love or friendship, and I feel sorry for you," Harry says to Voldemort in *Harry Potter and the Order of the Phoenix.*

BIBLE PASSAGE

"We know love by this, that he laid down his life for us—and we ought to lay down our lives for one another." (1 John 3:16 NRSV)

Harry and his friends at times articulate the ultimate idea of self-sacrifice: giving up one's own life for another.

DISCUSSION QUESTIONS:

1. How is friendship such a spiritual force in the film(s)? What friends have been the most spiritually influential to you?
2. What mentors does Harry have? How are they effective? Who have been the most valuable mentors in your life?
3. What qualities does Voldemort have that make him such an evil character?
4. How does Harry confront the potential for evil in himself? How do you resolve this feeling in yourself?
5. What examples of self-sacrifice stand out to you the most in the film(s)?

THE HUNGER GAMES

Series of four films 2012–2015

CATEGORIES: Apocalyptic, Christ figure

SUMMARY: The country of Panem is divided into districts run by an authoritarian government. Each year, a lottery is held to put young people in a televised death match called the Hunger Games. After her sister is selected, Katniss (Jennifer Lawrence) volunteers to take her place and later joins a rebellion against Panem's tyrannical ruler President Snow (Donald Sutherland).

The Hunger Games begins as a postapocalyptic film in dystopian North America and shifts to an apocalyptic film after rebellion escalates. Like other dystopias, the futuristic conditions represent contemporary social problems such as political corruption, social class divisions, and the tyranny of the media.

The film also bears traits of the young adult novel, which draws from several literary genres, including the coming-of-age and romance genres.[1] However, *The Hunger Games* is unconventional because the romance central to young adult texts is largely subordinated to its moral, social, and political content.[2]

What places *The Hunger Games* in the spiritual film category and sets it apart from young adult novel adaptations and non-spiritual apocalyptic films is the messianic and Christ figure characteristics of the main character Katniss Everdeen. Like Neo in *The Matrix*, Katniss is initially a reluctant messiah. Unlike Neo, who needs to be indoctrinated in wisdom first, Katniss embodies messianic qualities from the outset, although she does not think that her morality, ethics, and motivations are anything special. And like the *Harry Potter* series, the highest value is self-sacrifice.

This distinguishing characteristic of the Christ figure condition occurs early in the first film when Katniss volunteers to take her sister's place in the Hunger Games. Katniss is marginalized as being from an outlying district just as Jesus was dismissed with "nothing good can come out of

The Hunger Games features a messianic Christ figure Katniss Everdeen (Jennifer Lawrence) in both apocalyptic and post-apocalyptic settings. The film series also shows how political solutions can't solve the problems of baser human tendencies. Photo courtesy Lionsgate/Everett Collection

Nazareth." Katniss responds most to the vulnerable and suffering. As a Christ figure, she is threatening because she provides hope. "Fear does not work when there is hope," the tyrannical President Snow laments.

In *Catching Fire*, she sees other characters participating in the games sacrifice themselves for her. After Peeta says he would, if necessary, die instead of Katniss because she has her family to care for, her feelings grow stronger for him, effectively ending her passion for her hometown boyfriend Gale. Katniss's deepest love is not romantic. Rather, her definition of love derives from her desire to protect others and manifests itself in caring for suffering characters such as Rue, Prim, and Peeta.

Perhaps the most striking symbolism of Katniss as Christ figure is near the end of *Catching Fire*. She shoots an arrow at a force field in the heavens, separating the Hunger Games arena from the outside world. Lying on the ground in what appears to be peaceful contentment, a light in the heavens is revealed to be an aircraft that raises her up. She is lifted up with arms outstretched in a cruciform posture in Christ-like ascension.

What the film series does afterward is show how the political sphere cannot implement the morality of this Christ figure. The subsequent resurrection and ascension of the Christ figure does not transform or liberate the world. Instead, Katniss is called the Mockingjay and is exploited for the gain of the rebel leaders. Either a political system tries to destroy her as President Snow desires, or it co-opts her for political gain as the rebels do.

The series is filled with names, allusions, and imagery that recall Roman films in the spiritual movie genre. In this variation, the Panem rulers are the Romans, and the Hunger Games participants the Christians. However, Snow is not a leader like the stereotypical neurotic, psychotic, or infantile screen emperor. Instead, he is a calculating satanic figure. "He corrupts everyone and everything," Katniss says about him. When Peeta is held captive, he is altered as if possessed by a demonic force.

BIBLE PASSAGE

"In humility value others above yourselves, not looking to your own interests but each of you to the interests of the others." (Philippians 2:3–4 NIV)

Living for the interest of others rather than self-interest is a subversive idea to the power structure in *The Hunger Games*.

DISCUSSION QUESTIONS

1. What characteristics of a Christ figure does Katniss have?
2. Why is self-sacrifice so central to the film? How important is that concept in small and large ways in your own life?
3. Why is the political sphere unable to integrate Katniss's morality? How does the current political climate allow for spiritual principles to be enacted?
4. Why is the public so interested in the Hunger Games? What in contemporary culture attracts this kind of attention?
5. What resolution and consolation does Katniss ultimately find at the end of the series in *Mockingjay Part 2*? Is it a satisfactory one? Why or why not?

I CAN ONLY IMAGINE

2018

1 hour 50 minutes

CATEGORIES: Redemption story

SUMMARY: While growing up in a small Texas town, Bart Millard (J. Michael Finley) is tormented by his violent father Arthur (Dennis Quaid). Bart realizes he has a talent for singing and, after graduating high school, he leaves to join a Christian rock band. Recognizing he still feels unresolved anger at his father, however, he returns home to confront his past and finds his father a changed man who says he's now a devout Christian.

I Can Only Imagine features a Christian redemption story framed within a specific type of coming-of-age story. Singer Bart Millard of MercyMe is a protagonist with a troubled childhood whose creativity becomes an outlet for his pain.

Bart's artistic expression is both a gift and a burden. It generates talent but also a detrimental fixation on worldly success. The longing to be recognized for his music becomes more about validating his pain than spiritually reaching others.

The basis for this storyline comes from the *Künstlerroman*, a category of the literary coming-of-age story that focuses on the development of an artist as a special individual who undergoes a particular type of struggle.[1] The artist understands how life can be converted into art, but the process can also destroy life because the artist withdraws from the world to create art.[2] Thus, a tension develops between the spiritual calling of the artist's mission and the natural desire to participate in life.[3]

In film versions of this narrative genre, the conflict is often resolved by the protagonist expressing their authentic self through creativity. Because their art engages with universal spiritual themes about suffering and transcendence, audiences relate to the artist's pain. This bridges the gulf between the artist's isolation and other people.

In some ways, *I Can Only Imagine* is similar to Prince's *Purple Rain*, which also features an abusive tormented father, a misunderstood protagonist who self-isolates by creating music, and a culminating song expressing the hope for transcendence of suffering. However, *I Can Only Imagine* goes deeper than secular movies like *Purple Rain* by making spiritual realizations the catalyst for artistic expression.

I Can Only Imagine does this by utilizing the redemption story, a spiritual film category that replicates the Christian concept of spiritual transformation. The movie features two redemption stories: one of a father, the other of a son. It also adheres to a pattern in recent Christian films of one major character deepening his faith (Bart) and another major character (Arthur) converting from non-believer to believer.

Arthur's story is the redemption of a non-believer. In his initial flawed state, he is bitter, self-destructive, and violent because his life did not live up to his glory days of being a star football player in high school. Bart's initial flawed spiritual condition is a pursuit of success that leads him to extreme individualism. Both characters are similar in their mistaken desire to find happiness through worldly recognition.

On the surface, Bart follows the noble call of performing Christian music. However, his music is afflicted by insincerity because of Bart's preoccupation with success and his inability to enact forgiveness. This creates a false self. "All I see is a mask," his girlfriend observes about him. Only when Bart's mentor and manager asks him, "What are you running from?" does Bart realize he must confront his shadow self, which is immersed in his troubled relationship with his father.

When his father initially asks for forgiveness, Bart says, "God can forgive you, I can't." He must change this viewpoint to achieve redemption. If God is expected to forgive, humans must as well. After this realization, Bart writes the song "I Can Only Imagine," which marks his music's thematic transition from escapism and worldly concerns towards deep spiritual realizations. He only achieves success after he abandons an unhealthy desire for it.

BIBLE PASSAGE

"Repent therefore, and turn to God so that your sins may be wiped out." (Acts 3:19 NRSV)

In Christianity, redemption requires acknowledging and repenting for one's sins, which God forgives. This results in receiving grace and a new better self emerges.

DISCUSSION QUESTIONS

1. Why does the song "I Can Only Imagine" have such a powerful effect? What songs have had a powerful spiritual impact on you?
2. Is it possible to imagine what heaven is like? What is your idea of heaven?
3. Since Arthur's conversion largely occurs off screen, what do you think he experienced as he changed? When have you ever seen someone change in such a way?
4. Why is forgiveness an important spiritual quality? When have you had difficulty forgiving someone? Or are you in the process of trying to forgive someone?
5. How does the film show the significance of expressing one's personal spiritual story or feelings? Why is that so important?

I ORIGINS

2014

1 hour 46 minutes

CATEGORIES: Search for God, Westerner seeking Eastern wisdom

SUMMARY: Molecular biologist Ian Gray (Michael Pitt) works to prove how the eye evolved in order to discredit an intelligent design argument against natural selection in evolution. He meets a mysterious woman named Sofi (Astrid Bergès-Frisbey) who says the two knew each other in a past life, which Ian dismisses as nonsensical. However, after discovering a database with millions of scanned images of eyes, he investigates if matching irises can prove reincarnation.

The indie film *I Origins* produces a new protagonist in the spiritual movie genre: the anti-spiritual hipster scientist. With gentrified Brooklyn as a backdrop, the molecular biologist Ian Gray is aloof and emotionally remote. His fixation on what he calls the "data points" of life leaves him disconnected from other people. However, his hubris is challenged when he meets Sofi, to whom he is attracted but views as childish because of her belief in reincarnation.

Like *Contact* (1997), *I Origins* contains thoughtful conversations about the apparent disparity between science and religion, despite the film's flaws. Unlike *Contact*, it does not explore a backstory about why the protagonist disdains religion. But like Jodie Foster's character Ellie in *Contact*, Ian dismisses religion and spirituality because he is looking for empirical proof of God's existence. However, religious faith is the antithesis of the verifiable evidence that scientists in films are often depicted as demanding.

The movie can be divided into two halves. The first follows Ian's relationship with the mystical Sofi. A flaw of the film is that her character leans more toward manic pixie dream girl than someone on her own spiritual journey: Sofi adheres to the stereotype of a woman teaching a brooding man to embrace life and its mysteries.[1] However, at her most penetrating, Sofi tells Ian that, like some of the animals he is modifying, some humans acquire something beyond the five senses. "Perhaps some humans, rare humans, have mutated to have another sense, a spirit sense," she says.

Although the phrase is not mentioned in the movie, Ian's mission is to disprove the concept of "irreducible complexity" in intelligent design which disputes some of the precepts of evolution. The phrase, popularized by Michael Behe, compares this notion to a mousetrap in which all parts are necessary to make the whole work.[2] Because of the complexity of the parts, Behe questions how Darwin's idea of modifications from simpler forms could happen through natural selection.[3] The intricacy of the eye is perhaps the most pronounced example of this tenet of intelligent design.

The second half of the film shifts to the conventions of a thriller and entertains the possibility of merging science and spirituality. Does a database of matching irises in eyes show proof of reincarnation? Because the eye is connected to the brain, does that leave traces of a past life in memory?

I Origins, like *Contact*, does not so much come down on the side of religion as much as it warns scientists that their perspective is too narrow. At one point, Ian says science is superior to religion because it is flexible, asserting that this contrasts with the more fixed idea of the holy words of scripture. However, the film shows that it is Ian's scientific viewpoint that requires flexibility.

I Origins also contains elements of a redemption story, although it falls short of being a full-fledged redemption story. Like many unredeemed figures, Ian prioritizes his career at the expense of personal relationships. As part of Ian's mini-redemption, he also confronts events that look like coincidences but seem to be something more. At two key points, Ian is compelled to consider a sequence of numbers and a mathematical symbol both leading him to Sofi as non-rational, transcendental events.

SPIRITUAL TERM

Intelligent design—belief that life forms were created by an intelligent maker through evolution but not by natural selection alone. This differs from **creationism** which adheres to a Biblical account of creation. In *I Origins*, Ian tries to refute **irreducible complexity**, a principle of intelligent design that states complex organs such as the eye cannot be reduced to small components that randomly evolve.

DISCUSSION QUESTIONS

1. Why does Ian have so much contempt for spirituality? How do you reconcile science and spirituality?
2. Why does evolution seem to be so incompatible with religion? Is evolution congruent with your spiritual beliefs?
3. What incidents happen in the film that seem to be (good or bad) coincidences that may be more than coincidences? Have you had similar experiences in your life? What happened?
4. How does the film reinforce the major theme among scientists in the Search for God category of the spiritual film that they must be more open-minded?
5. Does the ending of the film validate reincarnation? Why or why not?

IDA

2013 (Poland)

1 hour 22 minutes

CATEGORIES: Transcendental, Clergy figure

SUMMARY: Before the novice nun Sister Anna (Agata Trzebuchowska) takes her final vows, the convent's Mother Superior tells Anna she must leave to visit her only living relative. After seeing her Aunt Wanda (Agata Kulesza), Anna learns her real name is Ida and that her parents were Jews killed during the Holocaust. The two women seek out more information about Ida's family, and Ida sees more of life's challenges outside of the convent.

With its stark black-and-white photography and meditative pacing, *Ida* is perhaps the finest recent example of what Paul Schrader calls the transcendental style in film. The film is not only remarkable for its film style but its content. It shows the journey of a prospective nun into 1960s Poland's secular society as both a test of her faith and an opportunity for her faith to grow.

Ida is a rarity among movies about nuns because it features very little of convent life. Less than five minutes into the film, the convent's mother superior instructs Anna to leave to visit her aunt. The movie reverses the narrative arc of the spiritual pilgrimage. Instead of a journey to a sacred site, it is an expedition into the secular world. Ida's spiritual journey occurs not in the convent but within society. She must explore her family identity and what society offers before making a final commitment to a religious order.

Initially, Ida distances herself by wearing her religious clothing as a kind of protective uniform, saying little, and frequently retreating into solitude. A turning point comes when Ida sees a stained-glass window while visiting a barn in a former family home.[1] "Fancy stained glass next to cow dung," her aunt derisively says. The secular and the spiritual are

Films featuring clergy figures are a fixture of the spiritual movie genre. *Ida* features a novice nun who undergoes a pilgrimage in reverse from a sacred site into a deeply flawed secular world. Photo courtesy Music Box Films/Everett Collection

side by side, and God is found in unexpected places and often in the messiness of the world—not just in the isolation of the convent.[2] It also recalls the nativity story, where a birth in a manger manifests God's grace in the grittiness of the world.[3]

Wanda later tells the reserved and distant Ida that "Jesus didn't hide in a cave with books but went out into the world" and "this Jesus of yours adored people like me." But Wanda is a lost soul cloistered in her own way in a lonely life of alcoholism, casual sex, and self-destruction. However, Wanda is correct that Ida's spiritual education requires that she immerse herself more into the world. Later, Ida emulates Wanda's lifestyle to experience firsthand the despair Wanda feels and the ultimate emptiness of unholy sensual experiences.

This is consistent with movies about nuns, which often depict a conflict between spiritual and worldly desires. Because nuns reject societal expectations as wives, mothers, and workers, they typically experience a test manifesting in restlessness, doubt, and temptations.[4]

Ida is the best clergy-based film released in years partly because it represents a striking update of the filmmaking techniques outlined in Paul Schrader's *Transcendental Style in Film*, including long takes, ambient sounds, and preference of visuals over dialogue that create a contemplative experience for the viewer. Ida's facial expressions also enhance contemplation, as her lack of dialogue allows the viewer to study her expressions.

The film also frequently shows characters low, small, or fragmented in the frame with space above them, creating a kind of cathedral effect and the sense of a divine presence.[5] It reminds the viewer there is more at work in the film's world than the viewer can perceive.[6]

BIBLE PASSAGE

"On hearing this, Jesus said to them, 'It is not the healthy who need a doctor, but the sick. I have not come to call the righteous, but sinners.'" (Mark 2:17 NIV)

Jesus's statement recalls Ida's spiritual growth through observing the reality of sin and distress. Although sometimes disturbing and demanding, it can be more spiritually instructive than sheltering with the righteous.

DISCUSSION QUESTIONS

1. How is Ida's immersion into the world outside of the convent necessary to her spiritual growth? What was a time you spiritually benefited from exposure to things that first repulsed you?
2. How does the film handle the separation between worldly and spiritual desires? Is this a divide that you feel or have felt in your life? What is the ultimate resolution to this?
3. Why does Wanda feel such despair? When have you seen a similar despair in your own life? When have you seen it in someone else's life?
4. What role does guilt play in the film? Which characters feel guilty and why?
5. How do you interpret the end of the film?

IKIRU

1952 (Japan)

2 hours 23 minutes

CATEGORIES: Redemption story

SUMMARY: City Hall worker Kanji Watanabe (Takashi Shimura) is diagnosed with terminal cancer. With just months left to live, he feels regretful about much of his life—particularly wasting so many years in an unfulfilling job. Eventually, he finds purpose and meaning in the time he has left.

Ikiru shows the spiritual erosion that comes after years of what the film's narrator calls the "meaningless busyness" of an unfulfilling job. Although work is a central activity and concern in most people's lives, cinema tends towards unrealistic, uncritical depictions of the workplace.

However, some spiritual films demonstrate how discernment about vocation becomes a spiritual act. The hero's journey films *Wall Street* and *The Devil Wears Prada* show how the lessons young adults learn in the workplace shape moral and spiritual formation. *Ikiru* shows the effects of an inconsequential job on someone nearing retirement age.

More than spiritually harming him, Watanabe's job perpetuates a bureaucracy that obstructs the social good. The government office Watanabe works at is representative of a political and economic system preserving the status quo and not helping the disadvantaged. "Doing anything is considered radical," one coworker later says.

Ikiru questions the possibility of meaningful individual action in the modern world.[1] It shows how an insignificant job can lead to alienation and a paralyzing crisis of meaning.[2] Although it warns about the dangers of compliance, the movie ultimately provides hope about breaking out of a deadening routine.[3]

Although Watanabe's illness is a physical one, his real illness is spiritual.[4] But before he experiences a spiritual awakening, he goes through a series of emotional stages after his cancer diagnosis: confusion/shock; depression/regret; pleasure seeking/escapism; longing to be young again. This yearning for youth perhaps occurs because he has no present and certainly no future, so he becomes lost in the past.[5]

During the final phase, Watanabe spends time with the young female coworker Toyo. The relationship is awkward and misplaced, but perhaps needed, because he cannot connect with either his daughter-in-law or son. But the altruism he shows her anticipates the pivotal turnaround moment of the redemption film, which occurs after Toyo says she likes making toy rabbits because she imagines she is making children happy. She then asks Watanabe whether he might be able to experience a similar joy.

This combination of innocence and a sense of mission makes Watanabe realize he can produce and initiate something instead of being a passive worker. He will use his position to resurrect a mother's long-stalled request to build a playground in a poor neighborhood. This restores to him a childlike state of wonder, gives him a sense of purpose, and generates possibility of community.[6]

This expresses the main component of the redemption story: a resolved will to do good. Benevolent love becomes the answer for the problem of human existence.[7] Like Christ, Watanabe will sacrifice himself for others—he will spend his last days serving others.[8]

For decades, he lived a life of exile due to his passivity.[9] So, to change, he must act. Redemption comes from not just internal realization but assertive actions that benefit the community.[10] Watanabe shifts from yearning for youth to thinking about the generations that come after him. The meaning of "Ikiru" in Japanese is "to live," interpreted in the film as having a cause, a purpose, and a sense of legacy.[11]

"This man bears a cross called cancer, he's Christ," a young writer says about Watanabe. But rather than a Christ figure, Watanabe becomes a "holy fool" character whose gentleness, humility, and concern for others enables him to overcome the powerful.[12] His childlike simplicity is fully realized in his decision to build a playground.[13] Watanabe succeeding as a fool character also resolves the film's central dilemma: the conflict between how people live in the modern world and a spiritual perspective.[14]

BIBLE PASSAGE

"Why, you do not even know what will happen tomorrow. What is your life? You are a mist that appears for a little while and then vanishes." (James 4:14 NIV)

The mournful song Watanabe sings in the movie reflects the idea in the Book of James about the brevity of life.

DISCUSSION QUESTIONS

1. How does Watanabe's impending death change his attitude toward life? Is there a way you can contemplate your own death as a motivation toward what's important in life?
2. Why do you think Watanabe slipped into such a deadening work routine? When has this happened to you? Is it currently happening to you?

3. Why does Watanabe search for pleasure and youthful companionship?
4. Why is Watanabe's legacy so important to him? What do you want your legacy to be?
5. How do you interpret the ending of the film, when the workers are back in the office?

INTO THE WILD

2007

2 hours 28 minutes

CATEGORIES: Hero's journey (variation), search for God (pilgrimage variation)

SUMMARY: After graduating college, Chris McCandless (Emile Hirsch) gives away his savings of $24,000 to charity before taking a cross-country trip. He tells no one of his whereabouts, abandons his car, and renames himself Alexander Super-tramp. His goal is to go to the Alaskan wilderness, where he hopes to find life at its most spiritually revealing.

Into The Wild is Chris McCandless's pilgrimage to find a spiritual identity outside of family and societal expectations of success. "I don't need money, it makes people cautious," he boldly says. His character's lack of caution imbues his character with a complexity that is the distinguishing mark of the film. His search for spiritual knowledge is both highly admirable and too severe, although the film stops short of being a cautionary tale.

McCandless's search for god is a pilgrimage to a natural place, and the Alaskan wilderness becomes a spiritual beacon. He hopes to find spiritual revelation there because he believes that its distance from society will strip life to its essential components. His declaration to "kill the false being within" by experiencing revelation recalls the Trappist monk Thomas Merton's identification of a lower "false self" that spiritual contemplatives must destroy.

Like so many American stories about forming a new identity, it depicts a journey west. The movie blends the myth of the frontier with the idea of the sublime experienced through nature.[1] McCandless believes the ills of modern society can only be escaped by returning to a more simplistic way of living in the primal state of the natural world.[2] *Into The Wild* is also a hero's journey influenced by the road movie genre with its themes of liberation from and critique of societal expectations and norms.[3]

Another major influence is transcendentalist American literature, with its longing for escape from the congestion of urban life and a return to nature where transcendent moments can occur.[4] This is a theme in the works of Thoreau and Jack London—two of McCandless's literary inspirations. In keeping with the hero's journey narrative, Chris finds mentorship, but in this case it is in the works of authors who inspire them and whose works become akin to religious texts for him.

The other mentor guides he meets on this trip to Alaska also become substitute family members, including a surrogate father (the wheat farmer, Wayne Westerberg), mother (the aging hippie, Jan Burres), grandfather (the leather craftsman, Ron Franz), and sister (the teenager Tracy). But the good-natured, curious, and hardworking McCandless also has a transformative effect on those around him. He provides insight, motivates them out of complacency, and solves some of their problems. At times, he becomes a liberating figure because of his free-spirited and persuasive personality.[5]

Rather than the long takes associated with the transcendental style, *Into the Wild* features an regularly moving camera, montages, and juxtaposition of images somewhat reminiscent of the films of Terrence Malick. This style shows the elation of a young person exhilarated by the world. Yet, at times, the ominous and dour soundtrack music implies a conflict between the jubilant and the tragic, highlighting the narrative's ambivalence towards its protagonist.

Ultimately, the film's structure becomes a puzzle about McCandless's identity composed through a series of storytelling techniques including landscape shots, ambient sounds of nature, literary texts, the responses of people he meets, the music of Eddie Vedder, and his sister's voiceover.[6] It consistently reveals that McCandless's most complicated and anti-heroic aspect is his abandonment and severance of human connections in favor of individualistic spiritual achievement. He finally receives a spiritual revelation about this part of himself in the Alaskan wild.

BIBLE PASSAGE

"God said, "It isn't good that the person should be alone. I will make for him a companion suitable for helping him.'" Genesis 2:18 (CJB)

Although it is about Adam and Eve, this passage shows the perils of too much solitude, one of the themes of *Into the Wild*.

DISCUSSION QUESTIONS

1. Is it irresponsible for McCandless to rename himself and not let anyone know where he goes on his spiritual journey? Why or why not?

2. How important is nature to McCandless? What does he find spiritual about nature and humble labor?

3. What are the key relationships McCandless makes on his journey?

4. What advice does McCandless receive about forgiveness from Mr. Franz? Do you agree with it? And does he ultimately follow that advice?

5. How does the ending of this film make it a variation on the hero's journey and not a strict adherence to it?

IT'S A WONDERFUL LIFE

1946

2 hours 10 minutes

CATEGORIES: Divine intervention

SUMMARY: After years of being disappointed and frustrated because of unfulfilled ambitions, bankruptcy and scandal threaten small-town banker George Bailey (Jimmy Stewart) after one of his employees misplaces some bank funds and the money is taken by Bailey's nemesis, the ruthless businessman Henry Potter (Lionel Barrymore). The distraught Bailey is suicidal, so a heavenly entity summons the angel Clarence (Henry Travers) to assist him.

In the Bible, the suffering Job wishes he was never born, a sentiment also expressed by the prophet Jeremiah and the author of Ecclesiastes. They not only want to end their lives but annihilate their entire existence—as if their lives were a cosmic mistake or an exercise in pain and futility. In *It's a Wonderful Life*, the beleaguered George Bailey also wishes he had never been born.

Although George at times recalls other Biblical figures like Joseph or Jesus, he most resembles Job, who cries out to God in anguish and anger after his children are killed, his business is obliterated, and he is afflicted with painful sores. Both George and Job serve their communities well, express devotion to family, win the admiration of others, and are considered righteous.[1] However, their commitment, sacrifice, and righteousness fail to protect them from catastrophe and despair.[2] They question why their faith in God and devotion to family and community cannot spare them from misfortune.[3]

As a movie in the divine intervention category of the spiritual film, *It's a Wonderful Life* presents a lesson given from a heavenly being to a troubled human. An angelic intervention corrects George's view that life is a burden and a series of humiliations and broken dreams.

George Bailey's despair is so deep that the angel Clarence must alter reality itself to rectify his perspective. George only realizes the value of his life when Clarence shows him a version of his hometown in an alternate reality in which he'd never been born. George had originally felt that he had lost his true nature by suppressing his own dreams by staying in his hometown, but this sequence shows that by fulfilling his dreams of travel, he would have ended up abandoning his true identity by forsaking the community.[4]

Despite the uplifting ending, most of the film focuses on George's frustrations and unfulfilled dreams. He experiences spiritual conflict between his individualistic goals and his family and community responsibilities. George has a romantic imagination and longs for travel and new experiences. However, a series of temporary commitments becomes for him a permanent trap.[5] This produces an almost constant state of desperation in George.[6] He repeatedly comes to the rescue of the community, but seems to never receive recognition for his sacrifice.[7]

The conflict Bailey experiences reflects a deeply American theme in literature and culture that reveres the adventurer over those who perform quiet steady work in a community.[8] *It's a Wonderful Life* corrects that opposition.[9] The movie acknowledges that domesticity requires giving up adventure; yet, the film asserts, it is within domesticity and responsibility that spiritual meaning emerges.[10] True happiness is attained by what is forgone rather than what is indulged.[11]

Ultimately, George's myths of adventure are unrealistic and self-centered, and he ultimately comes to embrace his wife Mary's romantic view of everyday life. Her veneration of stability and rootedness is antithetical to the escapist romance George feels.[12] While an unknown ideal appeals to George's imagination, a lifelong connection to what she knows most appeals to Mary.[13]

George is worn down not only from the inner conflict between adventure and responsibility but by the external threat of the ravenous businessman Potter. The Bailey family business is based on accommodating human needs and a belief in human goodness, while Potter is motivated by greed and has no faith in human nature.[14] George learns through a divine lesson that giving in to the desires of the self is to live in a world ruled by people like Mr. Potter.[15] Unlike other villains who reform, such as Ebenezer Scrooge in *A Christmas Carol*, Potter never changes. He remains a consistent force of evil.

In the end, George realizes choices have consequences beyond one's own existence.[16] He arrives at the insight that life derives its value not from materialism and individuality, but from tending to the needs of others.[17] What on the surface appears to restrict actually liberates and enriches.[18] George's encounter with the divine enables him to no longer yearn for freedom through escape; he instead finds meaning through connections that come from stability and community.[19]

BIBLE PASSAGE

"Why did I not perish at birth, and die as I came from the womb?" (Job 3:11 NIV)

Like Job, George Bailey wishes he was never born and receives a divine response.

DISCUSSION QUESTIONS

1. How does George's frustration affect his life?
2. Why are unfulfilled dreams so painful to George? How have you handled your unfulfilled dreams?
3. How is prayer portrayed? What are the key scenes when it is shown?
4. Do others truly understand George? Could they have been more helpful and understanding of him before the ending scene? If so, how?
5. What does the movie define as true success? What is your definition of success in life?

Jesus of Montreal

1989 (French Canada)

2 hours

CATEGORIES: Christ figure

SUMMARY: A group of unemployed actors in Montreal revise a church's annual Passion play performance to add historical context and address modern moral and social dilemmas, but church authorities threaten to shut the play down after it becomes an unexpected success. As the play precedes, Daniel (Lothaire Bluteau), the actor who plays Jesus, finds that his life increasingly parallels the story of Jesus.

Jesus of Montreal blurs the identities of the actor playing Jesus in the Passion play and the persona of Jesus, generating a perspective on how Jesus might operate in contemporary society and engaging with how events in the Gospels have similarities to the present day.[1]

Aside from the innovative and creative use of a Christ figure, *Jesus of Montreal* has three major objectives. It criticizes the inadequacy of contemporary cultural depictions of Jesus, adds supplementary material to the Passion Play story to make it applicable to contemporary audiences, and, most memorably, draws direct comparisons between the gospel story and modern contemporary life by using the Christ figure actor's life to mirror the Gospels. Instead of reconstructing a traditional historical Jesus, the Passion play presents the story in a modern context that points out how the Gospel's morality conflicts with contemporary values.[2]

Recalling Jesus's gathering of his disciples, Daniel recruits the actors in the beginning of the film. Aside from Daniel and his mysterious origins, the actors are largely defined by their social positions and their jobs within the power structure of the media. They find redemption by rejecting these roles to become creators and disciples of something holier.

They spread the gospel in their own way by writing and acting out the Passion play. Like many Christ figures, Daniel has a privileged relationship with women.[3] In the film, these women are the play's actresses, who at times recall the Virgin Mary, Mary Magdalene, and Martha and

Mary from the Gospels. The play itself takes place at night with city lights glimmering in the distance—making the setting appear like a modern Golgotha.

After the play is first performed, Daniel's life follows that of Jesus in the Gospels. High atop a skyscraper, in a variation of Satan's temptation of Jesus in the wilderness, a businessman sees the commercial potential of the Jesus story and tells Daniel, "This city is yours if you want it." In another scene, Daniel knocks over a table and camera equipment during an audition for a commercial, a variation on Jesus turning over the tables of the moneychangers in the temple.

The death and resurrection motif so critical to the Christ figure film is preceded by Daniel's apocalyptic speech, which recalls a descent into the underworld (the subway) before an ending resurrection that is both ethereal and physical. To show that he has found a way to give life to others, Daniel donates his vital organs, which illustrates a common theme in the Christ figure film: living on in others.

Aside from establishing connections between contemporary culture and the Gospels, the film shows how some current cultural definitions of Christ are false and inadequate. They include the New Age-influenced Christ follower (the librarian), the excessively cerebral view (the academic), and an overly emotional response (the audience member who disrupts the play).[4] Daniel rejects these conceptions of Jesus and stands by the version of Jesus in the Passion play.[5]

The ability of the actors to successfully revise the Passion play on their own reveals the declining authority of the Catholic Church and how economic factors and greed supersede morality in Quebecois culture.[6] The play also represents a movement from institutional orthodox teachings to liberation theology, which emphasizes how power structures oppress people and encourage sin.[7]

BIBLE PASSAGE

"Then Jesus told his disciples, 'If any want to become my followers, let them deny themselves and take up their cross and follow me.'" (Matthew 16:24 NRSV)

The actors deny themselves careers and relationships. They are, in their own way, followers of a gospel message who end up carrying a cross because of their convictions.

DISCUSSION QUESTIONS

1. Which parallel in the film between the Gospels and the contemporary world was most striking to you?
2. What definitions of Jesus in current society does the film present? What are some current definitions of Jesus in society now?
3. How does adding historical context to the Passion Play change the message? Is it important for you to do Biblical historical research for your own spiritual life?
4. What does the film say about the role of the commercial world of advertising and the media?
5. How does the film carry out the Christ figure pattern of death and resurrection?

JOAN THE MAID (JEANNE LA PUCELLE)

1994 (France)

Part 1: The Battles 2 hours 40 minutes;
Part 2: The Prisons 2 hours 56 minutes

CATEGORIES: Religious figure, Christ figure

SUMMARY: After saying she received a divine revelation, French peasant Joan (Sandrine Bonnaire) travels to see the King of France. She convinces him to let her command an army against invading English forces and leads the French to a crucial victory. Eventually, she is captured and executed.

Joan of Arc is probably the subject of more movies than any other saint. Part of her story's appeal is its romantic view of an illiterate peasant challenging institutional power.[1] All major films about her depict her as a mixture of mystic, virgin warrior, and androgynous figure.[2] This combination makes her a threat to religious and political authority.

However, within those consistent characteristics, filmmakers alter her character to define a martyr figure through a particular time period's cultural lens.

The Passion of Joan of Arc (1928) portrays her as a mystic to such an extreme that she appears to reside in a supernatural realm. In *Joan of Arc* (1948), a miscast Ingrid Bergman unsuccessfully attempts to create an epic heroine. Bresson's *The Trial of Joan of Arc* (1962) features a heroine as the voice of 1960s youth culture. *The Messenger* (1999) presents an unhinged Joan of Arc and suggests her visions may result from insanity, reflecting a growing cultural skepticism about supernatural aspects of religion. In the seventy years since the groundbreaking *Passion*, portrayals of Joan of Arc had radically changed from elevating her with an otherworldly transcendence to turning away from the theme of divine revelation.

Joan the Maid, which in its restored uncut two-part version totals more than five-and-a-half hours, is the most complex and well-rounded presentation of the fifteenth-century saint on film. It is a landmark movie not only in the Joan of Arc category but in the spiritual movie genre.

While its length and breadth make it epic in scope, it is in many ways an anti-epic film. The movie avoids episodes most associated with Joan of Arc such as extended mystical encounters, bloody battlefield scenes, and Joan's interrogation at an exhausting trial. Perhaps because of the exhaustive emphasis on the trial in *Passion* and *The Trial of Joan of Arc*, the director of *Joan the Maid* chose to circumvent it. The movie adds pauses between segments, as well as extended takes, rather than rapidly editing in action sequences or intercutting during more static scenes.[3] Characters also directly address the camera between some scenes, giving it an episodic feel rather than the pacing of a religious figure epic.

Eschewing historical biopic clichés, the film emphasizes Joan's spiritual transformation of the soldiers and her construction of the war as a religious one. Her peasant status combined with her spiritual charisma make her both down-to-earth and sacred.[4] Underneath her armor, she is a righteous force who forbids her soldiers to gamble, swear, or pillage.[5] "You want to win? Then be pure," she tells them. Unlike the removed mystic of other Joan of Arc films, Sandrine Bonnaire's multidimensional presentation shows a woman with a sense of humor, vulnerability, and courage grounded in the belief that she is following God's will.

Joan also is a screen Christ figure. She is of humble birth divinely guided on an important mission, leaves home, acquires a following, and performs miraculous deeds—after which authorities order a trial and brutally execute the savior Christ figure.[6] She tells the Dauphin that her voices call her "Daughter of God," echoing the New Testament phrase "Son of God." She asks for forgiveness to all while being led to the stake, recalling Jesus's prayer that his killers be forgiven. Joan calls out to Jesus before her death, just as Christ called out to his heavenly father.[7] Before her execution, she undergoes a Garden of Gethsemane moment, asking, "This deliverance, when will it come?" She also warns others like the prophetic Christ, commanding one clergy member, "For this I call you before God, you shall answer before him."

BIBLE PASSAGE

"Do not suppose that I have come to bring peace to the earth. I did not come to bring peace, but a sword." (Matthew 10:34 NIV)

Joan of Arc uses a sword to bring what she hopes will be religious-fueled justice.

DISCUSSION QUESTIONS

1. How do you think this movie compares to other Joan of Arc depictions in popular culture?
2. What qualities make Joan of Arc a Christ figure?
3. Why do the soldiers obey Joan? What qualities does she have that would make you want to follow her, if any?

4. Joan is not a pacifist and believes God is on one side of this war. Do you agree this can sometimes be the case? Why or why not?

5. How does Joan react to her impending execution and how does she confront it?

JOURNEY TO ITALY

1954

1 hour 37 minutes

CATEGORIES: Search for God

SUMMARY: Troubled married couple Katherine (Ingrid Bergman) and Alex (George Sanders) go to Italy to sell a family home, during which the two increasingly go their separate ways. After a mutual trip to Pompeii, however, their marriage reaches a turning point.

Roberto Rossellini directed several important films in the spiritual movie genre. His neorealist movie *Rome, Open City* (1945) features a heroic priest fighting against the Nazi occupation. *Flowers of St. Francis* (1950) is an episodic film about the spiritual teachings of Francis of Assisi. A trio of films featuring Ingrid Bergman started with *Stromboli* (1950), about a woman undergoing a spiritual crisis on a volcanic island, followed by *Europe '51* (1952), in which a wife leaves her self-indulgent bourgeois life to help the poor.

But Rossellini's most influential film in the spiritual movie genre is the third Bergman film *Journey to Italy* (1954). Rossellini redefines the narrative arc of a cinematic spiritual journey, which makes it a groundbreaking film.

Instead of a pilgrimage, redemption story, or hero's journey, the two main characters go on a less intentional and more ambiguous spiritual search. Modernism and materialism produce restlessness, boredom, and frustration, creating a spiritual vacuum that the characters attempt to fill by a search for meaning.

Italy provides an ideal landscape for this journey because the English couple is immersed and vulnerable in a foreign culture, forcing them to reassess their values.[1] The loneliness and wandering in *Journey to Italy* influenced similar existentialist journeys in Fellini's *La Dolce Vita* (1960) as well as Antonioni's *L'Avventura* (1960) and *La Notte* (1961). While Antonioni's existentialism is psychological and postmodern, Rossellini's is Catholic and romantic.[2]

Rossellini is most associated with gritty realist films depicting war-torn Italy, but *Journey to Italy* is a step toward another kind of spiritual realism. At the time of the film's release, Italians were no longer experiencing the physical hardships of the 1940s, but they were losing a sense of moral and ethical certainty during the postwar boom years, creating a societal spiritual crisis.[3] The escalation of materialism and modernism resulted in disillusionment and disengagement. It also created a newly established protagonist in modern cinema: the isolated and alienated individual.[4]

This is reflected in the two main characters, a socialite and a lawyer, who go through a profound existential crisis after remaining spiritually unconscious and burying themselves in business and the futile details of modern life.[5] Besides seeming to know little about each other, they don't know much about themselves because they prioritize money, status, and material comforts.[6] They live a life opposite of what is shown in Rossellini's *Flowers of St. Francis*, where materialism and status are abandoned.[7]

The film portrays two different spiritual conditions to illustrate the malaise of modernism. Alex is materialistic, business-minded, and rational, while Katherine is overly aesthetic, emotionally vulnerable, and otherworldly.[8] For the superficially suave and controlled Alex, a search for romantic affairs that ultimately don't work out makes him emotionally remote.[9] He worries about the time he is wasting while in Italy, a country he views as the epitome of laziness.[10] Katherine shows her weak spirituality by simply going to locations her poet friend wrote about rather than implementing her own spiritual path.[11] While Alex follows an amorphous itinerary without finding anything to truly connect with, Katherine immerses herself emotionally and aesthetically in the reality around her shown by alternating between closeups of her face and fragments of the external world.[12]

Although less dramatic than Dreyer's *Ordet*, a miracle occurs at the end of the film. Alex and Katherine see a religious procession with a statue of the Virgin Mary from which a miracle is expected.[13] The couple miraculously reconnect here,[14] and they are pulled out of their withdrawn intellectual realm into a set of emotions apparently new to them.[15] They finally discover spiritual meaning by confronting mortality, gaining a sense of time (after seeing ancient ruins), and realizing the supernatural capacity of religion.

BIBLE PASSAGE

"Meaningless! Meaningless!" says the Teacher. "Utterly meaningless! Everything is meaningless." (Ecclesiastes 1:2 NIV)

The married couple are in a state of despair because they feel a lack of meaning, a condition the author of Ecclesiastes wrote about.

DISCUSSION QUESTIONS

1. What are the biggest spiritual differences between the Northern European culture of the married couple and the Southern European Italian culture? Have you ever traveled somewhere where you saw a pronounced difference in spiritual outlook?
2. Although not a traditional religious pilgrimage, how does the movie become a spiritual journey for the married couple?
3. How do the characters embody a sense of loneliness? Why do you think this is a condition of modern living?
4. Why does the visit to Pompeii have an effect on the couple? When is a time you visited someplace that had a powerful impact on you?
5. What do you make of the ending miracle? Do you believe such miracles can occur?

THE KEYS OF THE KINGDOM

1944

2 hours 17 minutes

CATEGORIES: Clergy figure

SUMMARY: Following a tumultuous childhood and a failed romance in early adulthood, Francis Chisholm (Gregory Peck) becomes a priest. After failing in his first two churches, he is assigned to establish a Catholic parish in China. He finds adverse conditions but does his best to follow his faith and make his mission succeed.

This groundbreaking film is often erroneously grouped together with a series of Catholic clergy films, including *Boys Town* (1938), *Going My Way* (1944), and *The Bells of St. Mary's* (1945). All of these films engage with the Depression or Second World War and the desire for religious figures to help solve social problems. However, *Keys of the Kingdom* is a spiritual biography rather than a variation on the social problem film. It is also innovative for its tolerance and acceptance of other religions, cultures, and even the non-religious.

Unlike other classic Hollywood clergy films, *The Keys of the Kingdom* features an extended backstory covering the protagonist's life before becoming a priest as well as his decision to enter the priesthood. The typical clergy film often shows the self-assured priest already working in his vocation.

This multidimensional portrayal casts Chisholm as sometimes vulnerable, doubtful, and confused. After problems in his first two clergy assignments, he asks, "Am I so ill-equipped to give what's in my heart to give?" But underneath this vulnerability is a humility, dignity, and strength that Peck displays in some of his other films. One writer describes this persona as "earnest intensity."[1]

Heroic clergy figures in classic Hollywood films such as Francis Chisholm (Gregory Peck) were once a staple of the spiritual movie genre. *The Keys of the Kingdom* is notable for being an early version of the portrayal of a priest who seems to believe in a type of universalism. Photo courtesy 20th Century Fox/Everett Collection

Accordingly, he comes to expect honesty from others, particularly when posing questions about religious tolerance. While attending seminary, Chisholm is accused of exhibiting "unorthodox doctrine" because of a question he poses about religious exclusivity. His religious tolerance is a result of having grown up in Scotland with a Protestant mother and a Catholic father who experienced discrimination. Seeing his parents' devotion to each other despite their religious differences creates a religious open-mindedness that extends into his religious mission as a priest. This openness to people of all beliefs can be seen in an ongoing friendship he maintains with the atheist Willie Tulloch, who helps Chisholm in his mission. The film ultimately has a more universalist perspective on religion than a Catholic one.

As a result, some of Chisholm's most severe conflicts are with rigid religious figures—including Mother Maria-Veronica, who derisively calls him the "peasant priest." Later, though, she tearfully apologizes to him for her arrogance. "I knew that yours was a true humility and that mine was a duty," she says. She confesses how difficult it is to practice true humility, a theme important in the spiritual movie genre but seldom espoused in other films.

The movie also reproaches the conceit that institutional religious figures can sometimes possess. This manifests in Angus Mealey, a childhood friend of Chisholm who moved up in the church hierarchy and visits Chisholm in China. The contrast between these two figures is the catalyst for Mother Maria-Veronica's epiphany about recognizing spiritual modesty. Mealey represents a somewhat pompous institutional figure with a sense of expectation and entitlement that differs from Chisholm's modesty.

In *Keys of the Kingdom*, true religiosity is based on generosity and humility. Mother Maria Veronica's spiritual breakthrough is not through spiritual discipline or mysticism but humiliation and insight. "How strange that the moment of my greatest humiliation should bring with it the only peace I've ever truly known," she says.

Keys of the Kingdom also shows an important and lifechanging mentorship that is more common in the hero's journey or Westerner seeking Eastern wisdom spiritual films. Hamish MacNabb, a clergy mentor, sees the value of Chisholm's humility, tenderness, and inquisitiveness. MacNabb says he has affection for "the stray cat" quality he sees in Chisholm. He says it will prevent him from being what he calls "an ecclesiastic mechanic." And, as the film shows, Chisholm is anything but a priest just going through the motions, particularly for the time of the film's release.

BIBLE PASSAGE

"When pride comes, then comes disgrace, but with humility comes wisdom." (Proverbs 11:2 NIV)

Humility is sometimes mistaken for meekness, but the film contrasts it with the sin of pride.

DISCUSSION QUESTIONS

1. How does Francis exhibit humility? How is that different from meekness?
2. What characters are prideful? Why is pride such an obstacle to spiritual insight?

3. How does Francis view characters of other religions or no religion? How would you like to do this in your life?
4. What is Francis's approach to gathering members for his mission? How is that different from a traditional approaches to gathering church members?
5. How would you describe Hamish MacNabb's mentorship of Francis? Who was an important mentoring figure in your spiritual formation?

KING OF KINGS

1927 (Silent)

2 hours 40 minutes

CATEGORIES: Bible epic (Gospel film)

SUMMARY: Mary Magdalene (Jaqueline Logan) is enraged at Judas Iscariot (Joseph Schildkraut) for becoming a disciple of Jesus (H.B. Warner) and neglecting her. But after Jesus removes evil spirits from her, she too becomes a follower. Jesus heals, teaches, and aligns himself with the needy, but the high priest Caiphas (Rudolph Schildkraut) wants Jesus arrested.

In a remarkable non-Biblical color sequence that begins the film, Mary Magdalene reclines among Roman admirers at a decadent banquet. Coquettish, vain, and at one point petting a leopard, she explodes in anger when she hears Judas Iscariot has abandoned her because he is now a disciple of Jesus. She drives a chariot pulled by zebras to go see the man she calls the "vagabond carpenter." Suddenly uncomfortable when facing him, Jesus performs an exorcism that removes demons representing the seven deadly sins from her.

Director Cecil B. DeMille's employment of such spectacles entrenched in the Bible epic genre, finding iterations in extravagant sets, period costumes, special effects, and scenes with massive crowds. DeMille's blending of fictional historical and romantic plotlines with the gospel also shows how the so-called Jesus film could appeal to non-religious audiences as well.

DeMille also juxtaposes the sensual and the spiritual to achieve this end. He infamously used this technique later in his career in *The Ten Commandments* (1956), when the Jewish people participate in a mass orgy while Moses ascends Mt. Sinai to receive the Ten Commandments from God. *King of Kings* immediately establishes tension between religion and sexuality. It contrasts the worldly, self-indulgent lifestyle of Mary Magdalene with the selfless, noble spiritual lifestyle of Jesus, his followers, and the peasants who surround them.[1]

As with most Bible epic films, additional non-Biblical material indicates contemporary cultural problems that the gospel-based story attempts to alleviate. Mary Magdalene, for example, represents excess and the erosion of moral values of that era.[2] Another contemporary anxiety is reflected in Judas Iscariot's desire for power. "Would he but shun the poor and heal the rich we could straightaway make him king, with me as his right-hand man," Judas says.

Unlike other Bible epic films, the villains are neither the Romans nor the Pharisees but two individuals: Judas and the high priest Caiphas, who "cares more for revenue than religion."[3] Judas represents ambition and Caiphas the desire for money, while Mary Magdalene symbolizes cultural anxiety about overly sexual women (the director even goes so far as to visually align her with animals).

The film will appear antiquated in some ways to present day audiences, but it conveys an ethereal reverential image of Jesus unmatched in any Gospel-based film since. Without hearing Jesus's voice, the title cards containing Bible verses give the words a sense of authority.[4] The dramatic frame compositions also make *King of Kings* one of the most notable gospel films. The compositions and poses come from Victorian spectacular theater and its tradition of creating living representations of famous paintings.[5] The centerpiece of the film is the crucifixion, a stunning piece of filmmaking with its moody black-and-white photography and near-apocalyptic storm.

An immediate reaction of contemporary audiences to the film is that this screen Jesus is older. Most screen Jesuses are in their thirties, but H.B. Warner was fifty at the time of filming. This gives him the aura of a father figure in a film that emphasizes his affinity for women and children.[6] The omission of early Gospel material such as the birth narrative and John the Baptist conveys an unchanging image of Christ, thus further emphasizing this father figure persona.[7]

In addition to being older, this screen Jesus looks otherworldly. Dressed in a white robe, Warner's Jesus appears to be slightly overexposed with less shadow and contrast on him in soft focus, which sets him apart from his environment both physically and metaphorically.[8] In some ways, this makes him passive and patriarchal.[9] In other ways it gives him a persistent sense of melancholy.[10]

BIBLE PASSAGE

"Jesus said, 'I'll come and heal him.'" (Matthew 8:7 The Message)

Gospel-based films emphasize different attributes and interpretations of Jesus. In this film, he is portrayed primarily as a fatherly healer.[11]

DISCUSSION QUESTIONS

1. Gospel films create an image of Jesus reflecting the times. What does this film say about the 1920s?
2. What did you think of the silent film format to illustrate the gospel story? In what ways does it succeed or fail?
3. How does this screen Jesus suit your image of Jesus? What film version of Jesus is closest to your image?
4. What scenes regarding Jesus's connection to women and children stand out to you? Why do you think Jesus has an affinity for women and children?
5. What does the ending shot of Jesus's figure superimposed over a modern cityscape symbolize?

KUNDUN

1997

2 hours 14 minutes

CATEGORIES: Westerner seeking Eastern wisdom,
religious figure, difficulty living out faith

SUMMARY: In the 1930s, Tibetan Buddhist monks set out to find the reincarnation of the Dalai Lama. They discover a boy they believe is the reborn sage and guide him in the ways of Buddhism. However, as a young adult, the Dalai Lama faces a spiritual crisis after China invades Tibet.

Unlike *Gandhi* and *Malcolm X*, *Kundun* is not an epic-style film. *Kundun* also contains few extended dramatic sequences and little interior psychological development.[1] Instead, its themes and film style express a Buddhist perspective on perception and spiritual evolution.

The Buddhist sense of an inexpressible reality is conveyed in the film's structure, which creates confusion about time, place, and identity.[2] The film's pacing and observations of the everyday world in the use of closeups also emphasizes the Buddhist idea of focusing on the present moment and the interconnectedness of all beings.[3]

Kundun focuses on two eras of the Dalai Lama's life. The first begins at the age of two, when Tibetan monks determine a child in a remote village is the reincarnation of previous Dalai Lamas. The second begins when he is an older teenager and ends after the young spiritual leader is forced to leave his home country of Tibet.

These two sections of the film feature two major spiritual themes. The first is a child's spiritual development from selfishness to compassion. The second features a young adult steadfast about his spiritual commitment to nonviolence.

The first half is a journey out of the egoism of a child into selfless-ness.[4] The insights the young Dalai Lama gains are in many ways incompatible with American film standards.[5] Instead of conventional acting, *Kundun* presents a Buddhist principle of non-action, with the actor's face a non-expressive mask that conceals the actor's emotions and thoughts.[6] Nonetheless, the film emphasizes Buddhist ethics by showing a child deepening his compassion.[7]

The second half of the film features the Dalai Lama's nonviolent spiritual response to the invading Chinese military force. This conflict places the film partly in another category of the spiritual film genre, which is the difficulty of living out spirituality in a secular world. It shows the challenge of practicing nonviolence in a society that uses violence to resolve conflict and dominate others.[8] However, the Dalai Lama holds firm, and pain and suffering only strengthen his nonviolent convictions.[9]

On the surface, directing a movie so profoundly nonviolent in its message may appear incompatible for Martin Scorsese, who is best known for crime and mobster films. However, the film is consistent with Scorsese's critique of the dominance of violence. Violence in *Kundun* leads to destruction and corruption as it does in other Scorsese films. In using the Dalai Lama, *Kundun* reflects on the positive aspects of humans, whereas most Scorsese films reflect fallen or broken aspects of humans.[10]

The movie avoids the cliché of a flawed Westerner acquiring wis-dom through a journey to the East, as in *Seven Years in Tibet* (1997), another film that depicts a young Dalai Lama. However, like many Westerner seeking Eastern wisdom films, *Kundun* creates a generalized and simplified dichotomy between Eastern and Western values. In *Kun-dun*, the imperialist Chinese army is a metaphor for the convention of Western institutions. The hegemonic power takes over the territory of the other, making the Easterners submissive to its norms and values.[11] The Chinese are atheistic, militaristic, and imperialistic, which clashes with the Tibetans, who are community-minded, non-materialistic, and religious.

In the end, heroism is depicted not as combating violence, but flee-ing it. The Dalai Lama's journey out of Tibet to India is a Christ-like journey of suffering. Instead of a movement into a crucifixion, though, it leads to ascension. At the end of the film, the Dalai Lama appears in an elevated spot observing the mountainous Tibet through a telescope like a deity observing an earthly paradise. At the same time, he is a spiritual symbol of the condition of exile, cut off from his true community and life source.

SPIRITUAL CONCEPT

Ahimsa: the conduct of nonviolence and not killing, which is the first of the five Buddhist precepts.

DISCUSSION QUESTIONS

1. How does the film show spirituality from a child's point of view? How is it effective?
2. What are the key spiritual lessons the Dalai Lama learns in his young years? What spiritual lessons stand out from your own childhood?
3. Many Westerner seeking Eastern wisdom films feature a Western character learning from an Eastern wise man. How is this film different and how does that shape its spiritual message?
4. Why does the Chinese leader Mao Zedong tell the Dalai Lama "religion is poison"? Does this sentiment still exist in contemporary culture?
5. Did the Dalai Lama make the correct decision by leaving Tibet? Why or why not?

LES MISERABLES

1998

2 hours 14 minutes

CATEGORIES: Redemption story

SUMMARY: A bishop's act of kindness transforms Jean Valjean (Liam Neeson) from a hardened criminal into a virtuous person. But years later, even with a changed identity and a respectable position, Valjean is relentlessly pursued by police inspector Javert (Geoffrey Rush). Valjean flees with his adopted daughter Cosette (Claire Danes) to Paris, where they live unrecognized while a revolt against the government grows.

At the center of *Les Miserables* are two spiritual worldviews. The reformed thief Jean Valjean believes anyone can potentially be redeemed if mercy is shown to them. The other viewpoint comes from police inspector Javert, who rejects mercy and redemption, believing instead in secular law and a scientific view of human nature.

More than the 2012 musical film or the 1935 version, this screen version of Victor Hugo's novel highlights the duality between Valjean's emphasis on mercy and Javert's unyielding adherence to law as a measurement of justice. It also shows how grace can either be accepted, as Valjean does, or rejected, as Javert does.

The film also contrasts with others in the redemption story category. Usually, the redemption process unfolds in three phases: unredeemed self; the divided self; the redeemed self. The second act is often the critical period in which the protagonist experiences spiritual conflict and is unable to return to the old self yet still incapable of embracing a new self.

However, in *Les Miserables*, the redemption story jumps from the first to third stages. The bishop quickly redeems Valjean by refusing to send him back to prison for stealing his silver and even gives it to him as a gift. "You no longer belong to evil," the bishop says. "With this silver, I've bought your soul." This is an inversion of Faust's bargain with

Satan.[1] It also illustrates a Christian concept of salvation, as the bishop recovers Valjean's soul through his own self-denial.[2]

The bishop's act is more than an act of kindness; it is a demonstration of a Christian view of redemption.[3] Valjean learns from the bishop that he must conform to a Christian code by sacrificing survivalism and immediate gratification for a higher form of fulfillment by serving others.[4] Valjean manifests this through changing his life by becoming a responsible business owner and by following the example of the bishop by attempting to redeem others.[5]

This occurs after the unwed mother Fantine is fired from her job at Valjean's factory and forced into prostitution. Valjean must correct his error and sets out to redeem Fantine. After she is ostracized for being an unwed mother and is ashamed of being a prostitute, she continues to be defined by her past just as Valjean experienced as a convict. Identification with past sins contradicts the concept of redemption and grace so central to Christianity and what Valjean believes in. However, the admission of sins is a crucial step in the process of redemption. At a crucial point, Valjean asks a nun for reassurance that Fantine repented, which convinces him that she is redeemed.

Javert doesn't believe in redemption. He says, "reform is a discredited fantasy" and instead promotes a materialistic view of life in which "people are by nature lawbreakers or law abiders." When he thinks he has done wrong, he tells Valjean, "You must punish me or my life will have been meaningless," and later says, "The rules don't allow me to be merciful." He represents a legalistic view of spirituality. But Javert later sees that God cannot be defined through law and order.[6] However, this discovery is such a shock to Javert's worldview that he chooses to destroy himself rather than adapt to his new insight.[7]

Valjean not only believes that God is not legalistic, but that God does not advocate violence even in fights for a just cause. Valjean pursues a reformist agenda when he reinvents himself as the penitent Madeline, yet he never joins the rebels during their revolt.[8] He may empathize with their sensitivity to injustice, but Valjean realizes the solutions to life's problems are ultimately spiritual, not political.

BIBLE PASSAGE

"Because judgment without mercy will be shown to anyone who has not been merciful. Mercy triumphs over judgment." (James 2:13 NIV)

By juxtaposing Javert and Valjean, the movie shows the difference between judgment without mercy and mercy prevailing over judgment.

DISCUSSION QUESTIONS

1. Why do the bishop's actions have such a profound influence on Jean Valjean? When have someone's actions or words had a life-changing effect on you?
2. Who are the people most redeemed or changed by Jean Valjean?
3. Why did Jean Valjean spare Javert's life? Do you think Valjean expected Javert to change?
4. Why don't Marius's political solutions work? Why aren't political answers more effective in overcoming injustice in contemporary society?
5. Why did Javert commit his final action? What does this show about his spiritual perspective?

LIFE OF PI

2012

2 hours 7 minutes

CATEGORIES: Hero's journey

SUMMARY: Piscine Patel (Suraj Sharma), known as Pi, lives at a zoo in India with his family. At the age of sixteen, he leaves for Canada on a boat with his family and their collection of animals. After a shipwreck, he tries to survive on a lifeboat with a zebra, hyena, orangutan, and a tiger named Richard Parker.

The spiritual film usually provides answers to a spiritual quest rather than producing ambiguity through fragmented narratives or creating uncertainty. *Life of Pi* has a unique place in the spiritual film genre because of its ambiguity. it is open to multiple interpretations and doesn't contain a singular concept of truth.[1] But rather than dismiss religion, as some postmodernist films do, the film opens space for spirituality, or at least acknowledges a need for humans to understand the world through a religious worldview.

Set in India, the first third of the film takes a postmodernist approach to religious pluralism. Pi follows not one religion but three: Hinduism, Christianity, and Islam. "Faith is a house with many rooms," the adult Pi says to a writer asking about his story. He not only accepts other religions but practices them all.[2] Various religious experiences shape him, and his multicultural view of religion produces harmony.[3]

This religious pluralism embraces the postmodernist view that truth is fleetingly uncovered in multiple cultural sources rather than one. In contrast, Pi's father is an absolutist, rationalist, and atheist. For Pi's father, the truth is found in reason and science, not the multiplicity of truth in religion that Pi believes. Pi realizes he can go beyond rationality and make a leap of faith toward religion.[4]

His spiritual journey culminates in an exile at sea with four animals. The animal most important to the film's message is the tiger. Initially, Pi peers into the tiger's eyes to explore the theological concept that animals have souls. Later on, the tiger seems to symbolize the divine that Pi is both fearful of and longs to understand. However, Pi seems to agree with the writer's assertion that the tiger represents Pi himself. If this is true, the struggle with the tiger is a spiritual battle with himself. But, consistent with postmodernism, there are multiple ways to interpret the tiger.

Pi's journey at sea is one of physical survival until the storm he believes is propelled by God becomes a turning point in the hero's journey.[5] He confronts God, represented by the storm, with the dueling emotions of fear and awe.[6] After this, he experiences deepening dissolution of the self into the unknown where the divine dwells.[7]

Life of Pi also follows the survival narrative, a genre that includes films like *Cast Away* and novels such as *Robinson Crusoe*. This genre goes beyond the mechanics of survival and into the protagonist's fuller realization of life's meaning when societal influences are severed and life is reduced to its most core components and impulses.

In *Life of Pi* as in some other works in this genre, the survivor is purged of the traumatic pain of the trials of survival by recounting their unbelievable story to another person.[8] But Pi's story goes beyond recalling details of survival and becomes a spiritual narrative. Pi processes being an exile at sea and copes with devastation by giving the story spiritual meaning.[9]

SPIRITUAL CONCEPT

Postmodernism—a cultural trend that resists single explanations in favor of **pluralism**, an idea that there are many ways to understand the world and experience it.[10] In postmodernism, worldviews are particularly constructed through culture.[11] Postmodernism also deconstructs universal beliefs.[12]

DISCUSSION QUESTIONS

1. How does Pi view suffering? When in your life have you felt God was with you during a time of suffering?
2. How can *Life of Pi* be interpreted as a postmodern film? Where do you see evidence of postmodernism in other films or in the culture in general?
3. What do you think is the film's ultimate statement on religion? How do you feel postmodernism has affected religious belief in your culture?
4. "You cannot know the strength of your faith until it's been tested," Pi says. Do you believe this? Why or why not?
5. At the end of the film, after the writer says he prefers the story of Pi's survival with animals, Pi says "And so it goes with God." What is the meaning of that statement?

THE LION KING

1994

1 hour 28 minutes

CATEGORIES: Retaining Indigenous community and culture

SUMMARY: The lion king Mufasa (James Earl Jones) tells his son Simba (Matthew Broderick) he will succeed him as ruler of the Pride Lands. However, Mufasa's brother Scar (Jeremy Irons) kills Mufasa to become leader and Simba is forced into exile. After growing up as an itinerant outcast, the renewed Simba returns to claim his role as king.

The Lion King begins by depicting a paradise of tribal harmony. The film's holy figure, Rafiki, anoints and marks the forehead of Mufasa's son Simba, the future king. This alludes to both the Christian ritual of baptism and the West African ritual of a naming ceremony.[1] High atop a ridge, Rafiki lifts Simba up to the heavens. Heaven responds positively with a ray of sunlight falling on Simba.[2] Even animals that are prey to the lions bow to them as part of a sacred ceremony.[3]

The movie's trajectory is a journey to restore this paradise state, and, in doing so, it follows the two major themes of films in the retaining Indigenous community and culture category. The first is honoring and acknowledging the traditions of ancestors. The other is aligning with the forces of nature, defined in this film as the "circle of life."

Although *The Lion King* adheres to these conventions, there are some allusions to the Old Testament. Simba is driven into exile by jealous family members as Joseph was, and Simba must liberate his tribe from a despot as Moses did.[4] But the most significant reference is the Fall in the Garden of Eden. In an analogy to God instructing Adam and Eve not to eat the fruit from a tree, Mufasa tells Simba not to go to the shadowlands.[5] In this case, the tempter is Simba's manipulative uncle Scar.[6] Both Simba and his female friend Nala know entering the shadowlands is wrong, but they proceed, which leads to the tribe's disintegration and a reign of evil.[7]

Like other films in the Indigenous religion category, in *The Lion King* there is an emphasis on a young protagonist aligning with an ancestral tradition. Simba (Matthew Broderick) realizes his destiny is to follow the example of his father Mufasa (James Earl Jones). Photo courtesy Walt Disney Co./Everett Collection

This unfolds during the first of three phases of Simba's spiritual journey: paradise that falls; Simba's exile; return and reintegration into community.

During the first stage, Mufasa instructs Simba that there is a "delicate balance" between living creatures. He explains that, after death, the body decays and is eaten by others as part of "the circle of life." However, spirits of ancestors live on in the heavens, which highlights the significance of family in the film.[8]

Mufasa's brother Scar is a villain because he is both an anti-family and anti-tribal force. He is an effete figure who shows no interest in producing any offspring and turns the tribal African paradise into an unfertile wasteland.[9]

Simba's exile begins with him crossing of a desert, where he experiences both a symbolic death—leaving all he knew and loved—and a near physical death.[10] He meets two similarly nomadic friends, the meerkat Timon and the warthog Pumbaa. While Simba was a victim of his uncle Scar's ambition, Timon and Pumbaa personify a lack of ambition represented by their carefree philosophy of "hakuna matata," which means "no worries" in Swahili. They reject social responsibility, which results in passivity.[11] As a result of spending time with them, Simba experiences a loss of motivation, community, and perspective.[12]

Timon and Pumbaa become Simba's new community and change Simba's perspective a bit, even if he realizes he can't live his whole life like they do. Perhaps most importantly, Timon and Pumbaa teach Simba how to distance himself from despair.[13] This opens the way for Simba to realize life is more than avoiding worries and responsibilities and that he must live up to his calling as king.[14] He also learns that responsibility is greater than the guilt he feels about his father's death.[15] This guilt is his shadow self that he must face head on.[16]

The turning point into the third phase of return and reintegration is activated by Rafiki, who is part priest, part shaman, part monk. He states the central question of the film to Simba: "Who are you?"[17] He leads Simba to rejoin the tribe by conjuring the transcendent experience of Simba's father reappearing in spirit form.[18] Mufasa tells him, "remember who you are," which demonstrates the connection of identity to family and tribe, not individualism and dismissal of responsibility.

SPIRITUAL CONCEPT

Exile—Simba doesn't undertake a hero's journey or a pilgrimage but is forced into exile. This is a severe form of spiritual deprivation because it removes him from home and community, the primary sources of identity and purpose.

DISCUSSION QUESTIONS

1. What are Simba's shortcomings at the beginning? What was your major spiritual shortcoming during your formative years?
2. How is the "circle of life" defined in the film?

3. Who are Simba's mentors? Does he listen to them?
4. What are the benefits and the flaws of the ethics of "hakuna matata"?
5. What is the importance of tribe in this film? What community do you belong to?

THE LION, THE WITCH, AND THE WARDROBE

2005

2 hours 23 minutes

CATEGORIES: Christ figure

SUMMARY: To escape bombing raids on London during the Second World War, a mother sends her four children to the safety of a professor's home in the countryside. There, the children discover a wardrobe that leads to the magical land of Narnia. In a place where it is always winter but never Christmas, they align themselves with the noble lion Aslan (Liam Neeson) against the evil White Witch (Tilda Swinton).

As J.R.R. Tolkien does in *The Lord of the Rings*, C.S. Lewis uses fantasy to convey spiritual themes. In his Narnia stories, Lewis expresses Christian beliefs through imagery, setting, and characters that would not work in a realistic setting.[1] This technique creates what Madeleine L'Engle calls "truth through fantasy," which manifests in what is now called speculative fiction: stories set in imaginative worlds, futuristic settings, or supernatural occurrences in existing worlds.[2] These stories are most often in the fantasy, science fiction, dystopia, horror, and apocalyptic/postapocalyptic genres, but sometimes also feature supernatural occurrences within existing worlds.

Fantasy stories such as *Lord of the Rings* and the Narnia series are set in locations resembling medieval Europe, where battles are fought with swords, arrows, and axes instead of technology as in science fiction.[3] Lewis and Tolkien were not the first to communicate Christian beliefs in the fantasy genre. Hans Christian Andersen incorporated Christian themes into his fairy tales, and Scottish clergyman George MacDonald popularized the Christian fantasy genre with his novel *Phantastes* in 1858.[4]

In *The Lion, The Witch, and the Wardrobe*, the fantasy realm itself becomes a symbol for faith and the supernatural. Lewis uses magic as a metaphor for the mystical.[5] After Lucy visits Narnia alone, the other children refuse to believe her story and decide to consult with the professor they are staying with. "There are only three possibilities," he says. "Either your sister is telling lies, or she is mad, or she is telling the truth." This parallels Lewis's famous statement in *Mere Christianity* that Jesus's claim that he is the son of God makes him either "liar, lunatic, or Lord."[6]

Although some people call his Narnia stories allegories, Lewis preferred to call them "supposals," an imaginative answer to the question of how God might manifest in other worlds.[7] The Narnia stories are not direct parallels to Bible narratives but intersperse elements of Christianity into a fantasy story. Lewis summarized the main spiritual themes in each of the seven Narnia books. In *The Lion, The Witch, and the Wardrobe*, the primary theme is the death and resurrection of Christ.[8]

The Christ figure Aslan commits to dying for the sins of another—although in this case, he does so explicitly for Edmund, not for all of humanity. Nonetheless, the film illustrates the doctrine of atonement: that Christ's death paid the penalty of sinful humanity.[9] Aslan is mocked and humiliated as Christ was.[10] The stone table on which Aslan is slaughtered is physically different from the cross but recalls the crucifixion as a sacrifice.[11] Susan and Lucy's presence is reminiscent of the women at the foot of the cross.[12] Aslan experiences a resurrection at the equivalent of an empty tomb. He attributes his resurrection to a force that "defines right from wrong and governs all our destinies" where "death itself will turn backwards."

He also brings back to life in a mass resurrection those turned to stone by the White Witch. Although Aslan goes away, the characters assure themselves they will see him again. These events make Aslan one of the best-known Christ figures in the spiritual movie genre.

Other Biblical parallels are embedded in the movie, particularly the lure of evil represented by the satanic figure of the White Witch. She deceives Edmund with Turkish delight, a candy symbolic of temptation toward what appears pleasurable at the expense of morality. She also entices Edmund by promising him power. The White Witch acts as a warning about how things go wrong when one indulges desires without regard to consequences.[13]

BIBLE PASSAGE

"Therefore put on the full armor of God, so that when the day of evil comes, you may be able to stand your ground, and after you have done everything, to stand." (Ephesians 6:13 NIV)

In Narnia, Father Christmas gives instruments of combat to the children, an allusion to this passage.[14]

DISCUSSION QUESTIONS

1. What Biblical parallels stand out to you the most? Why?
2. How does this story demonstrate spiritual truths in a way a story set in reality could not? What other fantasy or speculative movies do this?
3. How are the children active participants in a spiritual journey rather than just escaping to a fantasy realm?
4. How does the White Witch show how evil works?
5. Why is Edmund susceptible to the White Witch's temptations? What significant temptations have you faced?

THE LORD OF THE RINGS

The Fellowship of the Ring (2001) 2 hours 58 minutes;
The Two Towers (2002) 2 hours 59 minutes;
The Return of the King (2003) 3 hours 21 minutes

CATEGORIES: Hero's journey, Christ figure

SUMMARY: The evil Sauron creates a Ring with the potential to corrupt anyone who possesses it. The Ring comes to the hobbit Frodo (Elijah Wood) who leaves his homeland with it after receiving instructions from the wizard Gandalf (Ian McKellen). Later, Frodo volunteers to carry the Ring to the dark land of Mordor to destroy it and, after a fellowship forms to aid Frodo, to fight off Sauron's forces trying to recapture the Ring.

The Lord of the Rings centers on the danger, power, and lure of a Ring the hobbit Frodo hopes to destroy. This ring is one of the most remarkable symbols of Christian theology in the spiritual movie genre. The Ring represents two particular aspects of sin. The first is that sin manifests as a desire for individual power. The second is that sin is a force that controls and contaminates the sinner's basic nature. "The hearts of men are easily corrupted," the elf Galadriel says. This corruption is most fully realized in Gollum, who exhibits an unstable, fragmented, and tortured identity because of his obsession with the Ring. Gollum murders to seize the Ring and casts aside all relationships in his quest to obtain it.[1]

A crucial moment in each character's story is when they are tempted to use the Ring.[2] To refuse the Ring is to remain true to oneself by resisting power and a desire to be greater.[3] Strength manifests not in exerting power but declining power.[4] Only by accepting limitations to one's own power and influence can one overcome temptation.[5]

This desire for the Ring, which symbolizes sin, displays what St. Augustine calls an "inordinate desire," which forges a "wicked will" that is the cause of evil.[6] In *The Lord of the Rings*, noble people act or imagine themselves as drastically different because of that desire.[7] Galadriel envisions herself as a dominating Queen, Boromir is overcome with madness and tries to take the Ring, and even Frodo and Sam go through stages of reluctance to surrender possession of the Ring.[8]

The Ring is innately evil because the satanic figure Sauron created it. Although the Ring has powers like conferring invisibility on whoever wears it, its danger derives from the enormous power that it grants to whoever wields it.[9] Because of Sauron's influence on the Ring, it will always turn to evil, and good people will become evil themselves.[10]

Aside from the power of sin represented by the Ring, the film's other major theme is the heroic spiritual characteristics the characters show on their journey. It demonstrates the importance of friendship in collectively fighting evil, the sacrifice sometimes necessary for a higher good, and the recognition that evil manifests both internally and externally. When Frodo asks Sam why people persist in such adversity, Sam replies with what can be seen a statement of purpose of these films: "There's some good in this world, and it's worth fighting for."

The Lord of the Rings series features a trio of Christ figures including the hobbit Frodo (Elijah Wood). He carries the burden of the ring, a metaphor for sin. Photo courtesy New Line Cinema/ Everett Collection

One can easily outline Frodo's narrative as a hero's journey, but another spiritual movie category these films exhibit is the filmic Christ figure. However, the Christ figure in this case is split into three characters: Frodo, Gandalf, and Aragorn.

These characters signify major attributes of Christ. Frodo represents humility and endurance, Gandalf wisdom and guidance, Aragorn courage and valor. Although these characters exhibit Christ-like characteristics through the film, all undergo a critical death and resurrection or an encounter with death.

Frodo returns to life after being stabbed by a witch-king and later attacked by the demon spider Shelob. After being pulled down from a bridge and plunging into darkness, Gandalf returns illuminated, renamed Gandalf the White. Aragorn confronts the Army of the Dead in a kind of purgatory. He later releases the spirits from their torment in limbo and becomes a ruler who promises to establish peace.

BIBLE PASSAGE

"Now if I do what I do not want to do, it is no longer I who do it, but it is sin living in me that does it." (Romans 7:20 NIV)

This description of sin recalls how the Ring's power possesses the characters.

DISCUSSION QUESTIONS

1. How does suffering lead to Frodo's spiritual growth?
2. What characters are tempted by the ring and how do they react?
3. What creates a bond between the members of the fellowship? What has been a time in your life when you've connected with people to fight for a noble cause?
4. How is the nature of evil portrayed in the film? Do you agree with it? Why or why not?
5. How do you interpret what happened to Frodo and Gollum as well as the ultimate destruction of the Ring?

MALCOLM X

1992

3 hours 22 minutes

CATEGORIES: Religious figure

SUMMARY: While in prison for selling drugs, Malcolm Little (Denzel Washington) is introduced to the teachings of Nation of Islam leader Elijah Muhammad. After his release, he renames himself Malcolm X and becomes known for his writings and speeches on racism. After a separation from the Nation of Islam, he goes on a pilgrimage to Mecca and returns with a new spiritual perspective.

Although its protagonist is known in popular culture primarily as a political figure, Spike Lee's epic *Malcolm X* is a spiritual biography. The film traces a man's spiritual progression from street criminal to faith leader. Malcolm's spiritual journey unfolds in four phases: criminal life; imprisonment; speaker and representative of the Nation of Islam; spiritual pilgrimage to Mecca.

In the first phase, Malcolm is a street hustler whose dominant desires are drugs, money, and women. He has no ability to process the racism that ravaged his family when he was young and mistakenly seeks liberation by acquiring money through crime.

This is encouraged by the first of three major mentors/father figures in the film, the criminal kingpin West Indian Archie. During this period, Malcolm is "lost in the darkness," as his next mentor will say. This phase represents a spiritually ignorant state, a lack of consciousness of one's self-worth and spirituality, and the dangers of seeking fulfillment through money and pleasure.

His second phase is consistent with the major theme of the spiritual prison film. Physical imprisonment leads to spiritual liberation.[1] Malcolm's spiritual education is ignited by his second mentor/father figure, an inmate named Baines who instructs him to transcend the "prison of your mind." He tells him about Nation of Islam leader Elijah Muhammad and says, "the key to Islam is submission," explaining this as the reason that Muslims pray to Mecca five times a day. Malcolm finds himself unable to pray until he experiences a vision of Elijah Mohammad in his cell. Malcolm compares the experience to Paul on the road to Damascus hearing the voice of Christ.

Malcolm acquires spiritual knowledge, gains self-worth, and becomes self-disciplined. His intellectual growth occurs simultaneously with his spiritual growth. This is one of the themes of the prison-based Black redemption narrative, which replaces the glamorization of a criminal lifestyle with masculinization through education.[2]

The third part of his spiritual progress occurs after his release from prison. Now spiritually educated, Malcolm lives out his faith by giving lectures about racism. He meets his third spiritual mentor, Elijah Muhammad, in person. He represents the character in the Black prison-based spiritual film whose knowledge and passion rescues a lost Black man who has fallen victim to societal conditions.[3]

During this phase of spiritual growth, Malcolm integrates adult responsibilities into his life by finding a vocation, marrying, and having children. It also shows how self-restraint changes his lifestyle, empowers him, and even changes the ways he dresses.[4] Malcolm's new clothes indicate a new identity. This discipline, along with support from the Nation of Islam, provides a sense of brotherhood that gives him confidence.[5] However, his wife leads him into his next spiritual stage by opening his eyes to the shortcomings of his mentor. "Are you so committed you blinded yourself?" she asks him. To attain deeper spiritual truth, Malcolm must confront his near idolatry of his spiritual guide.

In the fourth part of his spiritual journey, Malcolm makes a pilgrimage to Mecca and converts to Sunni Islam. He finally gains a sense of peace. Closeness to God becomes a substitute for human spiritual mentors. After seeing people of all colors on the pilgrimage, he no longer believes in Black separatism because of what he calls his "spiritual rebirth." "I no longer subscribe to sweeping indictments of one race," he says. He now believes true religious practice is the real anecdote to racism.

SPIRITUAL CONCEPT

Pilgrimage—a journey to a sacred site where a pilgrim seeks spiritual knowledge. Malcolm X goes on a Hajj (pilgrimage) to Mecca, a journey that is one of the Five Pillars of Islam, which also include profession of faith (shahada), prayer (salah), alms (zakat), and fasting (sawm).

DISCUSSION QUESTIONS

1. Who are the mentors in Malcolm's life? What purpose do they serve? What mentors have guided you?
2. How does Malcolm acquire self-discipline? How important is it to the spiritual life? What are ways you can improve your spiritual self-discipline?
3. How does disillusionment lead to a spiritual search? Has this happened in your life? When?
4. A turning point for Malcolm X is his pilgrimage to Mecca. Has there been a pilgrimage in your life that has changed you? Or would you like to make a spiritual pilgrimage?
5. The film can be divided into four stages of Malcolm's journey. Can you divide your life into spiritual stages? What are they?

A MAN CALLED OVE

2015 (Sweden)

1 hour 56 minutes

CATEGORIES: Redemption story

SUMMARY: Grumpy fifty-nine-year-old Ove (Rolf Lassgard) continues to grieve over his wife's death and wants to end his life by suicide to join her. Every time he tries to kill himself, however, he is interrupted by one of his neighbors. As a result, Ove starts becoming involved in the lives of the neighbors he distanced himself from.

Like Walter Kowalski in *Gran Torino*, Ove is a man from another generation. He is blunt and direct, can easily build or repair things, and possesses a clear sense of right and wrong. He is disruptive and out of touch with contemporary culture, yet the community needs his values as much as he needs community.

A Man Called Ove is a redemption story of a lonely elderly man who gradually gains companionship through cross-generational and cross-cultural bonds.[1] Ove has no children, so his lack of close family relationships and intergenerational contact intensifies his loneliness.[2]

During the first phase of the redemption story, Ove is consumed with grief over his wife's death and his estrangement from his neighbors. During the second phase, which takes up most of the film's duration, he is conflicted between his cantankerous persona and an emerging desire to help others. After realizing he cannot fight his battles alone, he develops a redeemed self in the third phase. However, Ove believes in an afterlife where he trusts he will see his wife again. His need for eternal companionship and reconciliation transcends the standard redemption story.

What also distinguishes this particular redemption story is the film's use of flashbacks to key parts of Ove's life, which also serve as a kind of psychological catharsis. Although his community bonds are important to his transformation, he also heals himself by reliving his memories.[3]

These flashbacks show how his moral and spiritual development were shaped through his father's benevolence and his wife's ability to empathize. "Everyone said he was too kind, how can anyone be too kind?" he says about his father. "She fought for everything that was good," he says about his wife, who personifies creativity, learning, and sensitivity toward the misunderstood and marginalized.

This contrasts with what Ove defines as an evil force—what he calls "the white shirts" who "always get their way." These are the bureaucrats who cause Ove's family house to burn down because they feel it is not modern enough and who attempt to forcibly remove Ove's friend to a private health care facility. Contemporary society and institutions do not function well and create a feeling of oppression and helplessness.[4]

To help counteract this, Ove becomes a self-appointed supervisor, routinely checking doors, gates, and walkways in his housing development to make sure everything is safe and meets community standards.[5] This also becomes a way for him to feel like he is protecting himself and others from the tragedies of life. His father and wife were injured or died from accidents, making Ove hypervigilant about following rules to ensure safety.

This self-sufficiency is challenged after his neighbor Parveneh tells him that "no one manages completely on their own." Although Parveneh helps Ove and becomes a surrogate daughter, there is not one clear liberator of Ove from his isolation, because Parveneh's daughters, a young man, other neighbors, and even a cat all connect with Ove.[6]

The movie thematizes how older men can feel a lack of agency because of physical aging, isolation, and a decline of engagement, and how they must search for ways to compensate for that loss of control.[7] The film depicts a society that lacks civic engagement but offers a vision of how this can be overcome by breaking down barriers between people—barriers created by indifference toward others and an illusion of self-sufficiency.[8] Building a supportive community only happens when people reach out to others.[9]

BIBLE PASSAGE

"If either of them falls down, one can help the other up. But pity anyone who falls and has no one to help them up." (Ecclesiastes 4:10 NIV)

Isolation brings unhappiness but bonds between people create meaning and happiness.

DISCUSSION QUESTIONS

1. What are the good and bad qualities Ove exhibits that are representative of his generation?
2. Ove and Sonja are different from each other, yet they marry. What do they see in one other?
3. How does Ove process his grieving about the loss of his father and his wife? Have you had a similar experience or know someone who has?

4. At one point, Ove says, "There comes a time in everyone's life when you decide what you want to be." What does he decide to become? What did you decide to become? Are you still deciding?
5. What episodes in Ove's life are shown as most important? If you were reviewing your life what would be the most important incidents?

THE MATRIX

1999

2 hours 16 minutes

CATEGORIES: Christ figure, hero's journey

SUMMARY: The human race is subjugated to living their lives in the Matrix, a computer programmed virtual reality. The rebels Morpheus (Laurence Fishburne) and Trinity (Carrie-Anne Moss) contact office worker Neo (Keanu Reeves) and insist he is "the one," a messiah who will liberate humanity from the Matrix. Neo then goes on a deeper journey to understand his existence and purpose.

Not since the original *Star Wars* trilogy has a movie so deeply influenced concepts of spirituality in popular culture. Like *Star Wars, The Matrix* generated universal appeal by blending ideas from Western and Eastern religions, enabling people of different faith traditions to see their own religion in the film. Moreover, the combination of religious views appealed to a spiritual but not religious audience.

However, *The Matrix* went one step further by merging mythology, philosophy, political commentary, spirituality, and film genres. One writer described the movie as a "curious hybrid of Platonic metaphysics, cyberpunk science fiction, and martial-arts cinema."[1] This subordinated spirituality to part of the film's underlying ideology, which stands in contrast to the dominance of the Force in *Star Wars*.

As part of its philosophical eclecticism, *The Matrix* uses Biblical names, analogies, and Christian theology. The rebel ship, the Nebuchadnezzar, is named after the Babylonian king in the Book of Daniel who had dreams that must be interpreted.[2] And the last remaining human city is Zion, synonymous with the holy city of Jerusalem.[3] However, the most significant Biblical analogies are the four main characters. Neo is a messianic Christ figure, Morpheus represents John the Baptist, Trinity largely symbolizes the Holy Spirit (and, to a lesser degree, Mary Magdalene), and Cypher is a Judas-like character.

Morpheus anticipates and prepares the way for the messiah Neo as John the Baptist did for Jesus. Neo's messianic narrative culminates in his death and subsequent resurrection. The post-resurrection Neo accomplishes things unimaginable before, such as stopping bullets, jumping inside an agent's body and exploding it, and ascending into the sky.[4]

This resurrection is significant because the war could not be won unless Neo is killed and resurrected. It is not until after the resurrection that Neo reaches full actualization.[5] Trinity has a role in the resurrection, first—like Michelangelo's *Pietà*—holding the lifeless Neo, and then—like Mary Magdalene at Jesus's tomb—seeing him come back to life.[6] Before this, Trinity is largely analogous to the Holy Spirit. The first time they meet, she whispers in his ear as the spirit would reach someone to give guidance.

Cypher is the Judas Iscariot figure, a traitor who forsakes his friends for the sake of selfish pleasures.[7] Cypher knows that the Matrix is not real and that its pleasures are illusory, yet he prefers them to the truth.[8] By contrasting Neo and Cypher, *The Matrix* equates the good with the real, truth, authenticity, self-knowledge, and free choice, and the bad with artifice, falsehood, inauthenticity, ignorance, and determinism.[9]

Although the Biblical parallels to the four main characters are clear, the film's emphasis on knowledge's role in liberation from illusions draws heavily on the early Christian movement of Gnosticism as well as the pattern in Westerner seeking Eastern wisdom films of blending and generalizing different Eastern faith traditions.

In Gnosticism, salvation comes from knowledge's transcendence of an evil material world. Neo learns the true nature of reality, allowing him to break the rules of the material world.[10] This is similar in some ways to Buddhism, which also sees humans as trapped in the limiting world of illusion where a redeemer figure provides liberating knowledge.[11]

In Buddhism, sensory experience, ignorance, and desire keep humans immersed in illusion until they recognize a false reality and renounce a mistaken sense of identity.[12] And as much as Morpheus is defined as a John the Baptist figure, he also fulfills the role of the Buddhist monk mentor to Neo by indoctrinating him about the Matrix.

In the end, ignorance is the real enemy in *The Matrix*.[13] The film utilizes religious traditions primarily to show the solution as knowledge and awakening.[14]

RELIGIOUS TERM

Gnosticism—An early Christian movement that emphasizes gnosis (knowledge), giving one insight about a flawed material world that makes one ignorant.[15]

DISCUSSION QUESTIONS

1. What does the Matrix represent in the film? Is there a parallel of its ideology in contemporary society? What is it?
2. What does the red pill and blue pill choice mean for Neo? Did he make the correct decision? Why or why not?
3. Why would some people in the film rather have ignorance than knowledge of the real? How is this true in life?
4. Although the film uses imagery, names, and ideas from several religions, what themes from one religion stand out to you?
5. Does the movie have a cohesive overall spiritual or philosophical theme? If so, what is it? If not, what makes it disjointed?

THE MISSION

1986

2 hours 5 minutes

CATEGORIES: Religious figure (Catholic clergy), redemption story

SUMMARY: In the mid-1700s, Jesuit missionary Gabriel (Jeremy Irons) establishes a religious mission among the native Guarani in remote South America. He oversees a thriving Christian community that includes the reformed slave trader Rodrigo Mendoza (Robert DeNiro). However, Cardinal Altamirano (Ray McAnally) believes the Jesuits are too powerful and decides to destroy the Jesuit settlement.

The central conflict in many films about missionaries is between religious missionaries and Indigenous cultures. *The Mission*, however, revolves around the clash between the Catholic Church and the Jesuits in South America, who set up a successful mission among the Guarani people. The movie contrasts the needs of religious bureaucracy with the needs of religious living represented by the Jesuits and the Guarani.[1] Like many spiritual films, it juxtaposes the insincere religion of establishment figures with the more authentic religion of those considered outsiders.

In *The Mission*, three main characters demonstrate different aspects of the tension between worldly and spiritual values. All of them choose between conscience and obedience.[2] Cardinal Altamirano believes the Church must submit to worldly pressures in order for it to survive. While the cardinal considers himself a pragmatist, he realizes that abolishing Jesuit settlements he sees as threatening to local economies and the Church establishment would destroy something valuable. "A surgeon to save the body must often hack off a limb," he says. "But in truth, nothing had prepared me for the beauty and the power of the limb that I had come here to sever." The cardinal's spiritual life is corrupted by pragmatism.[3]

He is suspicious of the communal aspects of the Christian settlements and calls them radical, even though a priest points out that the early Christian church operated communally. The cardinal resists the idea of bringing the Kingdom of God to earth by establishing collective

Christian communities. "It may distract from that paradise which is to come hereafter," he says.

For the cardinal, there is a clear separation between how things will be in the kingdom to come and what is necessary in this world to survive. As a result, the Church abandons the call to reflect the spirit of Christ and allows evil to spread further in the world.[4] The Church is also shown to care primarily about its own self-preservation and power.[5]

The Jesuit leader Gabriel does not acquiesce to the Church establishment. He believes God's kingdom can come to earth, but he rejects joining the other Jesuits in using force to defend the community. "If might is right, then love has no place in the world," he says. "It may be so, but I don't have the strength to live in a world like that." Gabriel emphasizes the transcendental with an intensity of commitment to what he feels is God's will.[6] This is supported by his belief in redemption in seemingly impossible circumstances, which includes guiding the compelling salvation of the former slave trader Mendoza.

Mendoza's story follows the three-stage process of a redemption story. Initially a slave trader in a fallen state, he experiences an internal spiritual conflict in the second stage after murdering his brother and retreating into isolation. He emerges again when Gabriel convinces him to enact a harrowing act of penance, where he carries a cargo of armor and weapons across the rugged terrain. His new redeemed self emerges in the third stage after the Guarani forgive and accept him. The film shows how appropriate penance can produce divine forgiveness and reconciliation with God.[7]

However, Mendoza's reaction to the invasion of the settlement is to take up arms against the invaders and initiate violence on those attacking the mission. The film's ending is disturbing and almost apocalyptic in scope and mood.[8] The worldviews the three main characters represent collide, making the movie conclude in an epic-like tragedy.

RELIGIOUS TERM

Jesuits—Members of a Catholic religious order called the Society of Jesus founded in the sixteenth century by St. Ignatius of Loyola. They are known for the influential spiritual disciplines outlined in Ignatius's *The Spiritual Exercises*, as well as their success spreading the gospel to other cultures.

DISCUSSION QUESTIONS

1. How do the Jesuits bring the Indigenous people to Christianity? How do you feel about the way they did it?
2. How does the natural world become a character in the film? What does it symbolize?
3. Why is the penance Mendoza performs so effective? When have you had a powerful experience practicing a form of penance?
4. What are the two approaches Gabriel and Mendoza take toward the destruction of their settlement? Which do you believe is the correct approach? Why?
5. Why does the cardinal believe he's doing the right thing? What does that say about the nature of power?

NIGHT OF THE HUNTER

1955

1 hour 32 minutes

CATEGORIES: Clergy figure

SUMMARY: The sinister evangelist Harry Powell (Robert Mitchum) learns of a man who committed a bank robbery and hid the money. Powell tracks down the man's widow, Willa Harper (Shelley Winters), and marries her, hoping to attain the money. However, her two children John and Pearl leave with the cash on a perilous trip down a river, and Powell relentlessly pursues them until they find protection from the kindhearted Rachel Cooper (Lillian Gish).

Many films in the spiritual movie genre forge a contrast between an institutional religious figure and an outsider religious figure. The institutional figure is typically hypocritical, manipulative, and insincere because of their affiliation with power, while the sincere religious figure is an outsider admired by the oppressed but scorned by authorities.

The Night of the Hunter plays out this dichotomy within the framework of revivalist Christianity. Both of the contrasting figures recall evangelical revivalist Christianity, which is based on revival meetings in tents (largely in rural America) with itinerant preachers rather than formal religion in churches. It is a Bible-based, spirit-filled evangelical form of Christianity.

In *The Night of the Hunter*, Rachel Cooper is a fulfillment of revivalism's true values, while the preacher Henry Powell is a perversion of it.[1] Powell is a preacher who manipulates others, whereas Rachel sincerely and quietly lives out her faith by taking in wayward children. Powell represents a neurotic, narcissistic, and punishing view of religion, while Rachel represents religious traits of forgiveness, humility, and compassion.

This duality gives the movie a Manichean quality between good and evil forces embodied in themes of light and dark, innocence and experience, male and female, and God and the devil.[2] The film's cinematography emphasizes that polarity. The use of shadows, unusual camera angles, and distorted perspectives creates a visual contrast of light and dark that owes much to German Expressionism and the American Southern Gothic genre.[3]

Powell contains the neurotic and psychotic elements of both film noir and horror films. He has found in Christianity something that appears to support his dark obsessions.[4]

Powell, though, is not a swindler like Burt Lancaster's sham revivalist preacher in *Elmer Gantry* (1960). Gantry is a salesman who uses revivalist Christianity as a means to apply his skills to manipulate people. Powell reveals his belief in God by talking to Him when no one is present, whereas an absolute hypocrite would not.[5] Powell views himself as the instrument of divine punishment without any concept of love, despite the sermon he routinely preaches using the words "love" and "hate" tattooed on his knuckles.[6]

Robert Mitchum plays a terrifying country preacher with the words love and hate tattooed on his knuckles. This character ushered in an era of troubled clergy figures in cinema. Photo courtesy United Artists/Everett Collection

The other side of revivalist Christianity is represented by Rachel Cooper, who is a protector of the vulnerable and provides direction to the lost. She is ostracized from her son, although the narrative does not explain the cause. As a result, she shelters and protects ostracized children. "I'm a strong tree with branches for many birds," she says. Her home is an oasis, a protective space that keeps the children from an outside world fraught with temptation, danger, and sin. In an ending soliloquy, she says children are the most spiritually resilient, which gives the movie a sense of hope.

Set during the Great Depression, economic survivalism drives the film's conflicts. Economic collapse causes the characters to show their true nature.[7] Both of John's fathers are consumed by a desire for money and willing to commit crimes to acquire it. Ultimately, this emphasis on money is something John rejects, perhaps inspired by how Rachel is not motivated by money.

One of cinema's most majestic sequences—the journey the children make down the river—symbolizes a passage from one worldview of money and religion to another. It serves as a means for liberation, and it is no surprise that one of the Bible stories Rachel recites to the children is the infant Moses being sent down the river. Despite the danger, it is a magical journey that ultimately leads to safety and a new beginning.[8]

BIBLE PASSAGE

"Beware of false prophets, who come to you in sheep's clothing but inwardly are ravenous wolves." (Matthew 7:15 NRSV)

The appearance of overt religiosity makes people susceptible to the evil motives of the preacher Henry Powell.

DISCUSSION QUESTIONS

1. Why is Powell so capable of swindling people? How do you see that kind of manipulation today?
2. Rachel is not attached to any formal religion, yet she lives a spiritual life. What do you think makes her that way? How have you experienced people without formal religion living very spiritual lives?
3. What about the journey the children go on gives it a fairy tale or Biblical-like quality?
4. What is the movie's view on the importance of money? What do you think the spiritual perspective on money should be?
5. How does the film juxtapose beauty and horror?

NOAH

2014

2 hours 18 minutes

CATEGORIES: Bible epic (Old Testament-based film), apocalyptic/postapocalyptic

SUMMARY: Noah (Russell Crowe) experiences vivid and terrible dreams of a devastating flood. He believes God's will is to destroy the human race because of the proliferation of evil. Noah builds an ark to protect animals and his family, who will be the only surviving creatures.

Noah demonstrates a tension inherent in the Bible between divine justice and divine mercy. Rather than God embodying these seemingly conflicting tendencies, the film transfers the conflict to Noah.

In the story of Noah in Genesis 6–9, God provides explicit instructions to build an ark. However, in the film, Noah has disturbing revelations about a flood and the sinful nature of man. This happens through a dream, a substance inducing a vision, and a waking vision. Noah does not receive clear instruction, but rather bits and pieces of information from various experiences of God.[1]

For most of the film, Noah interprets these visions with his family members—including his wife and his grandfather Methuselah—but there comes a point where this collaboration ends.[2] After seeing an image of himself as a wicked person in a vision, he realizes the potential for evil is in all humans. He wants to destroy the human race to eliminate that evil. Noah then isolates himself from family members and the fullness of God by rejecting mercy.[3] "The time for mercy has passed, now our punishment begins," he later says.

After Noah loses his sense of mercy, his fixation on destruction makes him an anti-hero. His turn is demonstrative of how an exclusive focus on sin and evil can suppress the capacity for mercy. Previously, the merciful side of Noah was expressed through his efforts to nurture and protect his family, animals, and the earth, and his rescue of the orphan Ila.

The beginning of the film outlines the story of the creation and Fall and the continuing effects of sin and violence that Noah is so disturbed by.[4] However, the division between the descendants of Adam's sons demonstrates two forces working in the world. "We only collect what we can use and what we need," says Noah, a descendant of Seth. The Canaanite leader Tubal-Cain says God's absence means men can take what they want. "A man isn't ruled by the heavens, he's ruled by his will," he says. The Canaanites are associated with the city and the industrial machine that destroyed creation, while Noah is aligned with environmental stewardship and the traditional family unit.[5]

Ultimately, the film comes down on the side of mercy, with Noah sparing Ila's baby twin girls so humanity can continue. This is reinforced in Ila's speech ending the film, where she tells Noah that he has chosen mercy and love. The film adds weight to her speech by using a montage of maternal animals caring for their young.[6]

The film establishes gender roles in line with the Bible epic, with care identified with femininity capable of transforming the male warriors. Although humanity in *Noah* is male-dominated, the women at the periphery embody the ethical stance that Noah must eventually adopt.[7]

As in many biblical epics, love triumphs over duty.[8] However, the Bible epic convention of romantic love as salvation is replaced in *Noah* with the ideal of familial love.[9] The film reflects a cultural trend evident in other contemporary spiritual films, which is a longing for the sustenance of home and family.[10]

This occurs within a film also in the apocalyptic/postapocalyptic genre of the spiritual film. Consistent with apocalyptic films, *Noah* is a warning. Whereas past films had correlated the Flood myth with the Cold War, it has since the 1960s been associated with ecological issues as it is in *Noah*.[11] But the film also is postapocalyptic because it emphasizes the postdiluvian hope of starting over—"a second chance," as Ila tells Noah.

BIBLE PASSAGE

"The Lord saw how great the wickedness of the human race had become on the earth, and that every inclination of the thoughts of the human heart was only evil all the time." (Genesis 6:5 NIV)

This sense of evil pervading humanity is at the center of this film.

DISCUSSION QUESTIONS

1. How is this movie different from how Noah's ark is usually portrayed in popular culture?
2. How are justice and mercy embodied in Noah and his family members? How do justice and mercy fit into your definition of God?
3. What do you think of how Noah is affected by sin in the world? How have you processed the presence of sin in the world?
4. How do the female characters maintain their sense of goodness about humanity? How have you been able to maintain that perspective?
5. Do you feel that Noah has resolved the tension between justice and mercy by the end of the film? Why or why not?

THE NUN'S STORY

1959

2 hours 29 minutes

CATEGORY: Religious figure

SUMMARY: Gabrielle (Audrey Hepburn) leaves her family to become a nun. She goes through a process of spiritual formation at a convent, where she encounters serious challenges and conflicts about her commitment to the religious order.

Perhaps no other film is as revealing as *The Nun's Story* in portraying the initiation into the rituals and routines of the cloistered life and showing the spiritual formation that occurs in a convent, from entry to taking final vows. But that is only the first hour of the film. *The Nun's Story* contains three well-defined segments. The first is set in a Belgian convent, the second in the Congo, and the third back in Europe at the outbreak of the Second World War.

The first hour of the film, which depicts contemplative practices, may be the most relevant section. Some of the major spiritual exercises outlined in this section of the film have now become popular contemplative traditions practiced by people outside of convents and monasteries.

One practice is the cultivation of interior and exterior silence "to make possible constant conversation with God," as Gabrielle is told. Another is the cessation of unnecessary conversation, and a third practice is shown when Gabrielle (later known as Sister Luke) writes down twice a day how she falls short in her spiritual life. This is a variation on the examination of conscience St. Ignatius outlines in *The Spiritual Exercises*, a daily practice that includes assessing one's thoughts and actions as well as asking forgiveness for failings.[1]

Another practice is the attempt to eliminate pride to achieve humility. Sister Luke is told the amount of pride within her is measured by the degree of humiliation she feels. The movie emphasizes how this emptying of self cannot be achieved by will alone.[2] It requires submission to the discipline of spiritual practices.

Less satisfying (but still very watchable) are the other two parts of the film that occur outside of the convent. In the Congo, Sister Luke works in a hospital with an atheist doctor who insists she is too independent to be a nun. He functions as both a mentor and an antagonist.

In the third part of the film, Sister Luke faces her ultimate conflict. She is reluctant to obey the convent's pledge to be neutral in war and forgive one's enemies. Over time, she becomes increasingly opposed to pacifism and wants to aid the Nazi resistance.

As in most Hollywood films, pacifism is depicted as an unrealistic position. And for all the respect shown toward the spiritual practices, the convent's demands are also portrayed as extreme. American popular culture generally prefers spirituality embedded in the world rather than the rejection of the world and submission to a cloistered religious order. As a result, the viewer can interpret Sister Luke's cloistered life as both noble and oppressive.[3]

The major conflict Sister Luke feels throughout the film is obedience, particularly because she is filled with so much of her own individual will.[4] Throughout the story, she moves progressively away from communal spirituality to a more individualized spirituality.[5]

Ultimately, the film falls into a treatment of nuns that is consistent with films like *Black Narcissus* (1947) or *The Sound of Music* (1965), a trope that might be called the story of a transgressive nun.[6] The film critiques the old order of the monastic life as being out of touch with modern life and as an escape.[7] The film is also ambiguous in its conclusion, which can be interpreted as either a personal victory for prevailing over an institution or a personal defeat for having failed in a vocation.[8]

"I thought I'd reach some resting place where obedience would be natural and struggle would end," Sister Luke says. But another nun tells her "there is no resting place ever, but you must have patience with yourself." The conversation encapsulates the film's representation of the struggles inherent in the spiritual life, convent or no convent.

SPIRITUAL CONCEPT

Contemplative spirituality: a set of practices to promote spiritual development. Some popular exercises include centering prayer (where one meditates on a sacred word or concept); *lectio divina* (contemplating scripture phrases); and daily examen (examination of conscience).

DISCUSSION QUESTIONS

1. How does Gabrielle's entry into the convent cause trouble in her family? Has your spiritual life ever caused difficulty with your family or friends? If so, when?
2. What are some of the spiritual formation practices Sister Luke learns in the convent? How can you implement these practices in your own spiritual life?
3. How important is self-discipline to Sister Luke's spiritual life? When does she succeed and when does she not succeed?
4. How does the film portray monastic life as both appealing and oppressive?
5. Why does Sister Luke have difficulty forgiving one's enemies or staying pacifist while her country is at war? Has it been challenging for you to forgive enemies?

OFFICE SPACE

1999

1 hour 29 minutes

CATEGORIES: Redemption story

SUMMARY: Beleaguered office worker Peter Gibbons (Ron Livingston) is bored and frustrated with his corporate office job. Desperate for relief, he seeks help from a hypnotherapist. After a mishap, the hypnotherapist's trance continues, which empowers Gibbons to make changes in his life.

This office satire that has become a cult classic over the years may seem like an odd choice for a spiritual film. But it deserves to be in the spiritual movie canon for several reasons. First, it demonstrates how a movie with no overt traditional religious or spiritual components can still convey spiritual transformation.

Office Space uses an occupational hypnotherapist as the vehicle for office worker Peter Gibbons's spiritual awakening. After undergoing hypnotherapy, Gibbons remains in an elevated level of consciousness that becomes an ongoing transcendent experience, which ultimately transforms his life.[1] Later, a co-worker tells Gibbons, "I know you had this religious experience, or whatever the hell it was."

Instead of going to church or performing spiritual practices, Gibbons and his new girlfriend, Joanna, find out about a spiritual system through pop culture. They watch episodes of the TV show *Kung Fu*, which features an itinerant Shaolin monk with flashbacks to his time in a monastery receiving guidance from elder monks.

Office Space also belongs in the spiritual movie canon is because it is a variation on the redemption story. In his pre-redemption state, Gibbons's flawed condition is one of inertia, suggesting sins of omission. He can't stand up to his passive-aggressive boss, is too timid to ask a waitress on a date, and admits he's had no direction in life for a vocation or career. He's deeply aware that his job is making him miserable, but he doesn't possess the spiritual knowledge to find a solution.

After the surrogate spiritual experience of an ongoing hypnotic state, he enters the second phase of the redemption story. Perhaps inspired by Herman Melville's story "Bartleby, the Scrivener" about an office clerk who says "I would prefer not to" when asked to do his work, Gibbons also initially refuses to do his work.[2] Then Gibbons enters a more assertive phase in which he initiates a scheme to infect the company's computer system with a virus that will slowly steal money from its accounts and deposit it into those of him and his two co-workers. However, his sense of injustice about the workplace goes too far. In the final phase of his redemption, he does his best to take responsibility for his actions and is rewarded with a favorable, near apocalyptic resolution of his dilemma.

This leads to his decision to become a construction worker, which he finds more fulfilling than office work. The only way Gibbons can change his life and spiritually improve is to abandon office work all together.[3] However, his two co-workers go on to work similar office jobs and Joanna gets another job at a restaurant after quitting her job at a chain restaurant. They just exchange one corporate job for another one. Throughout the film, as much as they loathe their jobs, they are afraid to lose them. They haven't gone through the spiritual progression Gibbons undergoes. While his co-workers may dislike their jobs, Peter goes further by disdaining the corporate structure and even the act of working itself.[4]

Office Space shows the dehumanizing conditions of office work, but it also suggests that corporate culture is incapable of offering hope for change or healthy dissent.[5] There also seems to be no alternative to escaping having to work in general.[6]

Office Space recalls Akira Kurosawa's film *Ikiru*, which shows the paralyzing and disturbing spiritual crisis an unfulfilling job creates. This occurs because workers are disempowered by a corporatized, managerial business culture that disenfranchises workers, which results in them

In *Office Space*, the beleaguered corporate worker Peter Gibbons (Ron Livingston) undergoes a spiritual awakening. The film shows meaningless jobs as spiritual barriers. Photo courtesy 20th Century Fox/Everett Collection

feeling an almost ongoing repressed anger.[7] Alienation from their work is the starting point to spiritual collapse.[8]

Office culture denies them agency and control over what they do.[9] Performing tedious tasks, working for incompetent and oppressive managers, fear of losing one's job, and an inability to confront superiors makes the employees unhappy with work and life in general.[10]

BIBLE PASSAGE

"What gain has the worker from his toil?" Ecclesiastes 3:9 (NIV)

The author of Ecclesiastes asks this question that's at the center of the spiritual conflict in *Office Space*: what does one truly receive for one's labor?

DISCUSSION QUESTIONS

1. What incidents show how dehumanizing the workplace is in *Office Space*? Are there any dehumanizing elements to your current job or a job you once had?

2. How do the three main characters handle dissatisfaction with their jobs?

3. Why do the characters put up with their jobs? Do they have alternatives?

4. What is Peter Gibbons' spiritual progression in the film? Is the outcome a satisfactory one?

5. How much does work have to do with one's spiritual life? How does your job connect to your spiritual life?

OF GODS AND MEN

2010 (France)

2 hours 2 minutes

CATEGORIES: Religious figure (Catholic clergy), difficulty living out faith

SUMMARY: In an Algerian monastery, a group of Trappist monks help the sick and needy. However, as a civil war escalates, they find themselves under the threat of violence. They must decide if they will stay despite impending danger from both Jihadists and a corrupt government.

Of Gods and Men reverses decades of largely negative stereotypes of clergy figures in cinema, yet the monks are not idealized heroic figures. They disagree with each other, are fearful at times, are sometimes confused about God's calling, and even occasionally have doubts. However, they are committed to following their faith even if they risk their lives.

Their decision to avoid taking sides in a civil war and to condemn violence also places the film in the category of spiritual films showing the difficulties living out faith. But before that crisis, the film depicts Christianity as a combination of spiritual disciplines and helping the needy.

The daily life of the monks is devoted to prayer, study, and work.[1] The film initially moves slowly by showing small everyday activities.[2]

These images feature both order and silence, and the accompanying scenes of collective prayers and choral chanting create an atmosphere of purity.[3] The monks are united through prayer and singing the psalms.[4] Perhaps not since *The Nun's Story* has there been such convincing contemplative images of monastic life.

Worship, however, is not a separate devotional action; it shows the discernment process about the danger they face during a civil war.[5] Contemplation and action are not unconnected.[6] Their actions make the monastery not only a retreat for a small group of monks but a place of service for nearby Muslim villagers suffering from poverty, illness, and corruption.[7]

However, the monks must respond when their peaceful life is violently challenged.[8] The monks and villagers are caught between dangers described by one monk as "two opponents," with "one clutching onto power, the other out to seize it." The French are also responsible, with one government official reminding the monks that the country's colonization was essentially "organized plundering." What makes these monks so dangerous to political factions is that they do not make distinctions between these groups and remain considerate towards all.[9] They don't take sides, which makes all political groups suspicious of them.

The dilemma of whether the monks should stay at the risk of their lives is applicable to anyone living out a life of faith. What price will someone pay for their beliefs and sense of mission?

The movie depicts the dynamics of each individual monk and how they resolve this question.[10] Some are deeply frightened and conflicted, yet others are determined to stay. "We are in a high-risk situation, but we persist in our faith and our confidence in God," the monk Luc concludes. "It is through poverty, failure, and death that we advance toward him."

Ultimately, their Christian faith and identity within the religious community leads the group to stay.[11] The monks' acceptance of the possibility that they might lose their lives transforms their earthly pain into a promise of eternal happiness.[12] While cinema typically explores ideas of survivalism and ego, *Of Gods and Men* renounces them.[13]

This is emphasized in a scene toward the end of the film, an adaptation of the Last Supper. Luc plays a cassette tape of Tchaikovsky's "Swan Lake." Without saying a word, the men's individual expressions show them absorbing the music and pondering the mystery of their own possible deaths.[14]

This scene, and the movie as a whole, illustrates how death can be transformed into something beautiful when given in self-sacrifice.[15] It also shows how suffering is not in vain when enacted for noble reasons.

BIBLE PASSAGE

"For God did not give us a spirit of cowardice, but rather a spirit of power and of love and of self-discipline." (2 Timothy 1:7 NRSV)

In deciding whether or not to stay in Algeria, the monks face the ultimate test of courage: the possibility of their own deaths.

DISCUSSION QUESTIONS

1. Do the monks make the right decision by staying? What would you have done in that situation?
2. How do the monks define their sense of mission? What is your sense of mission in your life or career?
3. How do the Christian monks treat the Muslim faith? What example does this set for how to make inroads with people of other faiths?
4. How are spiritual disciplines an integral part of the lives of the monks? What are your spiritual disciplines?
5. How do the monks go through discernment as a group? Who is your group that you can discern together with?

ON THE WATERFRONT

1954

1 hour 48 minutes

CATEGORIES: Religious figure (Clergy), redemption story

SUMMARY: Terry Malloy (Marlon Brando) is a longshoreman carrying out the orders of a corrupt union boss. But after the murders of would-be informants, Terry begins to reevaluate his life. With the guidance of the priest Father Barry (Karl Malden), and the support of Edie (Eva Marie Saint), the sister of one of the mob's victims, he goes in a new direction.

Although the film's central trajectory is Terry Malloy's redemption story, the movie's moral compass is the priest Father Barry, who is Malloy's mentor and the catalyst for his spiritual awakening.

Barry compares the murders of working-class men seeking justice to Jesus's crucifixion and says being silent is similar to participating in the crucifixion. This made *On the Waterfront* a major advancement in cinematic depictions of the socially conscious priest. As likeable as Spencer Tracy is as the idealistic Father Flanagan in *Boys Town* (1938), and Bing Crosby as the easygoing Father O'Malley in *Going My Way* (1944) and *The Bells of St. Mary's* (1945), the movies fall to spiritually superficiality in their presentation of facile solutions to social problems.

On the Waterfront radically altered cinema's definition of the street-wise priest. Along with Raul Julia's portrayal of Archbishop Oscar Romero in *Romero*, Barry is a heroic Catholic clergy figure. Many portrayals of Catholic clergy after *On the Waterfront* often showed priests as troubled, morally ambiguous, or ineffectual.

Father Barry's story is one of three redemption stories in the film, which also include Terry and Edie. Redemption stories exhibit a three-stage progression: 1. Spiritually unaware, 2. The struggle between the old self and the new self, 3. Emergence of the new self. Barry rapidly progresses from stages one to three after Edie scolds him for uttering platitudes after her brother's death. In an epiphany that occurs offscreen, Barry tells Edie he redefined his parish as the waterfront. As a result, he becomes the agent of Terry's awakening, intervening decisively at crucial moments to change the course of events.[1]

Barry's spiritual worldview is presented most fully in what is essentially a homily at the scene of Kayo's death at the waterfront. Using the cargo hold as a pulpit and Kayo's dead body before him, Barry rages against a lack of moral courage and says there's a shared responsibility for Kayo's death.[2] Here, the film becomes more than just an invective against corruption in a longshoreman's union. It's a broader statement about greed. "What does Christ think about the easy money boys who do none of the work and take all the gravy?" he asks. The scene ends with the equivalent of an ascension, with Kayo's dead body and Barry lifted upward from the cargo hold.[3]

Edie's redemption also comes quickly. She decides not to return to the cocoon of school because she's seen too much to return to a world of books. She discards her passive self, which was conditioned by religious education and contemporary masculine codes.[4]

The first act of Terry's redemption story is manifested in what he calls his philosophy of life: "Do it to him before he does it to you." He lives through allegiance to mobsters, which creates a false sense of brotherhood.[5] This contrasts with the brotherhood Barry talks about during his waterfront homily. Terry's second act of conflict between a flawed self and an emerging better self makes up much of the film's power. Terry is wracked by guilt and the conflict between his developing sense of responsibility and the corrupt values he was living by.[6] He realizes he's been a prisoner of his own making, incarcerated by his denials like one of the caged pigeons he keeps.[7]

Terry's new self emerges in the third act after the death of his brother. This culminates in the ending scene on the dock with imagery of a suffering but triumphant savior, although the film stops short of making Terry a full-blown Christ figure.

BIBLE PASSAGE

"Take no part in the unfruitful works of darkness, but instead expose them." Ephesians 5:11 (NRSV)

A theme in the film is exposing inequality, not escaping from it or doing what the characters call playing D&D: being deaf and dumb to injustice.

DISCUSSION QUESTIONS:

1. What difficulties do the characters face standing up to corruption? Have you suffered consequences speaking up about injustice?
2. Father Barry compares the deaths of working-class characters to Jesus's crucifixion. Are there any contemporary groups you feel that way about?
3. Father Barry quotes from Matthew 25:40 that "if you do it to the least of mine, you do it to me." How does this apply to what happens in the film?
4. Terry says Edie is "the first nice thing that ever happened to me." But why is Edie attracted to Terry?
5. Do you think the ending of the film resolved the injustice? Why or why not?

ORDET

1955 (Denmark)

2 hours 6 minutes

CATEGORIES: Christ figure, transcendental style

SUMMARY: Set in Denmark, the Borgen family struggles with doubt, conflict, and tragedy. Mikkel (Emil Christensen) is stuck in an agonizing agnosticism, Johannes (Preben Rye) appears to have slipped into insanity believing he is Jesus, and Anders (Cay Kristiansen) wants to marry into the family of an opposing religious sect. After Mikkel's kindhearted wife Inger (Birgitte Federspiel) undergoes a difficult childbirth, a miraculous event resolves their difficulties and differences.

Carl Dreyer's *Ordet* is a quiet, subtle film accentuated by a transcendental film style that includes long takes, ambient sounds, and lack of a traditional dramatic arc. The film's static quality is one of its most distinctive features.[1]

The film's average shot length is sixty-five seconds, with many shots running over two minutes.[2] The action takes place almost exclusively indoors in a few rooms with a limited number of characters.[3] The sets are naturalistic, with no exaggerated lighting, camerawork, or acting.[4]

Within these confined settings, the characters undergo spiritual crises.[5] Each character represents a different outlook on faith in relation to the religious doubt that accompanies modernism. To counteract this skepticism, *Ordet* shows nothing less momentous than eliminating doubt by supernaturally reviving the dead.[6] Although often called a resurrection, this miracle is actually a return of the spirit to a body, not a spirit leaving the body.[7]

Before this happens, the characters—and particularly the three brothers—are divided in their spiritual conditions. Mikkel is an agnostic who must witness absolute proof of the supernatural before believing in Christianity. His wife Inger reassures him goodness is more important than faith. She represents another aspect of modernism: the patient tolerance of a more inclusive Christianity.

The youngest brother Anders's plotline exposes the rigidity inherent in the two patriarchs of opposing religious sects. The heads of the two families represent different forms of faith. Peter Peterson characterizes austerity and renouncing worldliness. Anders's father Morten Borgen exemplifies an earthlier religiosity that has been encroached upon by scientific materialism.[8] Borgen's minister represents a tepid institutional Christianity, and he appears aligned with the secularism of the medical doctor.[9] The modernist clergy figure rejects the supernatural, saying miracles would break the laws of nature and insisting Christ's miracles happened only "under special circumstances."

The most arresting character in the film is the third brother, Johannes, who, in what appears to be madness, believes he is Jesus Christ. Not only is he the countervailing force to his family's minister's detached faith devoid of miracles, but he also becomes a symbol of belief in Christ in the modern world, where believing can either be a passive enterprise or disavowal of the supernatural. "People believe in the dead Christ, but not in the living," Johannes says, adding later that "all of you blaspheme God with your lukewarm faith."

The other characters believe Johannes is closer to God than they are, yet they distance themselves from him.[10] But Johannes also is detached since he reacts primarily to the supernatural rather than his surroundings.[11] Like other mystical figures in films, he is misunderstood and mocked for madness that is actually a disguised divinity.[12] Johannes gains spiritual insight into the possibility of miracles that rationalism and modernism deny.[13]

Johannes embodies the "Holy Fool" category of the Christ figure by critiquing contemporary culture's attempts to dilute religion.[14] The basis for the Holy Fool comes from the Old Testament, in which the prophet at God's command engages in foolish, mad behavior as a sign of judgment on the disobedient who think themselves wise and view the prophet as a madman.[15]

The New Testament continues this prophetic notion of holy folly in the life of Jesus, who speaks in cryptic parables, performs extreme actions, associates with the marginalized, and stresses extreme humility and the need to become simple and childlike to enter the kingdom of heaven.[16]

Because the Holy Fool has the freedom to dwell on the margins of society, the fool is not tied to worldly concerns. This enables the fool to call into question social conventions.[17] By doing this, the Holy Fool of Johannes points out the discrepancy between human and divine wisdom.[18]

BIBLE PASSAGE

"Jesus said to her, 'I am the resurrection and the life. The one who believes in me will live, even though they die.'" (John 11:25 NIV)

The resurrection takes on significant meaning in this film about belief in physical bodily resurrection.

DISCUSSION QUESTIONS

1. Why is Johannes considered crazy? Can religious followers in contemporary society be perceived as irrational?
2. How is Inger also a Christ figure?
3. What is the religious dispute between the patriarchs? What contemporary comparisons are there to their opposing ways of life?
4. What spiritual statement does the ending make about religious faith?
5. How do Inger's experiences in the last part of the film change the other characters?

PALE RIDER

1985

1 hour 55 minutes

CATEGORIES: Religious figure

SUMMARY: A mining company terrorizes a group of prospectors to try to steal their land claims. The worried and harassed teenager Megan (Sydney Penny) prays for help, and a mysterious preacher (Clint Eastwood) arrives to inspire and protect the prospectors.

Many Westerns feature characters that use redemptive violence to restore social and moral order, which later influenced action movies and superhero films.[1] Violence is shown favorably because it eliminates evil characters as punishment and prevents them from doing more malicious deeds.[2] This is derived from Biblical stories in which God justifies the righteous to take vengeance on his behalf.[3]

Westerns explore the idea of redemptive violence by thematizing settlers threatened by malevolent figures invading an Eden-like paradise.[4] *Pale Rider* follows a common Western formula of a heroic unmarried outsider removing "uncivilized" forces threatening the community. Those forces in this film manifest in an alliance between outlaws and greedy businesses and ranchers.[5]

In the end, the hero cannot fit into the community he saves because he goes outside the law to enact justice. The ending symbolizes this by showing the hero riding off alone, an allusion to *Shane* (1953). The hero who rescues the community with restorative violence cannot remain within it without disrupting it further.[6] This creates a feeling of both salvation and mystery about the protagonist.[7]

While this loner Western protagonist is almost always a monkish spiritual character, *Pale Rider* gives the enigmatic Western hero another quality: the appearance of a supernatural being.[8] He is a supernatural manifestation of Megan's prayer for a miracle to help the oppressed prospectors. It is a response to the only character that appears to have a personal relationship with God.[9] After reading from Psalm 23, "And I shall dwell in the house of the Lord forever," she adds, "But I'd like to get more of this life first." The reading illustrates the desire for divine justice to come to earth.

The stream of light from the heavens appearing right after Megan's prayer seems to signify God has heard and is answering. The lone rider known as the Preacher then appears.[10] He later arrives at Megan's house on a white horse as she reads from Revelation 6:8: "And I looked, and behold a pale horse: and his name that sat on him was Death, and Hell followed with him." The movie is not in the apocalyptic genre of the spiritual movie genre but uses symbolism from the Book of Revelation to emphasize supernatural justice coming to earth.

The Preacher is given judicial authority by wearing an imposing top hat, greatcoat, and a black kerchief around his neck that hides his parson's collar.[11] He is frequently on higher ground, above those being judged, as he looks down on the conduct of humanity.[12] He is most often in a state of contemplation, weighing both sides of the issue as he separates right from wrong.[13]

Consistent with the Western hero, his origins, power, and goodness are largely unexplained. He reveals little or nothing of his feelings and does not put down roots into the community he came to save.[14] He is not interested in earthly power but instead comes to judge the conduct of humanity.[15]

The Preacher appears to be not just a divine avenger but a ghostly figure seeking revenge. He reveals six bullet holes on his back, seeming to indicate that he has returned from the dead. However, his Christ-like wounds and killing of the villain Stockburn seem not just to settle an old score but to symbolize Christ's final destruction of evil in the Book of Revelation.[16]

Pale Rider goes beyond elevating the gunfighter to divine status in his efforts to punish evildoers as revenge. The character inspires the victimized community by uplifting them spiritually.[17] The Preacher defends how the prospectors define the American Dream through roots, a home, community, honest work, and the chance to make something of oneself.[18]

BIBLE PASSAGE

"When justice is done, it brings joy to the righteous but terror to evil-doers." (Proverbs 21:15 NIV)

The idea of retributive justice on earth is a central idea in the Western.

DISCUSSION QUESTIONS

1. How does the movie portray violence as a corrective force? Is violence in the name of justice compatible with your spiritual beliefs?
2. How does the movie mark a clear designation between good and evil characters? Is this sometimes a fair way to designate people? Why or why not?
3. Why does Megan alternate reciting Psalm 23 with her own prayer? Is this an effective way to pray?
4. How does the Preacher not just defend the prospectors but give them hope?
4. Why does the Preacher say "You can't serve God and Mammon both." What does that say about his spiritual role in the film?

THE PASSION OF THE CHRIST

2004

2 hours 7 minutes

CATEGORIES: Bible epic (gospel film)

SUMMARY: Jesus (Jim Caviezel) is seized in the Garden of Gethsemane and taken before religious authorities. He is turned over to the Roman government and is sentenced to death. He suffers agonizing relentless torture before he dies on the cross in a painful crucifixion.

The Passion of the Christ (2004) takes the gospel film out of the biopic format. Instead of covering Jesus's ministry, the movie focuses on the last twelve hours of his life. This concentration gives the film a serious theological intent that contrasts with most gospel-based films.[1]

It presents Christ's atonement and the theological concept of reconciliation between sinful humans and God that is delivered by Jesus's sacrifice on the cross. The emphasis on atonement goes against many depictions of Jesus in popular culture, which highlight his ministry and teachings rather than an atoning death.[2] It also goes against what can be called the meek and mild depiction of Jesus in gospel films.[3]

The Passion also marks a successful comeback of the gospel film. The genre collapsed after the critical and commercial failure of *The Greatest Story Ever Told* (1965), and it completely unraveled with the gospel satire *Life of Brian* (1979) and the reimagining of Christ in *The Last Temptation of Christ* (1988), which de-emphasize or eliminate the divine attributes of Christ. *Last Temptation* shows an insecure human side of Christ who wavers in his mission. Unlike *Last Temptation*, *The Passion* presents a determined Jesus.[4]

The Passion predates cinema to the Stations of the Cross, a series of stages tracing Jesus's physical journey to the cross. Like the Stations of

The gospel-based film is almost a genre unto itself. Mel Gibson's *The Passion of the Christ* emphasizes the atonement inherent in Christ's suffering rather than the teachings of Jesus, which many gospel films primarily feature. Photo courtesy Newmarket/Everett Collection

the Cross and the Passion Play, to understand Jesus in *The Passion* is to understand him through his suffering.[5]

The extraordinary violence enacted on Jesus in the film has theological implications. Jesus's inner strength—coming in part from his divine nature—enables him to endure the torment and pain, and Jesus's commitment to the mission of suffering is absolutely fixed.[6] Even during his greatest pain, Jesus ensures the torture will continue, never begs for mercy, does not try to escape or gain release, and does not try to overcome his adversaries through argument or force.[7]

Because Jesus's death is the sacrifice by which Jesus atones for the sins of humanity through suffering, the sins of humanity are transferred to Jesus. Because these sins are so enormous, Jesus must suffer an extraordinary amount.[8] The movie becomes a profound deliberation on suffering by making the audience uncomfortable watching such anguish.[9] It brings to mind the tradition of meditating on Christ's suffering as a spiritual practice.[10]

Some characters are changed by Jesus's suffering while others are not. Pontius Pilate and his wife Claudia have a conversation about truth and take different actions. Claudia is changed by her perception of hearing the truth and, in essence, converts.[11] As with other characters who change, this manifests in compassion as she comforts Jesus's mother and Mary Magdalene.[12] Pilate chooses his personal truth over the divine truth of Jesus.[13] Conversion leading to courage and compassion occurs in Veronica, as she wipes the blood from Jesus's face; Simon, who carries Jesus's cross and intervenes to stop a soldier beating Jesus; and the centurion Abenader, who helps the women take the deceased Jesus off the cross.[14] Others who see Jesus's suffering, like Caiphas, the soldiers, and some members of the crowd, take a different path and add to the torment.[15]

Atonement is not just for human sins but a victory against Satan. The movie is framed by a cosmic battle with Satan at the beginning in Gethsemane and the devil being cast down at the end.[16] In Gethsemane, Satan taunts Christ, declaring that no person can bear the burden he is contemplating.[17] A serpent, a reminder of the sin of disobedience in the Garden of Eden, appears, which Christ stomps to death, destroying his self-doubt.[18] Whereas Adam failed and brought sin into the world, Jesus will not fail and will free the world from sin.[19]

RELIGIOUS CONCEPT

Atonement: In Christianity, the idea that Christ's sacrifice on the cross is an action that compensates for human sin.

DISCUSSION QUESTIONS

1. What was your experience watching the violence in the film? What spiritual idea is the filmmaker expressing through the graphic violence?

2. How is this screen version of Jesus different from other presentations of Jesus in popular culture?

3. Do you feel it was effective for the film to solely feature the last hours of Jesus's life?

4. What is the role of evil in the film? How is it personified through human and supernatural characters?

5. What did you think of the ending resurrection scene? Should it have been expanded?

PEACEFUL WARRIOR

2006

2 hours

CATEGORIES: Westerner seeking Eastern wisdom (variation)

SUMMARY: Dan Millman (Scott Mechlowicz) is a gymnast training for the Olympics. Late one night, he meets a mysterious man working at a gas station who he calls Socrates (Nick Nolte). Soon, the gymnast realizes he needs spiritual training more than athletic training.

Starting in the silent film era with D.W. Griffith's *Broken Blossoms* (1919), the Westerner seeking Eastern wisdom film is often constructed around an older wise Eastern man, often a monk, who serves as a guru-like figure.[1] Typically set in Asia, the films tell the story of an Eastern sage teaching spiritual knowledge to a Westerner. The Western character, a kind of substitute for a novice monk, lacks spiritual wisdom because he or she is a product of an overly rational, hedonistic, and materialistic Western culture. Eastern teaching becomes the anecdote to these shortcomings.

This Eastern guru/Western novice dynamic occurs in movies as diverse in setting and scope as *The Razor's Edge* (1946), *Seven Years in Tibet* (1997), and *Eat, Pray, Love* (2010). However, *Peaceful Warrior* shifts the Westerner seeking Eastern wisdom film in a new direction that, despite its strengths, dilutes Eastern spirituality.

This occurs by reconfiguring the Eastern guru-like character into a Westerner and setting the film entirely in the West. This shows how Westerners have assimilated and coopted elements of Eastern religious thought. The guru-like Westernized character also does not represent or seem to follow a formal religion or spiritual practice.

Possibly influenced by the spiritual-but-not-religious movement, *Peaceful Warrior* offers no instruction in religious theology, meditation, or formal spiritual practices. The only reference to Eastern religion is when the monkish character nicknamed Socrates casually calls another apprentice "little Buddha," while she calls him "big Buddha."

As seen in Westerner seeking Eastern wisdom movies like *Lost Horizon* (1937) and even in non-spiritual martial arts films, the monk/guru possesses not just spirituality, but secret wisdom connected to health and longevity, and even supernatural abilities such as levitation and reading the thoughts of others. Thus, the knowledge of the sage character manifests in physical and psychic powers as well as ethical and spiritual knowledge.

What makes *Peaceful Warrior* a variation on the Westerner seeking Eastern wisdom film, however, are Socrates's spiritual lessons. Socrates is a mischievous and unconventional spiritual teacher. This expands on the Eastern religion–influenced film by removing the stereotype of the dignified but somewhat aloof guru situated in a remote monastery and instead inserts him into society.

Socrates's teachings so dominate the film that it suffers shortcomings when he is not on screen. When deviating from the teacher/student dynamic, the film is a pedestrian sports drama, and Socrates's female apprentice Joy is a noticeably underdeveloped character.

Socrates's training of the gymnast Dan is based around specific practical demonstrations more than a guru-like recitation of knowledge. Socrates imparts spiritual lessons to Dan through mundane tasks like eating properly or cleaning a car windshield. The real center of Dan's training, though, is purifying the mind and focusing on the present moment.

In *Peaceful Warrior*, the spiritual battleground is in the mind. "People are not their thoughts" and "the mind is just a reflex organ; it reacts to everything" are some of the statements Socrates makes about the danger of misleading thinking. Socrates demonstrates how to override the deluge of thoughts, doubts, and paralysis of analysis by acquiring a deepening awareness of the present.

It is there that a mystical-like state emerges and brings peace and insight. In this way, the film narrows Eastern religious ideas from spiritual practices and ethical teachings to techniques to focus on the present as a site of spiritual liberation.

Peaceful Warrior also deviates from the Westerner seeking Eastern wisdom mold in that Dan does not initially seek enlightenment. He is drawn to Socrates because he thinks he can acquire knowledge to help advance his gymnastic skills. Rather than being an intentional seeker, Dan is initially filled with arrogance and self-absorption that must be eradicated through Socrates's unorthodox teachings.

SPIRITUAL TERM

Satori—A concept in Zen Buddhism of an intuitive or mystical experience that produces a sense of reality defying ordinary experience or language.[2] At several points in the film, Dan gains insight into the cosmic reality of being more aware of the present moment.

DISCUSSION QUESTIONS

1. How much is this movie about the process of mentoring? Do you relate more to the mentor or the person being mentored? Why?
2. Why is there so much emphasis on the present moment? How is that idea a part of your spiritual life?
3. What are some of the obstacles Dan must overcome to spiritually progress? What have been some of your greatest spiritual challenges?
4. Why does Socrates encourage Dan to become more inward focused than outward focused? How do you feel this is an important part of the spiritual life?
5. What do you make of the ending with an absent Socrates? What does that mean for Dan's spiritual growth?

PINOCCHIO

1940

1 hour 28 minutes

CATEGORIES: Hero's journey, redemption story, cautionary tale

SUMMARY: The craftsman Geppetto carves a marionette out of wood he calls Pinocchio. A blue fairy animates Pinocchio and tells him he will be a real boy if he is brave, truthful, and unselfish. Pinocchio vows to follow the straight and narrow path, but he is led astray by manipulative and exploitative characters.

Pinocchio depicts a Christian view of salvation by using conventions from the hero's journey, redemption story, and the cautionary tale spiritual film categories.

Pinocchio refuses to obey what the Blue Fairy, Geppetto, and the Jiminy Cricket direct him to do. This makes the film, on one level, a Bible-influenced cautionary tale that elucidates how disobedience generates moral catastrophe. By not going to school, Pinocchio disobeys the Blue Fairy's "straight and narrow" instructions (echoing Jesus's statement in Matthew 7:14 that "straight is the gate, and narrow is the way"). As a result, Pinocchio yields to two temptations: fame in Stromboli's marionette show and self-indulgence on Pleasure Island.

What appears at first to be freedom is actually a form of bondage. Stromboli locks Pinocchio in a cage, and, on Pleasure Island, Pinocchio starts to transform into a donkey. The most terrifying aspect of Pinocchio is the control that temptation exerts over the marionette boy.[1] In Pinocchio, freedom is entrapment and obedience is freedom, which echoes St. Paul's claim in Romans 6:16–21 that freedom to sin is an illusion of freedom and that sin is a form of slavery.

Pinocchio also possesses elements of the hero's journey. Jiminy Cricket serves as a guide/mentor, trials unfold, and there is the important return home after Pinocchio's spiritual awakening, which culminates in his resurrection-like restoration to life.

Because Pinocchio succumbs to temptations, he must perform an act of redemption in the last third of the film, during which he rescues

Geppetto from the belly of a whale. This proves he has become selfless. The episode is a reference to the Book of Jonah, a narrative where the protagonist is also disobedient. In *Pinocchio*, however, the rebellious person is not inside the whale. Geppetto is there because he went to look for Pinocchio as a result of Pinocchio's defiance, which Pinocchio must now correct. This completes Pinocchio's spiritual development after a painful period of trial and error.[2]

These three spiritual film categories combine to show a Christian-influenced story of salvation from sin that fulfills the spiritual promise of Pinocchio's supernatural birth.

A deity figure (the Blue Fairy) grants Geppetto's wish (the equivalent of a prayer) to bring Pinocchio to life. But Pinocchio is not a "real boy" (converted or saved in Christian terms) until he earns his salvation. The Blue Fairy tells Pinocchio that life is a choice between good and evil. To help him discern the difference, she appoints Jiminy Cricket to serve as Pinocchio's conscience, which the cricket links to the "still, small voice," recalling the description of how God speaks to Elijah in the book of Kings. The trials in Pinocchio's hero's journey are temptations that Jiminy Cricket calls "the wrong things that seem right at the time."

The Blue Fairy tells Pinocchio "it will be entirely up to you," indicating that Pinocchio possesses free choice for his salvation. However, he receives divine assistance at critical moments. The Blue Fairy returns to rescue Pinocchio from Stromboli's cage, grants Pinocchio another chance even after he lies, and takes the form of a bird to give Pinocchio a note telling him Geppetto is trapped inside the whale. Even after massive mistakes, the divine force does not abandon Pinocchio.

BIBLE PASSAGE

"The Lord was not in the wind; and after the wind an earthquake, but the Lord was not in the earthquake; and after the earthquake a fire, but the Lord was not in the fire; and after the fire a still small voice." (1 Kings 19:11–12 KJV)

The well-known phrase "still small voice" is how God spoke to Elijah. Not in the external fury of winds, earthquakes, and fires but from a quiet interior place.

DISCUSSION QUESTIONS:

1. In Pinocchio, the conscience is linked to a "still small voice." How does this work in the film? How has a "still small voice" worked in your life?
2. Who are the surrogate mentor figures who lead Pinocchio astray? Why do they appeal to Pinocchio?
3. Why does Pinocchio get sidetracked from his goal? How have you been sidetracked in your life, and how did you get yourself back on "the straight and narrow" path?
4. How is Jiminy Cricket on his own spiritual journey as a mentor? What are areas in your life where you can serve as a mentor?
5. Jiminy Cricket tells Pinocchio, "Go ahead, make a fool of yourself, then maybe you'll listen to your conscience." How does that take place in the film? Do you think this is sometimes true in life?

PRINCESS MONONOKE

1997

2 hours 14 minutes

CATEGORIES: Retaining Indigenous community and culture, apocalyptic (variation)

SUMMARY: In fourteenth-century Japan, Ashitaka (Yoji Matsuda/Billy Crudup) is seriously wounded—the result of a curse after defending his village against a boar—and leaves in search of a way to remove the curse. In a magical forest, he is caught in a battle for forest resources between Lady Eboshi (Yuko Tanaka/Minnie Driver), the leader of Iron Town, and San (Yuriko Ishida/Claire Danes), a human girl raised by wolves who lives in the forest.

Like other anime films such as *Spirited Away*, *Princess Mononoke* is influenced by the Japanese Shinto faith. This is particularly apparent in the film's portrayal of animism—the belief that the physical world embodies spirits. *Princess Mononoke* features apparitions called kamis that live in forests, assume many forms, can transform, and can even possess others.[1] Part of anime's appeal for Western audiences is its construction of a mysterious realm removed from Western reality.[2]

Princess Mononoke contains consistent themes of the retaining Indigenous community and culture category of the spiritual movie genre. One of its major themes is the restoration of harmony in the world by recognizing and appeasing natural forces rather than pursuing individual moral transformation.

The forest where spirits dwell becomes both a sacred space and a spiritual landscape.[3] The kami represent the non-rational world existing in opposition to the human realm.[4] They include boar spirits, who would rather die than share forest resources with humans; ape spirits, who want to become as powerful as the humans; and kodamas, tree spirits.[5] However, the most powerful kami is the forest spirit/deer god, who in the daytime is a deer and at nighttime transforms into a giant translucent being that is both a giver and destroyer of life.[6]

The sacred natural space of the forest is under siege by Lady Eboshi, who runs a weapons-manufacturing plant. Although the forest is protected by animal spirits, the workers destroy it to dig for iron, an example of human exploitation of the natural world.[7] Eboshi embodies the materialist priorities of modern society because she does not see nature in terms of interconnectedness and balance but as a source of materials for industry and profit.[8] She abuses technology (shooting innocent animals), runs a corrupt industry (profiting by exploiting the marginalized), and sells to uncritical consumers (the purchasers of Eboshi's iron do not care where their products came from).[9]

At the other end of the spectrum is San, a girl with an ecocentric viewpoint that counters Eboshi's anthropocentric viewpoint.[10] They both see nature as a separate entity from humans and reconciliation as impossible.[11] However, San belongs to both the human and forest worlds, which enables her to understand the will of the deer god/forest god, the film's prominent deity figure.[12]

Between these two poles is Ashitaka, an outsider whose attempts to end the conflict are viewed with suspicion or dismissed as ignorant interference.[13] He is excessively idealistic and naive in believing everyone can just compromise and get along.[14]

Because of the epic cosmic battle between the forces of human civilization and the natural world, the film is also a variation on the apocalyptic film. Consistent with that category, it portrays contemporary struggles—in this case how to reconcile ancient tradition and nature with the advent of new technology.[15]

Another trait the movie has in common with apocalyptic films is how the humans show their destructive power through greed and the abuse of technology.[16] The characters' ambiguous moral positions and the ending's lack of resolution, however, make it a Westerner seeking Eastern wisdom variation on the apocalyptic film.

SPIRITUAL TERM

Kami—ancient gods of the Japanese Shinto religion closely linked to the forces of nature.[17] In *Princess Mononoke*, the kami take form in beasts and supernatural spirits, whose war against the humans shapes the narrative of the film.[18]

DISCUSSION QUESTIONS

1. What major human characters contain good and bad qualities? How is this a realistic presentation of how people are?
2. Do you see any contemporary parallels to the division between those driven by the economics of civilization or by reverence for natural resources? What are they?
3. The film depicts animism. What is your view of spirituality and the natural world?
4. How do the deity figure and spirits in the forest differ from views of deities in films influenced by Western religion?
5. Does the ending show there can be peace between civilization and nature? Why or why not?

THE RAZOR'S EDGE

1946

2 hours 25 minutes

CATEGORIES: Westerner seeking Eastern wisdom, hero's journey

SUMMARY: Returning First World War veteran Larry Darrell (Tyrone Power) refuses a lucrative job. His fiancée Isabel (Gene Tierney) says she will wait for him while he goes to Paris to figure out what he wants out of life. A year later, she is exasperated with what she considers his idleness and breaks off the engagement, sending Larry on a spiritual search culminating with a pilgrimage to India.

This film is an example of American cinema's maturation after the Second World War. Movies adopted a more realistic and darker tone than during the Depression era and the war years. This shift in postwar films reflects a post-crisis mentality. When immersed in a difficulty, the focus is on navigating the crisis. Only after the crisis ends is it possible to process the traumatic experience and assess how it has changed one's character. Often, it becomes impossible to return to a former way of life or continue to endure a status quo that now appears oppressive and limiting.

These ideas are conveyed in *The Razor's Edge* by the film's protagonist. War veteran Larry Darrell exemplifies postwar disillusionment—a search for purpose and meaning that a white-collar job, material comforts, and social status cannot fulfill. Although the film is set after the First World War, it follows a returning soldier's feeling of alienation from society thematized in many film noirs and post–Second World War films. His solution to disillusionment is to disregard social pressures and expectations to seek answers to his spiritual questions.[1]

Larry is also the forerunner of a character repeated in many later Westerner seeking Eastern wisdom films. Because he cannot find satisfactory solutions in Western knowledge or priorities, he travels to the

East to seek answers. An older male guru character then guides the young, troubled, and restless protagonist to necessary spiritual insight that allows him to return with a new perspective back to the West. Larry's search served as a formula for later films such as *Seven Years in Tibet* (1997) and *Eat, Pray, Love* (2010).

His spiritual journey is also a variation on the hero's journey model that unfolds in three stages. His initial spiritual condition is a combination of disbelief, restlessness, and aimlessness. Larry is friendly on the surface but angst-filled on the inside. Neither withdrawing to a bohemian-like life in Paris nor voracious reading provides him with the answers he seeks. Instead, only a mystical experience in the East that occurs in the second act of the film can rescue him from his condition.

In India, an unnamed holy man emphasizes that books and teachings are ultimately inadequate and merely introduce a seeker to the spiritual life. Substantial spiritual transformation takes place after a powerful transcendental experience. Larry undergoes this life-altering experience in isolation on a mountain, which the holy man assures Larry was a revelation in which "you and God were one." Consistent with many accounts of mystical encounters, the event is fleeting but life changing, and the holy man advises Larry to return to society.

With Larry back in Paris, the third act shows the outcome of other characters with secular priorities that contrast to his newfound spirituality. Larry's friends are damaged from years of putting their faith in chasing what they cannot achieve or an inability to recover from loss. He ends up surrounded by characters who represent values he rejects.[2]

For Larry's affluent European friend Elliot Templeton, that value is praise in society. Templeton devotes himself to clothes, appearance, and the aristocracy.[3] American business and ambition are represented by Gray Maturin.[4] His dependency on career and money causes him to suffer a nervous breakdown after a stock market crash. Larry's former girlfriend Isabel has the desperate need to possess and dominate.[5] She chases the status that comes from marriage and money, and she is ultimately consumed by a futile desire for Larry's love. His friend Sophie cannot recover from the loss of her husband and child in a car crash and becomes an alcoholic. Ultimately, she cannot stand withstand the tragedies and realities of life.[6]

After attaining a certain degree of enlightenment through his mystical experience in the East, Larry's new spiritual state requires more anonymity and humility than his friends and former life can provide. Unlike many American films, *The Razor's Edge* sees success as unattractive and elevates a lack of conventional ambition.

SPIRITUAL TERM

Mysticism—contains four qualities according to William James, all of which are revealed in Larry's transcendental experience in India: directly experienced and cannot be adequately described in words; reveals deep insight the intellect cannot attain; transient and cannot be sustained; produces a feeling of being grasped and held by a superior power.[7]

DISCUSSION QUESTIONS

1. Why is Larry unsatisfied after returning from war? When have you experienced a similar feeling following a harrowing experience?
2. How does the mystical experience in the mountains change Larry? When have you had a similar experience?
3. Why are the other major characters besides Larry never really satisfied?
4. Why does Somerset Maugham call Larry's choice with Sophie an act of self-sacrifice? Do you agree?
5. What is your interpretation of the end of the film? Did Larry make the right choice? Why or why not?

Revenge of the Sith

2005

2 hours 20 minutes

CATEGORIES: Cautionary tale

SUMMARY: Anakin Skywalker (Hayden Christiansen) trains as a Jedi under Obi-Wan Kenobi (Ewan McGregor). However, Chancellor Palpatine (Ian McDiarmid) recognizes the ambition in Anakin and educates him about the dark side of the Force. After experiencing premonitions of his wife Padme (Natalie Portman) dying, Skywalker considers what power he can gain by fully embracing the dark side.

The Force in the original *Star Wars* trilogy changed spirituality and popular culture. It merged concepts from Eastern and Western religions, thus creating a spirituality accessible to people of various faiths. After *Star Wars*, movies increasingly featured characters defined less by a specific religion and more by a more universal spirituality.

The Star Wars prequels, though, altered the meaning of the Force. In *The Phantom Menace* (1999), Qui-Gon Jinn defines the Force as consisting of midi-chlorians, "a microscopic life form that resides in all living cells." A young Anakin Skywalker is connected to a machine that determines he possesses more midi-chlorians than even the Jedi master Yoda. This appears to limit the Jedi to a genetic few.[1]

Anakin is even said to be conceived from midi-chlorians without a father. Partly because of this, several characters believe Anakin is "the chosen one," a frequent term in spiritual films for a messianic figure. But this variation on a virgin birth does not make Anakin a Christ figure. He is not a redeemer but someone they hope will "restore balance to the Force."

This may connect to the Taoist idea of the coexistence of the yin and the yang (the Force is influenced by the Taoist belief of an underlying energy that is a life force), but exactly how an individual creates a balance in the Force is never adequately explained. Additionally, in the original trilogy, Obi-Wan Kenobi and Yoda are on the periphery of society teaching

Luke the ways of the Force independently, whereas, in the prequels, the Force is institutionalized through a Jedi Council that keeps order.[2]

Despite these alterations to the Force, *The Revenge of the Sith* earns a place in the spiritual movie genre because it is cautionary tale about how a person turns to a life of evil, or to "the dark side."

Spiritual films often show the opposite trajectory. Someone discards their flawed nature for a better self, like in the redemption story. Instead of the conversion experience of the redemption story, *Revenge of the Sith* depicts the loss of integrity of a once noble and selfless person. How this happens reveals spiritual ideas about the nature of evil and why people are susceptible to it.

Anakin's decision is of his own free will. If Anakin turned to the dark side because Palpatine used a Sith mind trick on him, Anakin would not be morally accountable for the evil he commits.[3] However, Anakin consciously makes a choice that recalls the Fall in the Book of Genesis. Palpatine is analogous to the serpent in the Garden of Eden who plays upon the pride and envy of those tempted to pursue knowledge of good and evil in defiance of a command not to.[4] Anakin is selfish because he chooses power for his own gain.[5]

Palpatine encourages Anakin to focus on his ambition and anger, which are emotions that lead him deeper into the dark side. Another reason for Anakin's downfall is that he fears the death of his wife Padme so much that he wants to control and manipulate events. Yoda counsels him that "the fear of loss is a path to the dark side." He also adds that "death is a natural part of life; rejoice for those around you who transform into the Force."

However, Anakin refuses to accept the natural order of life and death and is unable to courageously move forward, regardless of the consequences.[6] In the end, he believes power is more important than love. "Love won't save you, only my new powers will do that," Anakin tells Padme.

BIBLE PASSAGE

"There is no fear in love. But perfect love drives out fear, because fear has to do with punishment. The one who fears is not made perfect in love." (1 John 4:18 NIV)

Anakin's fear of loss prevents him from recognizing what is right and wrong.

DISCUSSION QUESTIONS

1. Why is Anakin susceptible to Palpatine? What does this say about the nature of evil?
2. Is Obi-Wan an adequate mentor to Anakin? Is he in any way responsible for Anakin's downfall? Why?
3. Why are ambition, anger, and fear a pathway to the dark side? How have you overcome feeling these emotions?
4. Why doesn't Anakin tell the Jedi about his marriage? When have there been consequences in your life for keeping something secret?
5. Why does Obi-Wan leave Anakin at the end of the film? What does this say about his character?

THE RIVER

1951

1 hour 39 minutes

CATEGORIES: Westerner seeking Eastern wisdom

SUMMARY: A British family lives near the Ganges River in India after the Second World War. A wounded war veteran called Captain John (Thomas E. Breen) arrives, which stirs the interest of three young girls, including the adolescent Harriet (Patricia Walters). As the Hindu festival of Diwali comes and goes, the Western characters encounter love, birth, death, and spirituality.

Although *The River* is framed as a coming-of-age story of an English girl in India, the Ganges River—or perhaps more broadly, the flow of life itself—is the main character.

The characters' lives are caught up in the transitory quality and passage of time represented by the river.[1] The intercutting of documentary

Jean Renoir's *The River* shows a clash between cinematic conventions of Eastern and Western spirituality. While the Western characters often fight against life's adversities, Melanie (Radha) emphasizes submission to what life brings. Photo courtesy Mary Evans/AF Archive/Everett Collection

footage of the river underscores Harriet's statement that "people depended on the river spiritually as well as physically." During Diwali, the celebration of the Hindu religious festival of lights, the river serves as a vital backdrop. Harriet says Diwali made her feel "as if I were being stretched" during a holiday that contains symbols of light and darkness, representing what Harriet describes as "the old eternal war between good and evil."

Although *The River* is in the Westerner seeking Eastern wisdom category, it doesn't adhere to the convention of an older male Eastern sage figure imparting wisdom. Instead, the film juxtaposes Eastern and Western worldviews.

The movie uses cinematic tropes, with the Western viewpoint depicted as a combination of continual longing for something better and resisting disagreeable change. This contrasts with the trope that Eastern religion sees life as less about becoming something new and more about realizing a renewable state of being with all of its fluctuations and changes.[2] The film's central conflict is the Western characters' inability to accept the inevitaly of undesired change which results in disappointment and disillusionment.[3]

The film centers on the passions of the Western characters, particularly the turbulent feelings of three adolescent girls.[4] Their desires are ephemeral in contrast to the timeless cycle of creation and destruction represented by the river.[5] As the film progresses, their emotions are directed into different areas, with Valerie representing the aesthetic, Harriet the ethical, and Melanie the religious.[6]

The Western characters are limited by their emotions and desires, including the Second World War veteran Captain John. Like the convention of the war-scarred veteran in postwar film noirs, he is a moody drifter. Harriet observes that he is "asking questions but never opening his heart." He admits he cannot accept the burden of having lost a leg in the war and is suffering from mental health issues. Captain John's character represents the damage caused by Western culture and its wars.[7]

Because Melanie is the daughter of a Western father and an Eastern mother, she represents the conflict between Eastern and Western ideologies. Initially unsure about her true identity, her dynamic dance sequence during the story Harriet tells about Krishna and Radha visualizes her discovery of meaning and identity by merging art and religion.[8]

During the reenacted story of Krishna and Radha, after a village girl discovers her father's wishes have converged with her own, Melanie is transformed into the goddess Radha. She identifies with a powerful female deity who expresses her creative force by dancing to reveal her love for a man who changes into Krishna.[9] The dance illustrates how her acceptance of life rather than being at conflict with it creates both passionate and divine love.[10] This reenactment is also important because it shifts to Melanie's viewpoint, allowing the film to escape being dominated by Harriet's perspective.[11]

In a later scene, a disturbing conflict between the Eastern and Western characters emerges as Valerie and Harriet quarrel and Captain John is humiliated by his handicap.[12] Cruelty and egoism drive the relations in this scene, and the harmonious and devotional love with creativity represented in Harriet's story is replaced by strife.[13]

However, a brief but important exchange toward the end of the film attempts to resolve the cinematic spiritual generalizations between Eastern and Western perspectives as well as to end what Melanie calls rebellious-ness and quarreling with life. Captain John asks Melanie what they should do. She tells him that they should "consent to everything."

The dialogue illustrates the spiritual perspective that the charac-ters employ to resolve their conflicts: the acceptance of reality even in its negative, destructive aspects.[14]

RELIGIOUS CONCEPT

Kali—The Hindu goddess of destruction and creation. Harriet says, "For Hindus, all the universe is God," which provides a multitude of symbols containing divine virtues and qualities including Kali, who sym-bolizes how "creation is impossible without destruction."

DISCUSSION QUESTIONS:

1. How are creative and spiritual power gendered in this film? How does it contrast female and male characters through these forces?
2. How is creativity connected to spirituality? How do you see this in your life?
3. How are danger and evil represented in the film? How does Bogey's death fit into this?
4. How are destruction and creation illustrated in the film? How do you see this as a spiritual principle in your life?
5. How have the three adolescent girls (Harriet, Valerie, and Melanie) changed by the end of the film?

THE ROBE

1953

2 hours 15 minutes

Categories: Bible epic, redemption story, difficulty living out faith

Summary: The Roman tribune Marcellus Gallio (Richard Burton) serves in Palestine where he oversees the crucifixion of Christ. He is tormented by participating in it and searches for the robe Jesus wore because he feels it cursed him. He finds the robe with the slave Demetrius (Victor Mature), who, along with other early Christians, tells Marcellus about the Christian faith.

In *The Robe*, Rome is a brutal military dictatorship and an example of how power produces corruption.[1] This Roman Christian film begins just before the death of Christ at the end of the rule of Tiberius and the beginning of Caligula's reign. Although a hypermasculine military force carries out the violence, the emperors are depraved, infantile, neurotic, overly emotional, and sexually ambiguous.

Caligula in *The Robe*, like Nero in *Quo Vadis* and Commodus in *Gladiator*, are perverse leaders. They rule over a pagan empire with an infinite number of gods that seem to make any behavior acceptable, which generates hedonism.

The movie is a clash of Roman decadence and Christian idealism.[2] As in *Quo Vadis*, the film establishes a contrast between crass Roman men and refined Christian women.[3] In *Quo Vadis*, the Christian woman Lygia converts the Roman military leader Marcus Vinicius to Christianity. In *The Robe*, Marcellus's conversion begins after conversations with the paralyzed Christian Miriam, and Marcellus's love interest, Diana, follows him in converting to Christianity. The film identifies the shift in religions with a shift from earthly passion to the love of the divine,[4] from pagan skepticism to Christian piety.[5]

However, Diana represents innocence and makes him more receptive to new influences.[6] In the end, she speaks for Marcellus and declares there is another king in Christ, telling Caligula he is "vicious, treacherous, drunk with power, an evil insane monster posing as emperor."

Contrasting with the Roman state that combines militarism and hedonism, the Christians form a utopian community based on charity and kindness. In this respect, *The Robe* also fits in the spiritual movie category of showing the difficulty of living out faith in an antagonistic culture.

In the end, the warrior culture of Rome is spiritually overcome by a higher law that triumphs through a passive heroism rather than an active one.[7] Instead of showing in a significant way the supernatural elements of Christian faith, Christianity is the result of an ethical resurrection that creates a compassionate community.[8] Acts of charity redeem the social world. [9]

Conversion is a central theme in the Roman Christian film, and in *The Robe*, Marcellus's redemption transpires in three acts.[10]

In the first act, he is a tribune following his duty, but he is also enough of a dissident to defy Caligula and show respect for the valiant slave Demetrius. The second act occurs after Jesus's crucifixion: Marcellus becomes mentally unstable, which stands in for the conflict between an old and an emerging new identity. He goes in search of the robe, which becomes a spiritual pilgrimage during which he learns about Christianity from marginalized and feminine characters.[11] The third act comes after he declares his allegiance to Christianity.

Redemption stories often include conversion experiences linking the second and third acts. In *The Robe*, this occurs when Demetrius tells Marcellus "You think it's his robe that made you ill, but it's your conscience, your own decent shame." After Marcellus overcomes his superstition about the robe, he says what many transformed figures in the spiritual film genre declare before moving into full-fledged redemption: "I am not afraid."

BIBLE PASSAGE

"Here is a trustworthy saying that deserves full acceptance: Christ Jesus came into the world to save sinners—of whom I am the worst." (1 Timothy 1:15 NIV)

In one scene, the apostle Peter and Marcellus both think they are the worst of sinners. But in *The Robe*, there is the opportunity for redemption even for those who feel that they have sinned against Jesus himself.

DISCUSSION QUESTIONS

1. What are the differences between the Roman Empire and the Christian way of life? Do you see a divide now between Christians and the prevailing culture?
2. How does the film work as a redemption story for Marcellus and for Diana?
3. What do you think makes Marcellus capable of change?
4. How do you think Marcellus overcomes his feelings of guilt? How have you overcome guilt about past wrongdoings?
5. This movie portrays the actual crucifixion of Christ. How did you feel while watching that part and does it in any way reflect how you picture the crucifixion?

ROMERO

1989

1 hour 42 minutes

CATEGORIES: Religious figure, Christ figure, redemption story

SUMMARY: In 1977, Oscar Romero (Raul Julia) is named archbishop of El Salvador. Authorities believe he is a safe choice who will support the government's suppression of a religious-fueled peasant uprising. Yet, as Romero sees more tyranny, he speaks out about government oppression and economic injustice.

The Christ figure Oscar Romero is concerned with justice, attracts loyal followers, and is misunderstood by authorities. He also experiences a poignant Garden of Gethsemane moment in which he must accept

God's will rather than his own—a critical component of the Christ figure narrative.

At this desperate moment, he drops to knees and succinctly prays, "I can't. You must. I'm yours. Show me the way."

Consistent with a Christ figure, he achieves a death as a martyr and undergoes a symbolic resurrection through his ongoing influence on the living peasants. Aligning with the poor and the marginalized becomes interpreted as a political act and a challenge to secular authority, which costs him his life.[1]

However, Romero doesn't begin as a noble clergy character fighting oppression like priests in films such as *Rome, Open City* (1945). As Romero increasingly embraces being a Christ figure, he works out his own redemption.

Romero's initial flawed, unredeemed state is not rooted in conventional selfishness. Instead, he is disconnected, overly cerebral, and spiritually moderate. At first, he criticizes his friend and activist priest Rutilio Grande. "You're going too fast, we in the church must keep to the center," he insists. However, the film elucidates how moderation shuts off empathy and sensitivity toward injustice. The detachment that comes with moderation hardens the heart. By remaining neutral and distant, the church aligns itself with the ruling elite and becomes an instrument of an oppressive status quo.[2]

Like all redemption stories, *Romero* contains a critical turning point that awakens the protagonist from a limited, flawed state and motivates them to change. After government forces assassinate Grande, who in some ways is also a Christ figure sacrificed and resurrected, Romero intensifies his commitment to the poor and becomes more outspoken about oppression. However, as he becomes more spiritually redeemed, he simultaneously feels more pressure from authorities.

"I believe economic injustice is the root cause of our problems," he says, reiterating the liberation theology Grande supported. Originating in Latin America, liberation theology espouses that poverty and injustice are contrary to the will of God.[3] So the church must play a role in changing oppressive institutions and policies to alleviate injustice.

In liberation theology, spirituality is not just interior transformation but a release from external pressures and oppression.[4] But this movement cannot be accomplished alone. Liberation theology encourages people to connect with a Christian community that studies, worships, and performs social activism together.[5] "Our faith requires that we immerse ourselves in the world," Romero says, demonstrating his progression out of detachment into connection with the oppressed.

While liberation theology was initially controversial during the Cold War era, the Catholic Church increasingly embraced these ideas in some situations as a way to implement social justice—marking a move toward systemic change rather than the more limited intervention of charity. There are similarities between Romero and Christ because both align themselves with the poor and oppressed rather than suggesting violent solutions.[6]

Proponents of liberation theology point out Biblical connections through prophets who called for justice, including Moses. They emphasize how God actively worked to liberate the Hebrews from slavery and oppression. Romero moves this idea to the present day, with the oppressed people of God redefined as the peasants of El Salvador.

SPIRITUAL CONCEPT

Liberation Theology—Peruvian theologian and priest Gustavo Gutierrez wrote in his seminal book, *A Theology of Liberation*, that sin takes the form of poverty and injustice implemented through institutions.[7] He believed some degree of liberation from this oppression must be enacted to remove that sin.[8]

DISCUSSION QUESTIONS:

1. Do the events in *Romero* call for moderate or systemic change? Where do you see the conflict between moderate and systemic change in the current culture? What is the solution between those two ideologies?
2. How does non-violent resistance work in the film? Is it an appropriate spiritual response? Why or why not?

3. How does Romero get to know the peasants and understand their lives? What are ways you can do this in your own life with people who are marginalized?

4. Romero says the church has to work out its own salvation by aiding the poor. How important do you think helping the poor is for a religious institution?

5. How does Oscar Romero's end reflect the death and resurrection theme in Christ figure films?

RUN LOLA RUN

1998 (Germany)

1 hour 20 minutes

CATEGORIES: Search for God

SUMMARY: Lola (Franka Potente) receives a phone call from her boyfriend Manni (Moritz Bleibtreu) who says he misplaced money intended for a crime boss. Manni tells Lola if she does not come up with 100,000 marks in cash in the next twenty minutes, he will rob a grocery store. Lola enacts three different scenarios of how to get the money for Manni.

Run Lola Run is a compressed version of *Groundhog Day*. Instead of an entire day recurring multiple times, a twenty-minute period of time repeats three times. Both movies present a repeating set of circumstances, a "we're going to keep doing this until we get it right" scenario.[1] Instead of the protagonist encountering obstacles to enlightenment in different circumstances, there are variations on the same set of obstacles.[2]

Shot in Berlin less than a decade after the fall of the Berlin Wall, the movie emphasizes the frenetic desire for money. This could represent anxieties about capitalism in reunified Berlin or the tumult of modern life in general. Within this chase for money against the tyranny of time, Lola finds her spiritual identity.

Unlike *Groundhog Day, Run Lola Run* is not a redemption story. Lola does not begin selfish and move toward altruism. Instead, she starts in selflessness and deepens into spiritual self-actualization.[3] At the beginning of the film, Manni reminds Lola, "You said 'love can do everything.'" The movie depicts a fragmented culture that makes people anonymous and alienated, which Lola and Manni try to offset through their love for one another.[4] The plot's driving force is not a desire for money but an act of love and devotion.

In the first two attempts, Lola fails to gain significant spiritual awareness, but she draws on powerful and mystical inner resources to shape her destiny in the final attempt.[5] The third scenario is distinguished from the others from the beginning, as Lola she leaps over the dog and growls at him during her dash down the stairs, which is emblematic of her amplified self-assertion.

However, the turning point comes when—unlike the previous two sequences—she fails to arrive in time at the bank to see her father. Instead of giving up, she recites a short prayer with her eyes closed as she runs. The rapid statements accentuate her directness and earnestness: "Come on. Help me. Please. Just this once. I'll just keep running, okay? I'm waiting." She makes a commitment to wait and see what life brings and prays with her eyes closed, demonstrating the trust she feels.[6]

After a truck comes to a screeching halt just before her, she looks around and for the first time sees the world around her as separate from her needs.[7] She then sees a casino sign that she puts her hope in, illustrating an openness to unexpected solutions.[8] She also aids a heart attack victim in an ambulance, thus broadening her sense of altruism. In the third segment, Manni also receives spiritual guidance though an oracle-like blind woman who directs him to a solution.

The film is also a theological exploration of free will and determinism. With both forces at work, life is a dynamic and ever-shifting terrain in which everyone's actions have effects on others. This idea is set up by the dominos falling at the beginning of Lola's run and reinforced by rapid fire shots of the futures of minor characters altered by their encounters with Lola during each episode.

Run Lola Run depicts the will of the individual against the power of coincidence.[9] Although it validates both, Lola's resolve and free will ultimately stand out.[10] The power of will is most visibly demonstrated by Lola screaming at the roulette wheel to force the ball to land on the number she places her money on. This counteracts deterministic forces working against her winning the game.[11] Lola's passion—the engagement of will with feeling—ends up being the motivating force of the film.[12]

RELIGIOUS CONCEPT

The movie covers the interaction of **free will** (the ability to make choices) with **determinism** (an external cause and effect affecting individuals), which can include spiritual influences like the work of a deity or karma.

DISCUSSION QUESTIONS

1. How much free will/choice does Lola exert? How much free will do you think humans have?
2. What is the role of determinism for Lola? Is there something divine or spiritual in external circumstances or are they just coincidences? Why?
3. How does the movie show that small encounters and actions can make a difference? What's an example from your life?
4. How are doubt and uncertainty expressed between Lola and Mannie during their conversations at the end of the first two segments?
5. What spiritual insights has Lola gained by the end of the film?

THE SACRIFICE

1986 (Sweden)

2 hours 29 minutes

CATEGORIES: Apocalyptic, transcendental style (variation)

SUMMARY: Alexander (Erland Josephson) criticizes the elevation of technology and the flaws of modern life. At his birthday gathering, he and his guests learn that a nuclear catastrophe is imminent. Alexander prays to God and vows to sacrifice anything to restore the world.

Some of the most challenging films in the spiritual movie genre are by Russian director Andrei Tarkovsky. He directed seven feature films between 1962 and 1986, most of which are spiritual films.

The pacing of his films can be perplexing for some movie viewers. Tarkovsky goes beyond transcendental style towards what scholars have termed "slow cinema."[1] Like transcendental films, Tarkovsky employs an austere style using long takes, little action, negligible camera movement, and minimal narrative to produce not only slowness but a sense of distance rather than empathy.[2]

However, Tarkovsky's slow cinema does not aim to guide the filmgoer to another level of consciousness like the transcendental style. Instead, it expresses Tarkovsky's own desires and concerns as an auteur director.[3] Tarkovsky's work is notable for blurring the distinction between reality and the fantastic, which makes his narratives confusing and disjointed.

Still, Tarkovsky's films are highly regarded for their spiritual themes. His movies exhibit a continual concern and care for the human condition.[4] They also consistently depict the struggle between the material and the spiritual.[5]

In *The Sacrifice*, the protagonist Alexander is an unusual main character because he is overly intellectual and not heroic.[6] Unlike conventional heroes that drive a narrative forward, Alexander is a man of many words and little action.[7] He lacks the decisiveness and stable identity of mainstream film heroes.[8] Like other Tarkovsky protagonists, he starts with an absence of moral strength.[9] However, he also displays an awareness of the world's spiritual shortcomings. "Our entire civilization is built on sin from beginning to end," he says.

The turning point for Alexander arrives at the midpoint of the film, when he prays during the imminent threat of a nuclear attack, which leads him to embrace the Christian concept of self-sacrifice.[10] "I will relinquish everything that binds me to life if only thou dost restore everything as it was before," he says. Sacrifice finally sets the main character in motion.[11] This makes it a unique film in the apocalyptic genre for emphasizing spiritual transformation far more than physical survival.

Nevertheless, the film's ambiguous structure leaves unclear whether there actually is a looming apocalyptic event. The film suggests it could be a product of Alexander's imagination or a dream. The gap between reality and fantasy widens after he falls down while playing with his son. However, another major blackout or fantasy sequence appears to take place later in the film after Alexander crawls onto a sofa to sleep.

As Alexander's actions and motivations become increasingly disordered, the viewer is left unable to distinguish between what is real and what is a product of his despair and alienation.[12] The apocalyptic imagery could be a metaphor for his inner turmoil.[13] But it could also indicate how civilization is at a cataclysmic spiritual juncture because it replaced Christian morality with a godless ideology based on technology.[14] This self-destructive element of living in a troubled post-Christian culture is captured in Alexander's ambivalent personality, as he wanders between dream and reality.[15]

The Sacrifice's presentation of an apocalyptic event subverts the classical linear plot.[16] It blends Alexander's internal and external worlds into one continuous reality without clearly separating the two, creating an ambiguous narrative.[17]

This ambiguity is most pronounced after Alexander wakes up in the sunshine with nothing indicating there was a war or any mention of it by the other characters.[18] Yet, whatever occurred to Alexander spiritually transforms him enough that he sets a house ablaze, keeping what appears to be his sacrificial promise to God.

BIBLE PASSAGE

"People will faint from terror, apprehensive of what is coming on the world, for the heavenly bodies will be shaken." (Luke 21:26 NIV)

The fear of death in an apocalyptic event creates terror and apprehension in *The Sacrifice*.

DISCUSSION QUESTIONS

1. What did you think of the film's structure and style? Was it innovative, difficult to follow, or a combination of both? Why?
2. How do the characters react when they believe death is near? Have you ever seen or experienced that kind of apprehension from possible impending death?
3. What is the connection between the painting of Mary in *Adoration of the Magi* and the housekeeper Maria? How are they both figures of salvation to Alexander?
4. What is the meaning behind Alexander burning his house? When have you ever sacrificed something valuable to demonstrate a spiritual transformation?
5. How does the movie come full circle at the end? What is the significance of the line that "Little Man" says?

SCHINDLER'S LIST

1993

3 hours 15 minutes

CATEGORIES: Redemption story, difficulty living out faith

SUMMARY: During the Second World War in Nazi-occupied Poland, Oskar Schindler (Liam Neeson) uses subjugated Jews, including the accountant Itzhak Stern (Ben Kingsley), to work in his factory to make his business more profitable. Schindler recognizes how endangered the Jewish people are under the command of the Nazi commandant Amon Goeth (Ralph Fiennes), so he takes bold measures to protect his Jewish workers from being killed.

Many Holocaust movies center on dramatizing a survivor's narrative, but the core of *Schindler's List* is the redemption of German businessman Oskar Schindler.[1] His transformation from self-centered industrialist to one who shelters Jewish workers demonstrates the universal potential of spiritual conversion.[2]

The film illustrates the mystery of grace; how sometimes the unlikeliest people are spiritually transformed. It also demonstrates how redemption is connected not just to internal moral development but outward to altruistic actions, and how redemption manifests in protecting and aiding the vulnerable.

The movie follows the three-act redemption movie structure, which begins with Schindler unaware of his unredeemed lost nature. He is self-absorbed but exhibits charm and charisma that he capitalizes on.[3] However, people are merely instruments for Schindler's business, which funds his self-indulgent lifestyle.

The turning point into the redemption story's second act and the emergence of a new self comes when Schindler is on horseback looking down on the city of Krakow as the city's Jews are forcibly driven out of their homes. Amid the chaos, he is moved by seeing a wayward child in a red coat (one of the few color elements in the black and white film). Why does he focus on this child? Is it her vulnerability? Does the red represent the blood of violence? Or does Schindler finally acquire the ability to truly empathize?

By learning the value of one life, Schindler transcends his narcissism.[4] He grows to view his workers as possessing an identity apart from their utility for his factory.[5] He changes from being self-focused to other-focused, from flesh to spirit, from false freedom to true freedom.[6]

The turning point in the final act, when Schindler grows in righteousness, occurs after he sees the girl in the red coat exhumed from a grave to be burned. Instead of leaving as planned with the massive amount of money he has accumulated, he uses it to procure the release of Jewish workers and to relocate them to a Czechoslovakian factory. The extraordinary scene that depicts Schindler leaving the factory wishing he could have done more to save others symbolizes how a spiritual awakening can shine light on the need to accomplish more redemptive work. The scene also conveys repentance as an ongoing and sometimes painful process.

Schindler's redemption also leads to his renewal and acceptance of religion and elucidates how obedience to love sometimes precedes obedience to faith.[7] In his unredeemed state, he attends church as a backdrop to make deals in the black market, but as a redeemed person he goes to church to reconcile with his wife. He encourages a worker who is a rabbi to celebrate the Sabbath. He crosses himself after asking for a moment of silence for Holocaust victims.

After his awakening, Schindler believes others can reform as he did. He tries to change the sadistic commandant Goeth by advising him to exert self-control and show true power by not killing arbitrarily.[8] Goeth temporarily tries but ultimately cannot exhibit mercy. In contrast to Schindler, he is irredeemable.

Schindler's List also falls in the category of spiritual films showing the struggle living out faith. It recalls the oppression and exile of the Jews in the Old Testament. The Jews' expulsion echoes the journey of Jews in the Book of Exodus, particularly when Amon asks Schindler, "Who are you, Moses?"[9]

BIBLE PASSAGE

"You see that faith was active along with his works, and faith was brought to completion by the works." (James 2:22 NRSV)

Schindler's List shows how both spiritual awakening and actions work together in redeeming Schindler.

DISCUSSION QUESTIONS

1. Why do you think the girl in the red coat changes Schindler so much?
2. How does Schindler's redemption progress? Why are other-focused actions so important to his redemption?

3. What does the movie indicate about the nature of evil personified by Amon Goeth? How does this match your definition of evil?
4. Why did Schindler tell Goeth refraining from punishment is true power?
5. What does the ending scene show about the lasting effects of one's actions? What would you like your legacy to be to future generations?

THE SHACK

2017

2 hours 12 minutes

CATEGORIES: Search for God

SUMMARY: Mackenzie "Mack" Phillips (Sam Worthington) goes on a camping trip with his children during which his five-year-old-daughter is kidnapped and murdered at an abandoned shack in the woods. Later, the devastated Mack receives a note in his mailbox signed by "Papa," his wife's nickname for God, inviting Mack back to the shack. He goes there and confronts God, Jesus, and the Holy Spirit with his deep grief and anger.

In the search for God category of the spiritual film, the protagonist tries to prove whether God exists. In *The Shack*'s variation, the protagonist doesn't initiate the search. It's God who puts a note in the mailbox of Mack Phillips, a grieving father whose young daughter was murdered. God seeks the unbeliever or doubter.

As in another search for God film, *Crimes and Misdemeanors*, the search for God relates to suffering. Both films attempt to resolve what theologians call the theodicy question: Why does an all-good all-powerful God permit suffering?

Reconciling God and suffering is one of two significant spiritual dilemmas the film confronts. The other is the desire for a more personal

In *The Shack*, physical manifestations of God, Jesus, and the Holy Spirit occur. In this variation in the Search for God category, Mack Phillips (Sam Worthington) must come to terms with the suffering intrinsic in human existence. Photo courtesy Summit Education/Everett Collection

experience of God. The deepening relational encounter with the divine occurs after Mack returns to the shack and faces Jesus and human manifestations of God and the Holy Spirit. As the film proceeds, acceptance of suffering comes through development of a personal relationship with God and the Trinity.[1]

A child being kidnapped and killed is one of the most painful and shocking injustices one can imagine. But the viewer of *The Shack* can likely substitute whatever suffering they've experienced to make Mack's journey their own. Although the circumstances and details of suffering may differ, the questions and reactions are similar. Mack tells God, "It seems like you have a bad habit of turning your back on those you supposedly love" and "you may not cause those things, but you certainly don't stop them."

The horror of the child killing also follows a Protestant tradition of "personal witness" narrative by depicting a graphic sin that shows depravity, suffering, and fallen human nature that can only be overcome by a recommitment to faith.[2] This sin ignites a crisis in the protagonist that destroys an illusion of self-sufficiency, followed by a period of despair, and finally finding peace through faith and grace.[3]

The deity must be humanized for Mack to complete this journey, putting the film into the realm of emotion rather than rationalistic theological explanations for suffering.[4] This humanization happens through dialogue with the three components of the trinity. The conversations are about humanity's most fundamental experiences: loss, grief, pain, suffering, death, recovery, and forgiveness.[5]

Mack achieves two important epiphanies. The first is about judgment. After the character of Wisdom allows him to judge humans, Mack says he'd condemn his daughter's killer to hell. But sin is too pervasive to have its trail end at any one person. Where does the cause and effect end? Not just to the killer's father who shaped him. "Doesn't the legacy of brokenness go all the way back to Adam?" Wisdom asks him. When asked to judge his two surviving children for their shortcomings and condemn one to hell and send another to heaven, he offers to go instead. "You judged your children worthy of love even if it costs you everything, now you know Papa's heart," Wisdom says in an allusion to Christ's sacrifice on the cross.

The second major epiphany is forgiving the murderer who God is working to still redeem. Mack's ability to ultimately forgive reinforces God's explanation that God doesn't orchestrate tragedies but works to make good out of them.

Through forgiveness Mack manifests what he's learned: God always works for good; it is not always possible to understand God; and the only recourse is trust because focus on one's pain makes one lose sight of how God is working.

BIBLE PASSAGE

"Do not judge, and you will not be judged. Do not condemn, and you will not be condemned. Forgive, and you will be forgiven." (Luke 6:37 NIV)

A turning point in the film is Mack realizing he can't adequately judge and condemn others.

DISCUSSION QUESTIONS:

1. How does Mack's idea of the Trinity differ from what he experiences? How do these representations match how you imagine the trinity?
2. Why is it so important for Mack to forgive the murderer of his child? Have you ever had to forgive someone for a terrible offense?
3. Why is Wisdom's lesson about judging so important? What's your approach to not being judgmental of others?
4. Why is it important for Mack to return to the place that created so much pain?
5. Does Mack find an answer for suffering? Or for evil? Have you?

SHADOWLANDS

1993

2 hours 11 minutes

CATEGORIES: Religious figure

SUMMARY: The dignified and reserved Christian scholar C.S. Lewis (Anthony Hopkins) forms a friendship with an unexpected companion: the blunt and outspoken American writer Joy Gresham (Debra Winger). As the relationship advances, Lewis starts to reevaluate his priorities in life. After Joy becomes critically ill, Lewis confronts his deepest beliefs about love, suffering, and grief.

At the time the film is set, C.S. Lewis is at a high point as a Christian philosopher. He is the acclaimed author of *The Screwtape Letters*, *Mere Christianity*, and *The Lion, The Witch and the Wardrobe*. He is also an admired religious intellectual and professor at elite Oxford University, an academic variation of a monastery.

Despite being the era's leading Christian thinker, Lewis must spiritually grow. The spiritual trajectory of *Shadowlands* is similar to *Ida*

(2013). The protagonist is forced out of the routine of an enclosed institution for a pilgrimage in reverse. Rather than a trip to a religious structure or sacred place, this pilgrimage is a journey into the disorder and
frailty of the real world the protagonist previously distanced himself from.

In Lewis's case, being an author and professor disconnects himself
from a more experiential faith. Lewis, like Ida, acquires wisdom and
insight by first observing and then experiencing suffering. This produces a painful but necessary spiritual maturity.

In real life, Lewis was not as isolated or passionless as portrayed in
the beginning of the film.[1] Although inaccurate at times, the movie
engages with a Christian intellectual's resolution of the conflict between
religious theory and practice.[2] This occurs in three key areas: love, suffering, and grief.

For the aging bachelor Lewis, love becomes a disruptive force.[3] The
writer Joy Gresham challenges him, yet his work colleagues disapprove
of her. Their conflicting opinions about Lewis's Narnia books show the
difference between them. Joy talks admiringly of the magic in the books,
but his academic colleagues chastise Lewis about it because they prefer
rationality over imagination.[4] Over the course of the film, Lewis increasingly distances himself from their dogmatic rationality.

At the beginning of the film, Lewis says, "The most intense joy lies
not in the having but the desiring." Love is distance and longing for
something that cannot be attained, making love an ideal or spiritual
abstraction. But in one of the film's crucial later scenes, Lewis tells Joy
that happiness is not longing for something different. The seriously ill
Gresham responds by telling Lewis that the happiness they are sharing
will not last. Transience, uncertainty, and death await. She tells him,
"The pain then is part of the happiness now."

Initially, Lewis lectures in public with an evangelistic zeal about suffering. He calls suffering a gift and an act of love from God. He talks in
aphorisms such as "pain is God's megaphone to rouse a deaf world" and
compares God to a sculptor: "the blows of his chisel, which hurt us so
much, are what make us perfect." At the end of the film, though, he
offers no such platitudes.

Instead, he concludes with a personalized view of suffering, saying, "The boy chose safety, the man chooses suffering." Distancing from the world may offer some protection, but being engaged in the world inevitably leads to a necessary suffering.

Finally, the film grapples with the enormous difference between lecturing about how to handle grief and actually enduring it.[5] Lewis learns grief is the more genuine spiritual response to pain than the detached and rational philosophical perspective he held at the beginning of the film.[6]

Yet grief does not destroy Lewis's faith, even if he can no longer intellectually explain suffering as he once attempted to. Instead, experience shatters Lewis's cerebral view of God, allowing for the emergence of a stronger faith and a more complete understanding of God.[7]

SPIRITUAL CONCEPT

Theodicy—The term for the question of why an omniscient, benevolent God can permit evil. In *Shadowlands*, Lewis wrestles with this question like so many other writers and theologians.

DISCUSSION QUESTIONS

1. How can over-intellectualizing be a barrier to feeling closer to God? Has this ever happened to you?
2. What makes Lewis capable of shifting from intellectualizing God to a more experiential view? Is this a journey we need to emulate? Why or why not?
3. Lewis finds Joy interesting despite the fact they appear to be so different. What do they find appealing about each other?
4. How does the film show that happiness and pain are linked? What is your outlook on the relationship between the two?
5. How does Lewis change his views about suffering during the course of the film? When have you changed your views of it in your life?

SHANE

1953

1 hour 58 minutes

CATEGORIES: Christ figure

SUMMARY: The mysterious Shane (Alan Ladd) arrives out of the wilderness and begins working for Joe Starrett (Van Heflin) and his family on their homestead. Shane wins the admiration of Joe's son Joey (Brandon De Wilde) when he fights back against the ranchers who threaten them. The arrival of the gunfighter Jack Wilson (Jack Palance) forces Shane to take further measures to defend Starrett and the other settlers.

Westerns can be spiritual films because they show a battle in an Eden-like wilderness between godly settlers and intruding evil forces. In some Westerns, the conflict highlights the struggle between homesteaders and an alliance of big ranchers and outlaws.[1] Others are more problematic, depicting settlers as forces of good and Indigenous people as malicious attackers. Regardless of the conflict, the Western hero resolves it. He is often a stranger with exceptional abilities who enters a community, defeats the villains, and moves on after the community is saved.[2]

Central to the Western is a battle between clearly designated good and evil characters. The decline of the Western may be because contemporary audiences are generally more comfortable with moral ambiguity rather than moral absolutes.[3]

In *Shane*, the protagonist's background is enigmatic. "You can call me Shane," he says, but the film never divulges whether this is his real name or not. Shane is a nomad not just because he is mobile and without a domestic sphere, but because he never tells anyone about his life before his arrival in the Wyoming Territory town.[4] Shane is the prototype of the enigmatic Man with No Name in Clint Eastwood spaghetti westerns.[5] Eastwood would also borrow heavily from *Shane* for *Pale Rider* (1985), although the protagonist is reformulated from a Christ figure to a ghost-like avenger.

Shane embodies Christ figure qualities because of his mysterious origins and his salvation of both individuals and the community. Shane removes his gun belt, leaving behind his power over life and death, but reassumes this power when his mission of liberation requires it.[6] Like the son of God descending into the messiness of worldly life, Shane joins and identifies with the farmers by living and working with them.[7] Like Jesus, Shane lives by an evangelical poverty and relies on the goodness of others.[8]

The couple he stays with are Joe and Marian, who, like their namesakes the Biblical Joseph and Mary, are raising a young child.[9] Shane becomes a strong spiritual guide to Joey because Joey's father does not have the time or inclination.[10] Evil is represented by the Rykers and the gunslinger Wilson, who discourage the homesteaders, destroy their hope, and ultimately weaken their solidarity and moral resolve.[11] The homesteaders exemplify communal and social goals, while the ranchers and outlaws pursue individualistic selfish gain.[12]

Defeating that evil requires a redemptive sacrifice from the Christ figure Shane.[13] His sacrifice brings salvation by fulfilling Marian's hope for a better future and Joey's desire for a spiritual role model. It also saves Starrett from self-destruction in a fight he cannot win.[14] Shane redeems the community, as well, serving as a vehicle to enhance familial, moral, and civic values rather than individualistic goals.[15]

What makes Shane distinctive both in the Western and the spiritual movie genre is the extent of his dark side and the damage it causes him. Rather than being a confident Christ figure, Shane suffers because of his itinerant existence. He is jumpy when he hears noises, seems to have no direction, and will not talk about his past as if he were ashamed of it. Shane's face expresses uncertainty and doubt—something not seen in Western heroes like John Wayne.[16]

However, Shane ultimately uses his shadow side for good.[17] As the wounded Shane ascends back into the mountains alone, he recalls Christ shouldering the burden of the cross. And the film's famous line from Joey about wanting Shane to come back displays the Christian expectation for Christ to return.

BIBLE PASSAGE

"Jesus replied, 'Foxes have dens and birds have nests, but the Son of Man has no place to lay his head.'" (Matthew 8:20 NIV)

Shane signifies the Christ figure attribute of being nomadic and seemingly unable to find a home.

DISCUSSION QUESTIONS

1. What indicates that Shane has been a drifter? When have you felt that way in your life?
2. Why is there conflict between the settlers and the ranchers? What is a parallel in contemporary society between two similar groups? Why do these groups have conflict?
3. How does the movie show that violence is sometimes necessary for a higher good? Do you agree with that? Why or why not?
4. Why is Joey so enamored with Shane? Has there been a similar spiritual guide in your life?
5. Why does Shane leave at the end of the film? Why doesn't he stay?

THE SHAWSHANK REDEMPTION

1994

2 hours 22 minutes

CATEGORIES: Christ figure

SUMMARY: Andy Dufresne (Tim Robbins) is falsely convicted of murder and receives two life sentences. Inside Shawshank prison, he maintains a calm demeanor but nonetheless becomes a harassed outsider. Over time, he placates the prison guards and develops a friendship with a seasoned prisoner nicknamed Red (Morgan Freeman).

Prison films are often spiritual films. Oppressive prison conditions characterize the pain, suffering, and injustice of the human condition. They show how hardships put walls around people—even if they are not physical ones.[1] Prison films are also about spiritual self-preservation under oppressive authority.[2]

But adversities are not just to be endured. Escape from prison represents a universal desire to transcend life's difficulties.[3] It also signifies breaking out to a transcendent realm that symbolizes spiritual fulfillment or even heaven.

In some ways, prison becomes a metaphor for life. In *Shawshank Redemption*, new prisoners enter the jail cells naked and endure a type of baptism by being doused with water.[4] Later, the fear of release from prison is akin to a fear of death, or what Red calls the dangerous outcome of being "institutionalized." In prison, the absence of hope in a productive life is akin to a loss of spirituality and belief in something better.[5] The result is a collapse into nihilism, with life reduced to nothingness and brutality.[6]

Like many prison films, *Shawshank* is influenced by Alexander Dumas's *The Count of Monte Cristo*. In the 1844 novel, Edward Dantes is falsely imprisoned and befriends a monk in prison who becomes a spiritual mentor. The novel created the prison film genre's three major themes: prison life mirroring societal injustices; forced confinement creating spiritual insight; and escape from prison representing a movement toward the transcendent. *Strange Cargo* (1940), *Brute Force* (1947), *Birdman of Alcatraz* (1962), *Cool Hand Luke* (1967), and *Escape from Alcatraz* (1979) are also prison films embodying these themes. Like Dantes, Andy Dufresne is falsely convicted and imprisoned. The protagonist in a prison film is often either wrongly convicted or severely sentenced for a minor crime.

Unlike many American films that espouse an American Dream mythology, though, the prison film details how the American Dream has failed.[7] The prison, in its symbolism of the larger social structure, is separated into a three-tier system. There are the equivalents of a corrupt

The prison movie is often a metaphor for spiritual entrapment. *The Shawshank Redemption* shows a hope for release from oppression centering on an authentic friendship between Andy Dufresne (Tim Robbins) and "Red" Redding (Morgan Freeman). Photo courtesy Columbia/Everett Collection

executive class (the warden and other leaders), sadistic middle managers (the guards), and oppressed workers (prisoners) who, nonetheless, benefit from solidarity, a work ethic, and education.[8]

Many human interactions in the prison are transactional, which is why the friendship between Andy and Red is so important. It is not based on a quid pro quo dynamic but on a sincere admiration and respect for each other. The two men represent two different spiritual states that complement each other: experience and hope. Red is world-weary and wise; Andy is more optimistic and ethereal.

Andy follows the Christ figure convention of exhibiting a mysterious aura and origin. He performs the equivalent of miracles—things that seem impossible—that give the other prisoners a sense of freedom. He rigs the prison PA system to play Mozart. The first miracle he performs is the equivalent of Jesus's first miracle at Cana: Where Jesus water turned into wine, Andy provides beer to the prisoners. And like Jesus, Andy gathers twelve disciples, the men chosen for the roof tarring detail.[9]

Andy is an outsider with true religiosity that contrasts with the religious authority figure of the warden, who associates the Bible with rigid rules and punishment. Andy has a different view and conceals a digging instrument in the Bible within the Book of Exodus. This signifies that his escape is liberation, as the Hebrews escaped captivity in Egypt.

Later, Andy's vacant jail cell is comparable to an empty tomb, and the now iconic shot of Andy in the rain recalls the resurrected Jesus with a liberation that is both agony and ecstasy.[10] Like other Christ figures, Andy's resurrected spirit carries on in stories others tell about him.

BIBLE PASSAGE

"Now faith is the substance of things hoped for, the evidence of things not seen." (Hebrews 11:1 KJV)

Because it is unseen, hope draws one into a spiritual realm. In the film, Andy says hope is "something inside that they can't get to" and that "hope is a good thing, maybe the best of things, and no good thing ever dies."

DISCUSSION QUESTIONS

1. How is the prison film universal? What in your life do you feel imprisoned or limited by?
2. Why does Andy lift up hope as a transcendent feeling? When has hope elevated you through a difficult situation?
3. Red says, "They send you here for life, and that's exactly what they take—the part that counts, anyway." What does he mean?
4. At a key point, Andy leaves a note saying, "You were right, salvation lies within." What does this mean?
5. How do you interpret the ending? What transcendent qualities does it reveal?

SLEEPING BEAUTY

1959

1 hour 15 minutes

CATEGORIES: Apocalyptic

SUMMARY: Three virtuous fairies give gifts to Princess Aurora at her christening. However, the evil Maleficent prophesizes Aurora will prick her finger on a spinning wheel and die before her sixteenth birthday. Spinning wheels are destroyed in the kingdom, and the fairies take Aurora away to a cottage deep in the woods to hide her. Still, Maleficent is determined to find Aurora.

No reader, it is not a mistake to see this film listed in the apocalyptic category. Often overlooked in the film is a mass resurrection, a terrifying confrontation with a satanic figure, and a climactic battle between good and evil forces with references to the Book of Revelation.

This all occurs during the last third of this film. Before the apocalypse segment, the story is reminiscent of *Snow White and the Seven Dwarfs*. Like Snow White, Aurora is aligned with nature, is separated from the world into bucolic safety, and undergoes a resurrection-like return to life. However, because she has much less dialogue than Snow White, Aurora is a weaker presence and personality.

But this is consistent in a film about the battle between the characters and supernatural powers, which in this case are Maleficent and the three fairy godmothers. *Sleeping Beauty* is a cosmic fight between good and evil, with the human characters largely unable to use their own agency against these forces.

Even Prince Phillip, who ultimately fights Maleficent, is aided by the three fairy godmothers in critical ways. They work through the prince rather than the prince operating on his own.[1] The fairies rescue him from prison, present him with a sword and shield, transform objects thrown at him by Maleficent, and concentrate magic upon the sword that Phillip uses against Maleficent.[2] The godmothers also characterize grandmother-like qualities to Aurora, in contrast to Maleficent, who is the antithesis of the maternal.[3]

Like *Snow White and the Seven Dwarfs* and *Pinocchio, Sleeping Beauty* is a classic era Disney film with Biblical allusions. Despite its resurrection-like sequences, the characters are not Christ figures. However, Aurora has some qualities of the Christ figure as a baby. Three fairies visit her instead of three magi. And, like the Christ child, she is exiled to another land because of a ruler's threat.

Aurora does not grow up to have other Christ figure qualities. She becomes a largely nondescript personality and is perhaps immature and callow from being so isolated. While many critics write about her passive qualities, all the human characters in the film are passive and somewhat one-dimensional. This is because *Sleeping Beauty* is a movie where the real action occurs in the supernatural realm, not in the world of humans.

The action culminates in the final confrontation against Maleficent, who declares she is "the mistress of all evil" aided "by all the powers of hell." She transforms into a dragon at a key point, referencing the dragon fought by the archangel Michael in chapter 12 of the Book of Revelation. It is also in this chapter where there is a direct connection between a dragon and Satan.

The movie, though, does not just refer to the Book of Revelation. Prince Phillip recalls not only the archangel Michael in Revelation but Peter, who was released from his chains in prison by an angel in the book of Acts. The fairies give Phillip a "shield of virtue" and a "sword of truth," recalling Ephesians 6, where Paul instructs his followers to "put on the full armor of God" to fight against evil forces. During a final battle with Maleficent, the fairies command that "evil die and good endure." The scene ends with a cross-shaped sword hanging over a dead body, signifying that Christianity has conquered evil.

Another important Christian theme in the film is resurrection. Aurora and later the entire kingdom are put under a temporary spell before being awakened in a mass resurrection. This reflects the intermediate state between death and resurrection in some Christian theology.

Afterward emerges the equivalent of a New Jerusalem, with brightness covering the once darkened kingdom.

BIBLE PASSAGE

"Put on the full armor of God, so that you can take your stand against the devil's schemes." (Ephesians 6:11 NIV)

The fairies that armor Prince Phillip make a similar statement that "these weapons of righteousness will triumph over evil."

DISCUSSION QUESTIONS

1. Why does Maleficent represent a satanic figure? What other characters in films also represent satanic figures?
2. How does this movie create a clear conflict between good and evil? How are good and evil presented in current children's films?
3. In what ways do the three fairies combat evil? Is it the appropriate response? Why or why not?
4. How does the film use resurrection as a theme? What are your ideas about resurrection?
5. How can fairy tales depict spiritual truths? What are the spiritual truths that stand out to you in this movie?

SMOKE SIGNALS

1998

1 hour 29 minutes

CATEGORIES: Retaining Indigenous community and culture

SUMMARY: After a family crisis, Arnold Joseph (Gary Farmer) leaves his wife, son Victor (Adam Beach), and an American Indian Reservation in Idaho, and he dies years later in a trailer in Arizona. Unable to pay for the trip to retrieve his father's ashes, Victor accepts money from the nerdy storyteller Thomas (Evan Adams). The two travel together to Arizona and recall a tragic event from their past.

This indie film is groundbreaking not only for its multidimensional presentation of Native American characters but for its spirituality. *Smoke Signals* achieves this without medicine men, peace pipes, vision quests, ghost dances, or other Native American spirituality clichés. This defies what the film's writer, Sherman Alexie, called the two most common stereotypes of Native Americans in movies: the warrior and the shaman.[1]

Still, *Smoke Signals* does adhere to some conventions of the retaining Indigenous community and culture film. It merges the past and the present, it recognizes tradition and ancestors, and the characters strive to find an identity outside of the dominant culture. The movie also emphasizes Thomas's storytelling, which uses Native American oral tradition to resist misrepresentation and reclaim history.[2] Overall, it places an emphasis on contemporary issues, such as life on the reservation and questions of identity.[3] The movie primarily deals with everyday spirituality rather than grand spiritual events.[4]

Protagonists Thomas and Victor must find their identities outside of a culture that does not understand them yet shapes their personalities. The film opens on July 4, 1976, during the American bicentennial celebration, as the Native Americans self-ironically celebrate their own domination, cultural demise, and subjugation.[5] The characters later talk about depictions of Native American in films from John Wayne Westerns to *Dances with Wolves* and how these instances of cultural appropriation affect how others perceive them and how they view themselves.

Most of the film is a road movie, with the road trip functioning as a surrogate pilgrimage that transforms character. Consistent with the road movie genre, the characters that the protagonists encounter along the way represent prevailing social problems. The bus they ride on, for example, evokes the Civil Rights movement of the 1960s, as most of the patrons on the bus are white and sometimes antagonistic.[6] However, rather than being victimized by the non-Indigenous society beyond the

The Native American film *Smoke Signals* features a spiritual pilgrimage from tribal lands into a non-tribal culture that stereotypes and marginalizes Native Americans. But redemption and understanding come from the difficult and challenging journey. Photo courtesy Miramax/Everett Collection

reservation, Victor and Thomas ultimately find healing through their encounters with the broader world.[7]

The spiritual trajectory of their road trip is toward Victor forgiving his father. The trip becomes a journey out of isolation and alienation toward acceptance and forgiveness.[8] Thomas and Victor's father's friend Suzy Song both help Victor appreciate some of his deceased father's redeeming qualities.[9] Victor's acceptance of his father does not develop out of a psychological narrative of introspection, but is facilitated through stories told by family and the community.[10]

As suggested by the film's title, the movie is about communication between father and son, between friends, and between the past and present.[11] The emphasis on communication reveals that people possess the capacity to be both destructive and suffer from others' destructive qualities through how they communicate or don't communicate. Thomas says that some children "are pillars of flame that burn everything they touch," while others "are just pillars of ash that fall apart when you touch them." Victor and himself contain both qualities, he says.

Although the film is in the retaining Indigenous community and culture category, Alexie and the film's director, Chris Eyre, note that key scenes were inspired by Biblical stories, including Victor's mom's acclaimed fry bread being a metaphor for communion bread.[12] Thomas tells the story of how she fed one hundred Native Americans with fifty pieces of bread, recalling how Jesus fed the multitude.[13]

Thomas also hopes for Arnold's resurrection when his ashes are finally released. However, this homecoming also honors Victor's father's life and his connection to Native traditions.[14] Victor achieves closure with his father and acceptance of himself when he releases his father's ashes into a river that once gave his ancestors food to survive.[15]

BIBLE PASSAGE

"Bear with each other and forgive one another if any of you has a grievance against someone. Forgive as the Lord forgave you." (Colossians 3:13 NIV)

Victor cannot spiritually mature until he can forgive.

DISCUSSION QUESTIONS

1. Why is storytelling so important in the film? Does it always reflect the truth? Why or why not?
2. How does the film mix the past and the present? What does that say about the role of the past in the present lives of the characters?
3. Why doesn't Arnold return home to his family even though he wants to go back? Have you ever not done something for a similar reason?
4. How is fire a central element in the film? What does it symbolize?
5. Why is forgiveness such an important spiritual quality? What was your biggest challenge in forgiving someone? Or do you still have someone to forgive?

THE SONG OF BERNADETTE

1943

2 hours 36 minutes

Categories: Religious figure (nun), divine intervention, difficulty living out faith

Summary: French peasant Bernadette Soubirous (Jennifer Jones) sees a vision of the Virgin Mary at a grotto in the village of Lourdes. Religious authorities are skeptical because they don't believe the mother of Jesus would appear to a young peasant girl. However, crowds gather at a spring containing miraculous healing abilities that arises at the site.

The Song of Bernadette honors a significant spiritual trait not often elevated in cinema: humility. It also thematizes how some people, including religious leaders, cannot understand why someone in a humble station in life might receive special grace, spiritual insight, and a heavenly visitation instead of those with stature and power.

The peasant girl Bernadette lives in a fallen world filled with poverty, unemployment, and family dysfunction. However, the conditions of life don't harden her heart, and she remains a gentle, ethereal person. She is ridiculed but does not retaliate, electing to instead withdraw into a quiet and resilient humility. Throughout the film, Bernadette expresses a childlike earnestness and innocence that, contrasts with the prevalence of eroticized females in many movies of the Second World War era.[1]

Bernadette's vision of an apparition of the Virgin Mary at a cave next to a garbage dump elucidates how, like Christ being born in a lowly stable, the most spiritual of events can occur in the most unlikely places. A major theme in *The Song of Bernadette* is that grace, represented by Mary's appearance to Bernadette, comes to those many may consider undeserving.

Grace is the Christian concept of comfort, love, humility, and confidence in God, along with self-imposed severity for ones' own shortcomings, and tenderness for those of others.[2] Grace is not rooted in a transactional system of merits and demerits, which means that it can sometimes be received by those some may believe unworthy. Bernadette is perceived as undeserving and spiritually ignorant because of her poverty and lack of understanding about formal religious concepts.

However, the bestowal of grace on Bernadette leads to the burden of suffering.[3] This situates the movie partly within the difficulty living out faith category, where there is conflict between her religious insight and the world. Bernadette confronts skepticism that only increases with her notoriety.[4] This condemnation is exemplified by the nun Marie-Therese at the convent that Bernadette later joins. Marie-Therese is tormented by the idea of unmerited grace being given to a poverty-stricken child who does not appear to show signs of suffering, asceticism, or struggling to achieve virtue.[5]

The movie's affirmation of the miraculous and its setting in an ancient, small country town recalls the medieval era and its belief in saints and visions.[6] It depicts Mary as a figure who intervenes to demonstrate the power of faith.[7] She, like Bernadette, was a humble young woman also chosen in what could be called unmerited grace.[8]

Although not a full-fledged Christ figure, Bernadette is a symbol of suffering. She is purified through pain and fulfills a Christ-like destiny of helping the ailing.[9] Yet, in the end, she cannot benefit from the healing others receive from the Lourdes spring. Like Christ, she takes on suffering to release others from their distress.

Bernadette's simple and pure faith allows her to overcome the disbelief of powerful figures who doubt.[10] Through her purity and integrity, the maligned peasant girl enacts the power to influence others.[11]

Some of the initial resistance comes from authorities demanding a level of proof for divine intervention that can never be attained. Over the course of the movie, the people who criticize her the most undergo a spiritual progression. The bishop initially dismisses her but over time becomes convinced because of her sincerity. The nun Therese-Marie is antagonistic but eventually repents for her pride. The lawyer who defines the miraculous event as just superstition realizes his selfishness and narrow-mindedness. However, not all grow spiritually because of Bernadette. The mayor continues to only see opportunism in the infamy of the spring.

BIBLE PASSAGE

"For all those who exalt themselves will be humbled, and those who humble themselves will be exalted." (Luke 14:11 NIV)

The Song of Bernadette is a rare movie featuring a humble protagonist who is ultimately revered, while those of higher stature are, in time, humbled.

DISCUSSION QUESTIONS

1. What qualities make Bernadette humble? How do you enact humility in your life?
2. Why are authorities so unwilling to believe Bernadette? When have you encountered skepticism about your religious beliefs?
3. One of the central spiritual ideas in the film is that grace can manifest in the unlikeliest of people and circumstances. When have you seen this happen?
4. Do you believe miracles can occur? How can they happen in this day and age?
5. Why doesn't Bernadette want to be healed by the spring in Lourdes?

SOUL

2020

1 hour 40 minutes

CATEGORIES: Divine intervention

SUMMARY: Piano player Joe Gardner (Jamie Foxx) is on the verge of what he feels will be a life transforming event: playing with legendary jazz saxophonist Dorothea Williams (Angela Bassett). However, he dies on the same day that he is supposed to be at his momentous gig. After a mix-up in the afterlife, Gardner returns to the living with 22 (Tina Fey)—a soul who doesn't want to be born.

Soul is an anomaly because it represents a recent high-profile American movie with overt spiritual themes. It directly confronts questions about the meaning and purpose of life and offers an extensive (albeit theologically non-specific) view of the afterlife.

The movie expands and deepens spiritual themes presented in two other Pixar films. *Up* (2009) also examines, in some moments, the true meaning of life and the disappointments that come from ambition. But much of the film is a more secular conventional variation of a hero's journey rather than a deeper evaluation of everyday life as in *Soul*. *Coco* (2017) features a view of the afterlife based on the Mexican holiday the Day of the Dead during which dead ancestors temporarily return. This, however, is mainly a plot device used to resolve earthly family problems rather than to portray spiritual conditions.

Soul adheres to conventions of the divine intervention category, which sometimes includes having a soul placed in the wrong body to learn lessons. Here, it happens to two individuals. The soul of jazz musician Joe Gardner is placed into the body of a cat, while the unborn soul 22 ends up in Gardner's body.

The film in this category that *Soul* most resembles (despite the absence of an angel acting as a mediator between divine and human realms) is *It's a Wonderful Life*. Similar to the 1946 film, the protagonist is torn between responsibility and individual ambition. However, unlike George Bailey, Gardner is not a married man with children and small-town social commitments. Joe Gardner is an urban unmarried loner who, like Bailey, suffers from the tyranny of having unfulfilled dreams that make him unsatisfied with his life.

But over the course of the film, *Soul* subverts the secular narrative in many films that individual dreams, and particularly career goals, are the primary purpose in life. Although Joe is advised in the afterlife that it is important to find his "spark," it later becomes clear that Joe made a mistake in believing his spark was his career goals.

In a key scene, the spark is revealed to be something else when Gardner recalls what has been most memorable in his life. What matters are connections with other people and the enjoyment of simple things. Joe dismissively tells 22 what she enjoyed most as a human were "not purposes, just regular old living." But, like *It's a Wonderful Life*, "regular old living" turns out to be more valuable than ambition.

A large part of the film is set in an afterlife that does not adhere to a specific religious view. Still, this section wrestles with questions about the meaning and purpose of life and depicts multiple spiritual conditions.

Because of increasing religious and political polarization, there are fewer spiritual films currently being made. Pixar's 2020 film *Soul* is a rare recent film with spiritual themes. Photo courtesy Disney+/ Everett Collection

Not-yet-born souls are stamped with personalities, although it is unclear if this is a reference to reincarnation or not. One scene centers on an ambiguous "Great Beyond" and an escalator leading to a white light, an allusion to the ascending staircase in *A Matter of Life and Death* (1946). The film also features a realm for lost souls that is meant for those, described by the mystic Moonwind, who "are obsessed with something that disconnects them from life." Moonwind dwells in The Zone, a place between the physical and the spiritual that humans on earth can temporarily go to. Ultimately, this is not enough for Joe, who can enter The Zone through his piano playing. However, to achieve a true spiritual breakthrough, he must perform an act of self-sacrifice similar to the quality of a Christ figure.

Soul also argues that genuine spiritual identity comes from the union of body and soul.[1] Like other divine intervention films, including *The Bishop's Wife* (1947) and *Wings of Desire* (1989), it elevates joy in the pains and pleasures of being human in a body. In *Soul*, jazz music functions as a metaphor for living where one must improvise to enjoy or withstand whatever life brings.

BIBLE PASSAGE

"Yet when I surveyed all that my hands had done and what I had toiled to achieve, everything was meaningless, a chasing after the wind; nothing was gained under the sun." (Ecclesiastes 2:11 NIV)

Even after a major accomplishment, Joe Gardner feels both let down and a sense of disillusionment in the same way the author of Ecclesiastes does.

DISCUSSION QUESTIONS

1. What effect does Joe's focus on his music career have on him?
2. What is the main lesson 22 learns about life to make her unafraid?
3. What puts people into the mystical state of "The Zone"? What puts you in that state?
4. Why is Joe ultimately disappointed by playing with Dorothea Williams? When have you ever experienced a momentous letdown?
5. What do you think Joe did at the end? How will he live his life after all he has experienced?

SPIRITED AWAY

2001

2 hours 5 minutes

CATEGORIES: Hero's journey, retaining Indigenous community and culture

SUMMARY: Ten-year-old Chihiro (Rumi Hiiragi/Daveigh Chase) is angry and troubled because her family is moving. On the way to their new home, they become lost and enter a supernatural realm where her parents are transformed into pigs. To end the spell, Chihiro must adapt and progress through a strange magical domain.

Like the use of Christian themes in the *Narnia* movies and *The Lord of the Rings*, *Spirited Away* and other anime films, like *Princess Mononoke* (1997), contain motifs from the Indigenous Japanese religion Shinto. What all these films have in common is their presentation of spiritual journeys within a fantasy realm.

Deities in Shinto are known as kami and are associated with natural phenomena.[1] In Shinto, all things possess a force that, when potent enough, allows them to manifest as spirits.[2] In *Spirited Away*, sudden disappearances are attributed to spirits transporting someone to the spirit world.[3]

The first indication Chihiro is entering a spirit realm is her glimpse of the torii, a wooden gate known for leading to a Shinto shrine, as well as small, house-like shrines and roadside statues.[4] She goes through a tunnel and a bridge that are demarcations between this world and the other.[5] Here, Chihiro first sees the disembodied kami in shadowy forms.

Later, Chihiro interacts with kami that take other forms.[6] These include the river spirit Haku and the stink spirit, which both change after they are purified.[7] The Shinto symbolism throughout the film shows that Chihiro's spiritual journey is guided by ancient spirituality, which counteracts the modernism and consumerism infecting her family.

To benefit from the kami, one must be sensitized to their presence. This occurs when one moves from the mundane everyday world into a liminal realm,[8] which is an in-between space before returning to the ordinary world.[9] This intermediate realm is characterized by disorientation and ambiguity.[10] Chihiro's positive, perceptive response to this unpredictable world makes her spiritually mature.[11]

Despite the irrational and sometimes bizarre qualities of Chihiro's adventure, *Spirited Away* also contains the structure of the traditional hero's journey. The protagonist undergoes trials with supernatural assistance to spiritually progress.

In the bathhouse, Chihiro undergoes a change that becomes an antidote to the modern, indulgent childhood that weakened her.[12] The bathhouse manager Yubaba fills the role of the mother for her rebirth, which sees the spoiled Chihiro regenerated as a devoted person who performs courageous duties.[13] Chihiro's progression is framed by her navigation of the precarious staircase, which she at first descends with terror but then later negotiates without fear.[14]

A strong element of her journey is the Shinto idea of purification, which[15] requires a cleansing or wiping away of external and interior pollution.[16] The most notable example of this comes when the stink spirit threatens to overwhelm the bathhouse, but Chihiro meets the challenge of bathing it.[17] As a result, the spirit returns to its natural state of purity.[18]

The story is not driven by a showdown between right and wrong.[19] Instead, the heroine is thrown into a place where good and bad dwell together, and, rather than destroying evil, she survives and adapts to it.[20] Rather than fixed opposites of good versus evil, the film reflects a Shinto outlook that events are either polluting or purifying.[21]

Although the film focuses primarily on spirituality, it does engage in social commentary on two of its major themes: environmentalism and greed. The stink spirit is a manifestation of a landscape affected by environmental degradation.[22] Chihiro's mother and father embody the Indigenous spirituality film's generalizations about Western-influenced consumer culture in which consumers act on impulse and are oblivious to the consequences of excessive consumption.[23] The character who most embodies this is No Face, a lonely spirit in black robes with an insatiable hunger whose overconsumption brings destruction and loss of identity.[24]

SPIRITUAL TERM

Shinto—An Indigenous Japanese religion that embodies animism, a belief that objects and places in the material world contain spiritual forces.

DISCUSSION QUESTIONS

1. How does Chihiro change from the beginning of the film to the end?
2. What is an example of a character that contains both good and evil characteristics? How does this differ from other animated or fantasy movies?
3. What does Chihiro do that changes No Face? How does this fit into the film's themes?
4. How does the film contrast modern Japan with ancient spiritual Japan? How does modernism invade the spiritual realm?
5. In general, what makes the anime film different in theme and structure from Western animated films?

STARS WARS TRILOGY

1977, 1980, 1983

Star Wars 2 hours 1 minute;
The Empire Strikes Back 2 hours 4 minutes;
Return of the Jedi 2 hours 11 minutes

CATEGORIES: Hero's journey

SUMMARY: Obi-Wan Kenobi (Alec Guinness) introduces Luke Skywalker (Mark Hamill) to the ways of the Force, a belief in a universal spiritual energy. With the help of the maverick pilot Han Solo (Harrison Ford), they rescue rebel alliance leader Princess Leia (Carrie Fisher) from the evil Darth Vader and the Imperial Army. After destroying the Empire's Death Star, Luke learns more about the Force from Jedi master Yoda before a final confrontation with Vader.

The hero's journey as outlined in Joseph Campbell's *Hero With a Thousand Faces* inspired George Lucas's shaping of the *Star Wars* characters and plotline. After the film's enormous success, many movies applied the hero's journey to the spiritual movie genre and others.

However, the original *Star Wars* trilogy is not just a notable and influential example of the hero's journey. *Star Wars* utilizes two new (at the time) ideas that had an enormous impact on religion and popular culture.

The first is that blending elements from both Eastern and Western religions creates a generalized spirituality that appeals to people of many religious beliefs.[1] Numerous films following *Star Wars* contain fewer references to specific religions and instead create a more universal and generalized spirituality. The second is the positioning of spirituality as more powerful than technology and science.

An important issue in many science-fiction films is the misuse of technology.[2] What distinguishes *Star Wars* is its resolution of this conflict through spirituality. Similar to contemporary culture, some characters in the series view religion as a relic that has been replaced by science. When Obi-Wan tells Luke about the Force, Han Solo echoes pre-redemption John Wayne in *Three Godfathers* when he says, "I've never seen anything to make me believe there's one all-powerful force controlling everything."

Within the technology-driven Empire, Darth Vader is shown as a peculiar, anachronistic person who believes in the mystical.[3] When an Imperial authority boasts, "This station is now the ultimate power in the universe," Vader replies that "the power to destroy a planet is insignificant next to the power of the Force."

The Force is the basis for the film's spirituality. The distinction between good and dark sides of the Force is a dichotomy between good and evil consistent with Christianity. Other Christian motifs in the trilogy include the self-sacrifice of Obi-Wan Kenobi in *Star Wars* and Luke's self-sacrifice leading to the redemption of Darth Vader in *Return of the Jedi*.[4] "If you strike me down, I will become more powerful than you can possibly imagine," Obi-Wan says, recalling a Christ figure's belief in the power of the resurrection.

Star Wars radically changed how spirituality is portrayed in films. Its mixture of Eastern and Western spirituality reflected the growing spiritual but not religious movement, which can blend different spiritual traditions. Photo courtesy LucasFilm/Everett Collection

Both Darth Vader and the Emperor ask Luke to reign with them, similar to Satan's temptation of Christ.[5] Individuals also appear to be resurrected and continue on in an afterlife as ghost figures and voices from beyond, as exemplified by Obi-Wan's voice instructing Luke. The conception of the afterlife depicted here does not clearly belong to any particular religion.

Yet, the Force contains important elements of Eastern religion. Obi-Wan and Yoda are both guru-like sages consistent with Westerner seeking Eastern wisdom films. Yoda teaches a Zen-like intuitive or non-rational understanding of being.[6] The Force also appears to hold an Eastern religious view of a unifying consciousness embodied in the Force. "It's an energy field created by all living things; it surrounds us, penetrates us, it binds the galaxy together," Obi-wan says.

Being connected with the Force also means draining oneself of passions, which is consistent with Buddhist teachings that emphasize detachment. When Luke asks how he will know to avoid the dark side, Yoda tells him it will happen "when you are calm, at peace, passive."

Those attuned to the Force manipulate both matter and the mind. They read thoughts, play mind tricks on the less spiritual, and move objects. In this way, the Force is like the Taoist belief that the universe consists of an energy called chi that can be harnessed.

SPIRITUAL TERM

Chi—In the Eastern philosophy of Taoism, chi means vital energy. To maximize chi, Taoists work on enhancing matter, movement, and the mind.[7]

DISCUSSION QUESTIONS

1. How would you describe the spirituality of the Force? Do you see anything of your own belief system in it?
2. What are significant ways spirituality is more important than reliance on technology? How do you see the spirituality and science conflict in contemporary culture?
3. What is the role of friendship in these films?
4. What is the meaning of what happens to Luke in the cave in *The Empire Strikes Back*?
5. Why is Darth Vader capable of redemption? When have you seen yourself or others redeem themselves after a long period of experiencing the "dark side" of life?

THE STRAIGHT STORY

1999

1 hour 52 minutes

CATEGORIES: Hero's journey (pilgrimage variation), transcendental style

SUMMARY: The aging Alvin Straight (Richard Farnsworth) finds out that his estranged brother is in failing health. Without a driver's license and with no other way to make the journey from Iowa to Wisconsin, he travels on a riding mower to see the brother with whom he has not spoken in a decade. Along the route, he recounts his past and meets people who benefit from his wisdom and advice.

Alvin's slow ride from Iowa to Wisconsin is a spiritual journey. Some of this is shown through the juxtaposition of his 250-mile trip on a riding mower with sweeping overhead shots of farm fields, luminous clouds, storms, star-filled skies, and sunsets. The scenes present an older man in relation to the passage of time, represented by seasons and the weather, as well as the immensity of life and nature. Alvin's autumn journey engages with a harvest time metaphor that reflects an assessment of what he has reaped in his life.[1]

The Straight Story is a movie about both advancing in age and the spiritual challenges of human relationships—particularly what binds and separates families, the weight of regret, and the need for forgiveness.

Like other movies featuring a modern pilgrimage, *The Straight Story* does not feature a traditional sacred site awaiting Alvin at the end of his journey. Instead, Alvin's commitment to reconciliation is represented by the home of his estranged brother. However, like all pilgrimage movies, *The Straight Story* is about transformation of character during a journey.

This transformation occurs in two major ways. First, Alvin's revelation of regrets from his past functions as a form of confession and repentance of sins. Second, Alvin transforms the character of those he meets in small and large ways.

Alvin's disclosure of his regrets and sins serves as a spiritual deliverance. Opening up to others becomes a cleansing process that prepares him for the end goal of his pilgrimage: an emotional meeting with his brother.[2] However, these confessions also liberate others. When Alvin reveals a war story that he has never told anyone else, it affects another veteran wrestling with his own demons. After expressing how he learned to swallow his pride to forgive his brother, two squabbling brothers appear to resolve their differences. Relating a story about a tragic event with his grandchildren inspires a runaway girl to return home to her family.

Alvin's confessions demonstrate how aging increases self-awareness. Wisdom is derived from remorse over past recklessness, and the lightness of insight and redemption arises from the darkness of regret.[3]

Alvin's memory serves as both a source of pain and a basis for wisdom. "At my age, I've seen about all that life has to dish out," he says. "I know to separate the wheat from the chaff and let the small stuff fall away." Yet, he also says the worst part of aging is remembering when he was young, which seems to indicate both regret and nostalgia for youth.

Although Alvin is a stoic character, darkness and regret appear to be always just below the surface (similar to Robert Duvall's character in *Tender Mercies*). Some of that regret relates to alcoholism in his past.[4] He also hints at being neglectful and wandering. He tells Rose he's "going back on the road," suggesting he once fled to escape family responsibilities.[5]

The film's use of long takes and undramatic narrative structure, which draws from the transcendental film style, is both stylistically and thematically reminiscent of the films of Ozu, a director also concerned with the destruction of family by modernity. *The Straight Story* illustrates the dangers of the breakdown of family and uses the road not to decimate family but to redeem it.[6] Like in Ozu's films, *The Straight Story*'s slow pace is a thoughtful reaction to the speed of modernity.[7]

BIBLE PASSAGE

"If you have anything against someone, forgive—only then will your heavenly Father be inclined to also wipe your slate clean of sins." (Mark 11:25 The Message).

Because Alvin believes he must be forgiven, he possesses the capacity to forgive.

DISCUSSION QUESTIONS

1. What does the film say about the importance of hospitality to strangers? How can you implement hospitality more in your life?
2. In what ways is the trip a possible redemption story for Alvin? What about his past do you think he has the most regrets about?
3. How is Alvin's journey/pilgrimage a metaphor for the life of faith?
4. Have you ever taken a journey or pilgrimage by yourself? If so, did you come to any realizations? If not, is there a journey or pilgrimage you'd like to make alone?
5. What do you think happened in the end between Alvin and his brother? Will they reconcile? Why or why not?

THE TEN COMMANDMENTS

1956

3 hours 40 minutes

CATEGORIES: Bible epic

SUMMARY: After an Egyptian pharaoh orders the killing of newborn male Hebrew babies, a Hebrew mother sends her baby boy down the river in a basket. The pharaoh's daughter finds him and raises him as her own child. Moses (Charlton Heston) becomes a great Egyptian leader who, after learning he is Jewish, joins the Hebrews and leads a movement to free them from slavery.

The Ten Commandments is the pinnacle of the Bible epic's Old Testament sub-genre. With extravagant sets, extensive extras, and special effects, *The Ten Commandments* presents religion as spectacle.[1] It shows Egypt as a totalitarian military dictatorship, similar to how the Bible epic genre characterizes Rome. The oppressive ruling state resonated with contemporary audiences as a regime representing fascism, communism, the segregated American South, or any tyrannical government.

But beneath the spectacle and political associations, the Old Testament Bible epic is driven by the accomplishments, trials, and encounters of great individuals.[2] At the center of *The Ten Commandments* is Moses's epic spiritual journey.

The spiritual life of Moses consists of three stages—ignorance, testing, and enlightenment—somewhat similar to the redemption story but with key differences.[3]

During the first act, Moses is not in the kind of flawed state typical of characters in the first stage of a redemption story. However, he is ignorant of the full extent of the suffering of slaves because he is too immersed in the Egyptian power structure. Fitting with the genre's convention of adding extensive non-Biblical material, the film delves into friction between Moses and Rameses, who are engaged in a sibling rivalry for the attention of the Pharaoh and Nefertiti.[4]

Instead of the Hebrews becoming too numerous, as in the Bible, Moses is sent down the Nile to freedom because of a star proclaiming his birth. This leads to the pharaoh ordering the deaths of newborn males, similar to Herod's execution of the infants in the Gospel of Matthew. Moses's birth occurs in humble surroundings, recalling Jesus's birth narrative. This adds a messianic characterization to Moses, although it is not as full-fledged as in most Christ figure films.

Unlike the typical redemption story, the second act of *The Ten Commandments* does not revolve around an internal conflict between an old self and an emerging self. Instead, it deepens a newfound identity. The turning point is Moses's banishment to the desert, a place "where holy men and prophets are cleansed and purged for God's great purpose," as the narrator states. After this trial, Moses's breakthrough comes from integrating into the desert community of Midian. "I am a stranger in a strange land," he says, symbolizing how a new identity can be forged in unusual and unexpected surroundings.

The third stage, enlightenment, occurs after Moses's encounter with God at the burning bush. Moses then possesses supernatural abilities, acting as an instrument of God to lead the Hebrews out of Egypt. His life is now one of action to liberate the Hebrews.

Moses's success in freeing the slaves is a spiritual act, which stands in contrast to the will of Rameses, who values power over others.[5] Rameses's clashes with Moses are a struggle between human will and divine will.[6] The Egyptians are idolaters, which in the Bible epic genre stands in for atheism and rationalism.[7] Like the redemption story, the protagonist proclaims a new identity. He tells Nefertiti that "the Moses who loved you was another man."

Moses's spiritual journey, enhanced by the film's use of special effects, reasserts the sacred and supernatural over the secular.[8] Faith triumphs over reason.[9] The literal depictions of Biblical supernatural events illustrate the spectacle associated with the genre, including the famous parting of the Red Sea.

The Ten Commandments is the peak of the traditional Bible epic. Its use of spectacle, special effects, and a heroic portrayal of Moses (Charlton Heston) typifies the genre. Photo courtesy Paramount/Everett Collection

This confirms religious awe to a contemporary society that tends to reject the supernatural.[10] It also shows freedom not as something individuals achieve on their own but as something God bestows.[11]

BIBLE PASSAGE

"The Lord said, 'I have indeed seen the misery of my people in Egypt. I have heard them crying out because of their slave drivers, and I am concerned about their suffering.'" (Exodus 3:7 NIV)

This shows God is concerned and sensitive to collective suffering.

DISCUSSION QUESTIONS

1. The Bible epic creates tension between rulers and the oppressed. How do you see that duality in contemporary conditions?
2. Moses is often depicted as a heroic individual. But what are his spiritual challenges?
3. Why did the Hebrews need the Ten Commandments? How do you think contemporary culture views the Commandments?

4. Why does Moses want to question God? When have you ever questioned God?

5. Why is the scene with the burning bush the turning point of Moses's spiritual journey? Has there been an awareness of God that was a major turning point in your life? When?

TENDER MERCIES

1983

1 hour 32 minutes

CATEGORIES: Redemption story, transcendentalist style

SUMMARY: After a drunken night in an out-of-the-way motel, down-and-out country singer Mac Sledge (Robert Duvall) offers to work for motel owner Rosa Lee (Tess Harper), the single mother of ten-year-old Sonny (Allan Hubbard). Mac and Rosa Lee later marry, but Mac must overcome his drinking, anger, and regrets. He progresses by attending church, getting baptized, and deepening his relationship with his new family.

The redemption in this film does not have the conversion experience turnaround moment of films such as *Groundhog Day*, *About a Boy*, and *Ikiru*. Instead, it follows a process that actor Tess Harper describes as a "quiet struggle."[1] The progression's gradual change covers the spiritual challenges of small-town characters often overlooked in American films. The film's pacing and cinematography emphasize this struggle by utilizing the transcendentalist film techniques of long takes and meditative shots.

Tender Mercies is also a unique film for its portrayal of the importance of church. The redemption figure protagonist Mac and his son Sonny are baptized on the same day, and both initially say they do not feel any different. The resulting redemption for Mac, though, is a measured one that occurs mysteriously off camera but is nonetheless transformative.[2]

The film tracks closely to the spiritual battle outlined in chapter eight of the Epistle to Romans, in which Paul defines life as a battle between the flesh and the spirit. Mac's alcoholism, anger, and desire to leave when things get challenging are fleshly earthly desires. His family, spirituality, and sincere music show his redemptive spiritual side.

Mac's redemption accords with Paul's discussion of conquering desires of the flesh. Mac begins as a wanderer, in some ways an exiled Cain.[3] He suffers a kind of death at the beginning of the film when he is laid out on the floor drunk.[4] The motel Mariposa—the name means "butterfly" in Spanish—is a symbol of the resurrection Mac experiences within it.[5] The motel itself is a symbol of transition, where visitors come as a refuge from the vast Texas landscape that seems to engulf them.

Consistent with a theme in traditional country music, redemption in the film is propelled by a devoted and loving spiritual woman.[6] Rosa Lee sings in the church choir, prays, and quotes scripture. A religious woman becomes a force of salvation for a wayward man.

Yet, hovering over redemption is death and the mystery of life's sufferings and blessings. Whether it is the death of Sonny's father in a war, Mac's daughter's death, or Mac's alcoholism, the film depicts a tendency in the human condition toward self-destruction.[7] While Mac works in a garden, he asks Rosa Lee why death comes to some and redemption to others.

Rosa Lee is silent. Happiness and suffering are both inexplicable.[8] In a spiritual paradox, the mystery of God's will is not solved, yet the characters embrace the tender mercies of everyday life.[9] What's most important is connection with others who also live with that paradox of happiness and suffering, as the film's moving ending scene shows.

The transcendentalist style resonates in both the actors' performances and the cinematography. Perhaps Mac and Rosa Lee are drawn to each other because they are both stoics. Their silent disposition throughout the film shifts the mechanism of character development to their facial expressions, which are similar to those of ruminating cow-boys in Westerns. A feeling of the transcendental is also expressed in the film's portrayal of everyday activities such as work, conversation, eating, and watching television at the expense of more action-oriented activities portrayed in conventional Hollywood films.[10]

BIBLE PASSAGE

"Remember not the sins of my youth, nor my transgressions: according to thy mercy remember thou me for thy goodness' sake, O Lord." (Psalm 25:7 KJV)

Rosa Lee recites this verse before she goes to sleep after Mac angrily leaves the house, but it also connects to Mac's redemption story.

DISCUSSION QUESTIONS

1. How does Mac's music contrast with his ex-wife's country music? How do their lifestyles differ?
2. How do Mac and Sonny's stories parallel each other? How do they help each other?
3. What institutions and people help Mac work out his redemption?
4. Rosa Lee prays from Psalm 25, which calls for redemption by both forgetting the past and waiting for instruction. How is this principle at work in the film? When have you seen it work in your own life or the lives of others?
5. When Mac asks about the reasons good or bad things happen, Rosa Lee says nothing. Have there been times in life when either you or someone else has asked that question? Is there an answer? If not, how can you live with not knowing "why"?

THREE GODFATHERS

1948

1 hour 46 minutes

CATEGORIES: Redemption story

SUMMARY: Three bandits, led by Robert Hightower (John Wayne), rob a bank and escape into the desert to evade the law. At a decimated watering station, they find a dying woman and promise to protect her newborn child. The three men struggle to make it back to civilization with the infant.

Director John Ford uses the frontier of the American West to explore some of the deepest American conflicts, including the nomadic and the settled, the wild and the civilized, and the masculine and the feminine.[1] Ford's westerns, including *Stagecoach* (1939), *My Darling Clementine* (1946), and *The Searchers* (1957), are American film classics because they encompass those struggles.

Three Godfathers not only features these cultural tensions but adds the most explicit Christian imagery of any of his Westerns. Ford goes beyond portraying the historical to presenting the mythical.[2]

Like *The Fugitive*, Ford's other film firmly anchored in the spiritual movie genre, *Three Godfathers* features overt Christian symbolism. In *The Fugitive*, the protagonist is a Christ figure, and other characters represent Mary Magdalene, Judas Iscariot, and Pontius Pilate. In *Three Godfathers*, the characters evoke the Nativity story, with the three outlaws representing the three wise men and the baby signifying the baby Jesus.

The three men are not traditional Western heroes. They are bandits who need redemption, which caring for a baby produces. Ford sees human nature as something weakened by original sin, but he sees redemption as possible through the exercise of free will.[3] Salvation or damnation are not predetermined in the film's theology, so choices take on paramount significance.[4] No matter how flawed, weak, proud, or sinful a character is, in Ford's films they can choose redemption—often through self-sacrifice.[5]

The three outlaws achieve redemption by promising a dying woman they will care for her child. The brutality and materialism that governed the robbers' past is then transformed into a responsibility that quickly alters their spiritual conditions.[6]

That the outlaws have the potential for this change demonstrates the moral density of Ford's films.[7] Although his moralism generally is rooted in the family, law, duty, and tradition, he also strongly identifies with the misfit and the maverick, stressing how society needs their energy and contribution.[8] Because Ford shows the perspectives of both insiders and outsiders, his films like *Three Godfathers* achieve a profound complexity.[9]

In *Three Godfathers*, redemption occurs in the desert, where life is stripped to its basics. As the bandits go deeper into the desert, they suffer more by losing their belongings. Yet, they are simultaneously purified by losing baggage from their past behavior.[10] The spiritual turmoil in this process is physically symbolized through sandstorms and an absence of essential shelter, water, and food. The bandits are on an involuntary fast and spiritual pilgrimage.

Their reformations, though, occur at different paces. William is the youngest and least corrupt, so his change is the swiftest. He reverts to an innocence and recognizes a grand design in his redemption. "You think this is all chance, just accidental?" he says. Before saying a child's prayer, he tells Pedro to read Psalm 137, with its homesick lament, "How shall we sing the Lord's song in a strange land?"

Hightower is the most cynical of the three, and his redemption requires supernatural intervention through voices and images that guide him back to society. His integration into society becomes his salvation. As a result, Hightower fulfills the other Biblical parable in the film besides the nativity story: the Prodigal Son.[11] Redemption means more to someone who had a choice and knew the attraction of sin but gained wisdom after becoming dissatisfied with a life of crime, cynicism, and immorality.[12] Hightower appreciates real values because he lived so long without them.[13]

This corresponds with the film's emphasis on self-sacrifice, as the woman, the Kid, and Pedro all die so that a child may live and Hightower may be redeemed.[14] The film is unusual in Ford's canon because it is not the individual who sacrifices for society but others who sacrifice for one man's redemption.[15]

BIBLE PASSAGE

"In whom we have redemption, the forgiveness of sins." (Colossians 1:14 NIV)

Three Godfathers shows redemption eliminating past transgressions. Hightower is accepted back into the community he once plundered and disrupted.

DISCUSSION QUESTIONS

1. What foreshadowing is there that hints the three outlaws might not be such bad men after all?
2. Why do the three men keep the dying woman's wish?
3. How does the movie contrast the outlaws with the authorities pursuing them? What does that say about the themes of individualism vs. community and the nomadic vs. the settled?
4. What is the film's view of redemption? How does it match your view?
5. How does the film show the spirituality of community? What communities do you belong to that you consider spiritual?

TOKYO STORY

1953 (Japan)

2 hours 16 minutes

CATEGORIES: Cautionary tale, transcendental style,
Westerner seeking Eastern wisdom

SUMMARY: An elderly couple travel from their small town to visit their grown children in Tokyo. However, they feel uncomfortable and perceive themselves as obstacles because their children are so busy with their own lives. The couple leaves early, and one of them becomes critically ill on the way home.

Regarded by some as one of the best films ever made (in a *Sight and Sound* poll among critics and filmmakers, it was voted the third best film of all time behind *Vertigo* and *Citizen Kane*),[1] Ozu's *Tokyo Story* is also a significant spiritual film. It is a cautionary tale and a notable example of the transcendental film style incorporating images of Eastern spirituality.

Tokyo Story presents a cautionary tale channeled through a narrative about how modern life destroys the traditional family. All but one of the aging couple's children have moved away to the city and are preoccupied with their jobs, homes, and raising children. They cannot meaningfully connect with their parents, who are resigned to being marginalized.

This reflects the major theme in Ozu's films, which is dissolution of the family.[2] The Japanese director's films often feature the estrangement of parents and children caused by the divisions in modern Japanese society.[3] The erosion of the family is disastrous because—unlike many generalized depictions of American families in Western cinema, where leaving the family is considered an act of maturity—rootedness in family is often a key component of self in presentations of the family in Asian cinema.[4]

Ozu is sympathetic to the older generation because they represent traditional culture, and their age shows the effects of time and the transience of life—two major themes in this film.[5] The journey the couple makes to see their children is a pilgrimage. They hope to confirm that their life's work of raising children has been worthwhile.[6] They return feeling disappointed but forgiving and accepting of their imperfect children.[7]

The film emphasizes the significance of compassion in Buddhism through the forgiveness practiced by the older couple and the kindness of their daughter-in-law Noriko.[8] Compassion distinguishes admirable characters from the less admirable.[9] However, the film also highlights the difficulty of being compassionate in modern culture. Noriko is the character most aware of this. After Kyoko is outraged at what she views as the selfish behavior of her siblings, she later despairingly says, "Isn't life disappointing?" Noriko admits it is, yet she kindly says how difficult it is to overcome self-centeredness. "I may become like that in spite of myself," she admits.

The film's transcendental style, which employs long takes and ambient sounds to place the viewer in a contemplative state. It focuses on commonplace activities, illustrating the Zen Buddhist idea that the transcendent finds expression in everyday events.[10] The film's pacing and style also mirrors how the characters in the film appear calm on the surface but contain deep, untapped feelings on the inside.[11] To maneuver through life, the characters take an attitude of detached awareness without passing judgment on others.[12]

Another use of transcendental techniques is found in Ozu's placement of a stationary camera at the level of a person seated in traditional fashion on a tatami (floor mat).[13] Ozu seldom cuts away from a speaking character, as if every person has the right to be heard in full.[14] The conflicts between characters occur in conversations indoors and are offset by shots between scenes of outdoor Japanese life, including empty streets, passing vehicles, a distant mountain, and a lake.[15] Ozu also includes symbols of transience and passage like smoke, trains, and bridges.[16]

The ending images show how the disparities and difficulties of life are not resolved but accepted.[17] They indicate a view of enlightenment that comes from epiphanies about the often painful realities and limitations of life.[18] This differs from a view of conversion that enables the transcendence of earthly limitations.[19] Instead of a permanent transformation, spiritual insight instead comes from flashes of awareness.[20]

RELIGIOUS TERM

Anicca: The impermanence and transitoriness of everything finite and recognition of the perishing of everything in the natural order.[21] This is a major theme in *Tokyo Story*.

DISCUSSION QUESTIONS

1. Are the parents too resigned? Or are they humble? Where have you seen these qualities in your parents or other important older people in your life?
2. Who are the most compassionate characters and what makes them that way?
3. What about modern living makes it difficult for the children to connect with their parents? What aspects of modern life make it challenging for you to bond with your family?
4. Is it inevitable, as Noriko believes, that one will focus on building one's own life away from their family and community of origin? Is this just part of life? Is that something you've had to do?
5. How do the cutaway shots between scenes make a spiritual statement?

THE TREASURE OF THE SIERRA MADRE

1948

2 hours 6 minutes

CATEGORIES: Cautionary tale

SUMMARY: Down-and-out American Fred C. Dobbs (Humphrey Bogart) meets another drifter, Bob Curtin (Tim Holt), in Mexico. They combine their money and, along with old-timer prospector Howard (Walter Huston), journey into the countryside to search for gold. They struggle with bandits, interlopers, and Dobbs's accelerating greed and paranoia.

Treasure of the Sierra Madre shows that greed is not just a temptation for the ultra-ambitious or evil. Anyone is susceptible. As a cautionary tale, the movie reveals how human nature makes people vulnerable to greed. Overcoming greed requires acknowledging it as a formidable temptation—particularly in a culture that does not do enough to provide economic stability.

The three main characters search for gold because they cannot find satisfactory work in the more conventional institutions. Dobbs and Curtin work what they think are legitimate jobs and are swindled. Their economic deprivation relegates them to lives on the fringes of modern capitalist society, radically alone and seemingly without identity.[1] They are dehumanized and alienated by institutions corrupted by greed, which they are powerless to combat.[2]

Rather than an archetypical quest for adventure, the prospectors are forced by desperation and confinement into a dangerous journey.[3] However, during this semi-subversion of the hero's journey, the main characters are shaped by how they manage greed. A physical search for gold turns into unexpected acquisition of self-knowledge.[4]

Even before beginning the journey, the older prospector Howard is aware of the weakness greed causes in himself and others, and he is committed to helping others develop that awareness.[5] Howard believes greed leaves people insatiable, and he knows it leads to corruption of the spirit.[6] The accumulation of wealth creates anger, distrust, insecurity, and a disintegration of human connections.[7]

Howard acts as a surrogate father figure to Dobbs and Curtin, with one son (Dobbs) more difficult than the other.[8] Initially, Dobbs shows too limited a perspective on greed and insists he will take only what he needs. His denial of his own vulnerability proves fatal because he cannot overcome what he will not face.[9] As Dobbs unravels, though, Curtin builds character. Over the course of the film, the lure of wealth and power destabilizes the friendship and solidarity between Dobbs and the other two men.[10]

Howard and Curtin do not disintegrate like Dobbs because they want to use money to find some sense of home, while Dobbs wants economic power.[11] Dobbs's downfall reaches its zenith when he rejects his conscience as an agent to determine his action. "If you got a conscience, it'll pester you to death," he says. "If you don't believe you got one, what can it do to you?"

The film advocates for two alternatives to the double trap of institutionalized greed and individualistic ambition. Howard seeks an escape from capitalist civilization. He goes to live with a tribe of Native Americans, where he finds freedom from individualism in community.[12] The pre-modern village represents a fantasy innocent society.[13] The sense of community it offers makes it a spiritual alternative to self-absorption and materialism.[14]

The other alternative is embodied in Curtin's plans to visit Cody's widow, who leads a humble domesticated life. She writes in a letter to her nomadic husband that "we've already found life's real treasure." Curtin learns from Cody, who leaves home for the wrong treasure and pays with his life.[15]

The catalyst to finding these two alternatives is what Howard calls "a great joke played on us by the Lord, of fate, or nature, or whatever you prefer." After they discover that the gold dust they accumulated is irrevocably lost to the blowing winds, their boisterous laughter signals their arrival at an understanding of life's deepest meaning.[16] Howard recognizes the futility of the search for wealth, which leads him to change his priorities.[17] Howard and Curtin achieve control by realizing how little control they truly have.[18]

BIBLE PASSAGE

"Those who want to get rich fall into temptation and a trap and into many foolish and harmful desires that plunge people into ruin and destruction." (1 Timothy 6:9 NIV)

The movie shows how desire for wealth can turn to destructive greed.

DISCUSSION QUESTIONS

1. Was it foreshadowed that Dobbs is capable of destructive greed? Or did you find it unexpected? When was a time in your life you were surprised by greed in yourself or others?

2. Why is greed so dangerous? Where do you see greed most in your life or within society?

3. What is Howard's philosophy about greed? How does it change during the movie?

4. What is the tragedy of Cody? Who is someone you know or have heard of whose life was sidetracked or devastated by greed? What happened?

5. Are the alternatives that Howard and Curtin find satisfactory? How have you found your own alternatives to greed and the search for wealth?

THE TREE OF LIFE

2011

2 hours 19 minutes

CATEGORIES: Search for God

SUMMARY: A grief-stricken woman (Jessica Chastain) raises questions about God after her nineteen-year-old son R.L. dies. The film flashes back to scenes of tension between her husband (Brad Pitt) and their oldest son Jack (Sean Penn) in 1950s Texas. In a non-linear structure, the movie becomes a meditation/prayer on creation, suffering, sin, beauty, and faith.

The Tree of Life does nothing less than probe for the meaning of life itself.[1] It is so bold and unconventional that it could be challenging for some viewers and may require several viewings to adequately understand and appreciate it.

The film grapples with multiple spiritual themes, but one of the most prevalent is suffering. The film begins with a quote from the book of Job in which God answers Job's questions about suffering, saying, "Where were you when I created the heavens and the earth?" Some interpret this as God sarcastically "pulling rank" on Job, but *The Tree of Life* shows a different interpretation in its emphasis on the miracle of creation.[2] This culminates in the segment showing the creation of the universe.

The film suggests that the way to understand sorrow is by immersion in the opposite—the beauty and comfort of creation.[3] It rejects reading Job's questioning as arrogance that needs to be silenced, asserting instead that humans can draw closer to God through questioning.[4] The two persons who most question God (Mrs. O'Brien and Jack) are rewarded with a meaningful communion with God.[5]

After the creation section, the film shows the O'Briens starting their family, revealing how the beauty of creation is reflected in everyday life. Human lives are not insignificant and reflect the grandeur of creation.[6] However, this creates a paradox because the beauty of creation is given by the same entity that, for unknown reasons, permits suffering.[7] There is no rational explanation for suffering, so one can only accept this paradox not through passive resignation but from an ongoing inner struggle with God.[8]

Another of the film's major themes is the Christian concept of the Fall. In an Eden-like suburb, Jack's Fall manifests in rebellious behavior. "What I want to do, I can't do; I do what I hate," he says, recalling Paul's declaration in Romans 7:15: "I do not do what I want, but I do the very thing I hate." Jack's father's Fall is caused both by frustration about not becoming financially and professionally successful and misguided disciplining of his children. He embodies nature in the dichotomy between grace and nature that Mrs. O'Brien outlines at the beginning of the film.

She says grace "doesn't try to please itself" and that it "accepts insults and injuries," while nature "only wants to please itself" and "finds reasons to be unhappy when all the world is shining around it." The famous scene in the creation segment in which the wounded dinosaur is spared by the stronger one depicts a moment of grace occurring within the order of nature.[9] The world, in the film's cosmology, is the history of grace and nature.[10]

The parents are physical manifestations of this conflict between grace and nature.[11] Mrs. O'Brien encapsulates grace through kindness, gentleness, faith, and a sense of peace, while her husband represents nature through harshness, obsession with worldly achievements, and his opinion of religion as a set of rules to follow to ensure success.[12] Jack struggles with these two worldviews and is unsure of which to emulate.[13]

This conflict is resolved in Jack's adult life when he experiences a vision of an otherworldly beach with people from his life embracing each other. The film shows there is life and reunion beyond the grave when Jack and Mrs. O'Brien see R.L.[14] The glimpse of future reconciliation in a scene of tranquility takes place on a beach seemingly outside of time.[15] Within this setting, Jack and his mother gain understanding and acceptance of the hardships that they have experienced.[16]

BIBLE PASSAGE

"Where were you when I laid the foundations of the Earth . . . when the morning stars sang together, and all the sons of God shouted for joy?" (Job 38:4,7 NKJV)

The film begins with God's response to Job's questioning by emphasizing the glory of creation.

DISCUSSION QUESTIONS

1. How did you feel about the film's non-linear structure? Why do you think the filmmaker used this technique?
2. What did you think about the film's use of voiceover? How is it different than voiceover is used in most films?
3. How is the division between grace and nature accomplished? Do you believe this is a central conflict of life?
4. What was your reaction to the creation segment of the film? Is it part of your spiritual life to reflect on creation? Why or why not?
5. What is your interpretation of the scene on the beach toward the end of the film?

V FOR VENDETTA

2005

2 hours 12 minutes

CATEGORIES: Apocalyptic, Christ figure, hero's journey

SUMMARY: A mysterious masked man known as "V" leads a rebellion against an oppressive totalitarian government. V plans to blow up the House of Parliament in London to incite rebellion, and, after rescuing her from attackers, Evey (Natalie Portman) assists him.

What separates *V For Vendetta* from more secular dystopian apocalyptic films is that the protagonist is a Christ figure and that Evey, who becomes a disciple of V, undergoes a hero's journey in a story within the story.

In some ways, V recalls postmodernist protagonists in superhero films. V's superhuman strength actually comes from the system he opposes.[1] While in a detention center, he is infected with a virus, a variation on the postmodern superhero whose power is created by an accident (such as Spiderman, who acquires power after a radioactive spider bites him).[2]

Like other cinematic Christ figures, V is concerned with justice, attracts followers, and experiences both a violent death and a symbolic resurrection through his followers. It contains a Pietà-like death scene and he realizes that he is more than just matter. "Why won't you die?" says one antagonist shooting at him. V replies, "Beneath this mask there is more than just flesh. Beneath this mask there is an idea, and ideas are bulletproof." V operates by an inner spirit that secular authorities don't comprehend.

Some viewers may initially have difficulty identifying the Christ figure references because of the film's violence. But the Christ figure in the apocalyptic dystopian film often exhibits violence because the genre is influenced by the violence in the Book of Revelation. And like V's favorite film, *The Count of Monte Cristo*, this movie tells a story of justice through revenge.

"Violence can be used for good," V bluntly tells Evey. Before one of his victims dies, he says forgiveness matters, but this insight does not change his actions. He views himself as an instrument of fate through which justice and vengeance operate. "I, like God, do not play with dice and do not believe in coincidence," he says. Consistent with a Christ figure, he sees his life as determined by a providence to which he surrenders. However, he differs from the Christ figure by enacting retributive justice and inspiring others to overthrow the government.

Similar to *Romero*, the film advocates liberation theology. The government is so corrupt and sinful that it must be changed. And, like *Romero*, there is a clear difference between institutional religion and religion as enacted outside of the power structure. In Vendetta, the bishop is not only subservient to the state but also a pedophile.

V also uses Biblical allusions as a Christ figure sometimes does. When Evey is in danger in the film's opening scene, one of her attackers quotes Proverbs 13:24 about not sparing the rod. V turns the quote on them when he retaliates with swords. Later in the film, he tells another character to put an X on his door if he agrees with his plan, a reference to the signal in Exodus that protects the Hebrews from afflictions God enacts on the Egyptians.

A prominent Christ-figure trait in the film is V's relationship with a Mary Magdalene-like character. In the graphic novel the film is based on, Evey is a sex worker. While the film does not maintain this characteristic, she still moves on the margins of society.

Ultimately, Evey becomes a disciple of V and experiences a hero's journey. This culminates in a spiritual awakening while she is jailed and tortured into revealing V's identity. After finding a letter from a former prisoner in her cell, she overcomes her fear of death. Through her suffering, Evey finds what V calls "freedom" and "something that mattered more than life." As a follower of a Christ figure, her spiritual awakening takes place when she realizes spirit triumphs over flesh.

BIBLE PASSAGE

"It is joy to the just to do judgment: but destruction shall be to the workers of iniquity." (Proverbs 21:15 KJV)

The Bible encompasses both justice and mercy. Passages like this emphasize justice and a warning to those who create inequality.

DISCUSSION QUESTIONS

1. Why does V believe violence is a way to enact social change? What is your opinion about violence as a means toward justice?
2. How does Evey grow spiritually by her time in the cell? When have you had to undergo deprivation of some kind to spiritually mature?
3. What makes Evey not afraid of death? How do you feel about death?
4. How does the death and resurrection theme in the Christ figure film play out in this movie?
5. The movie shows problems of 2005. What are the social problems of today that could be included in a dystopia film?

VOYAGE OF THE DAWN TREADER

2010

1 hour 53 minutes

CATEGORIES: Christ Figure, redemption story

SUMMARY: Lucy (Georgie Henley) and Edmund Pevensie (Skandar Keynes), along with their cousin Eustace (Will Poulter), are transported through a painting to an open sea in the magical land of Narnia. They are rescued and taken aboard a ship commanded by Prince Caspian (Ben Barnes). While traveling to different islands to fight an evil force, they face trials and temptations.

The successful cinematic adaptation of C.S. Lewis's *The Lion, the Witch, and The Wardrobe* (2005) was followed by *Prince Caspian* (2008), which became a critical and commercial disappointment. The lengthy movie and its gratuitous battle scenes emphasized action sequences over spirituality. It effectively killed the momentum of adapting Lewis's children's books into a film series. Only one more of Lewis's seven Narnia books, *The Voyage of the Dawn Treader*, was made into a film. Although often overlooked, *Dawn Treader* is a fascinating movie about spiritual development.

Lewis himself described the book as a story depicting what he called "the spiritual life."[3] He believed that spiritual progress is achieved through battling evil—which first manifests internally through impure desires.

However, the film plays on several other Christian themes. They are conveyed through a narrative structure influenced by Homer's *The Odyssey* and feature travels to strange islands and encounters with peculiar, sometimes threatening characters.[2] Lewis uses its episodic tales of visits to many different islands to explore Christian themes of redemption (Eustace's story), the unseen presence of Christ (characters relying on the Christ figure Aslan), the Eucharist (the feast at Aslan's table), and the reality of a heavenly kingdom (Aslan's Country).[3]

Spiritual advancement comes through acquiring courage and faith to fight evil. "To defeat the darkness out there you must defeat the darkness in yourself," the magician Coriakin says, warning that, because evil exists in the world, everyone will be tested. These tests come through temptations.

The major characters are susceptible to specific temptations that open them to evil activity. Lucy's temptation is vanity and the desire to be loved beyond the limits God sets.[4] Edmund's temptation is power, which he feels he can gain at one point by using a pool that turns objects into gold. The character who does not face temptation is the mouse Reepicheep, the embodiment of true courage and faith.[5] His courage never falters because he does not encounter the fears that cause the humans to waver.[6]

Although the major characters all spiritually progress, Eustace transforms the most. His narrative is a redemption story. He begins in the initial first flawed stage as a rationalist who reads books with what he calls "real information." He dismisses not only fairy tales but religion, which he calls delusional.

Three of C.S. Lewis's *Narnia* stories have been adapted into films including *Voyage of the Dawn Treader*. The lion Aslan is one of the spiritual movie genre's most blatant Christ figures. Photo courtesy 20th Century Fox/Everett Collection

His spiritual defect is an intellectual pride that separates him from other people and makes him feel both superior and cowardly. The second stage of the redemption story is the conflicted state between the old self and an emerging new self, which in this case takes place after Eustace is turned into a dragon and must work out his spiritual progress. The third stage reinforces the Christ figure Aslan as a redeemer, freeing Eustace's rebelliousness and transforming him into a new person.[7]

Aslan is less active in *Dawn Treader* than in the previous two Narnia films; his most prominent feat is changing Eustace from a dragon back into a boy.[8] However, despite not being physically present to the characters, he seems to be present often in a protective (although invisible) way.[9] This shows how faith requires belief in what is sometimes felt but not seen.

Regardless of his visibility, Aslan returns in a compelling ending scene on the edge of Aslan's Country, which leads to a heavenly realm. The atmosphere communicates a sense of loss because the magical childhood of the two Pevensie children is coming to an end and Aslan tells them they are too old to return to Narnia. However, they also harbor hope for an eventual reunion with loved ones as they realize eternity in heaven ultimately awaits them.

BIBLE PASSAGE

"Test me, Lord, and try me, examine my heart and my mind." (Psalms 26:2 NIV)

The Voyage of the Dawn Treader is about being spiritually tested. This occurs partly through temptation, and the movie shows how one can spiritually progress by recognizing temptation and resisting it.

DISCUSSION QUESTIONS

1. Why does Eustace have to go through a phase as a dragon to spiritually progress?
2. What spiritual qualities does Reepicheep possess? What does his small size say about the power of faith?
3. What does the film say about temptation? What specific temptations you are most susceptible to?
4. How is courage shown as a spiritual quality? What do you currently need to be spiritually courageous about in your life?
5. Why does Aslan tell the two children they are too old to return to Narnia? What does that mean for their spiritual lives?

WALL STREET

1987

2 hours 6 minutes

CATEGORIES: Hero's journey

SUMMARY: Corporate raider Gordon Gekko (Michael Douglas) requires insider information from stockbroker Bud Fox (Charlie Sheen) to do business. Fox initially hesitates but then relents. However, Fox later faces a moral crisis when Gekko's financial interests conflict with those of Bud's father (Martin Sheen), a union leader at an airline company.

Like *The Devil Wears Prada*, *Wall Street* is a hero's journey through the commercial epicenter of New York City. Like *Prada*, the protagonist constructs a new but faulty identity by receiving mentorship from industry moguls, penetrating the exclusive terrain of the rich and powerful, and yielding to a temptress/tempter. Both films conclude with the protagonists returning to the community whence they came with newfound wisdom after painful lessons. In *Wall Street*, the protagonist experiences a spiritual reunion within their innermost circle: family.[1]

Before this happens, however, Fox must decide which father figure in his life to follow. In Joseph Campbell's concept of the hero's journey, atonement with the father is a critical element of the narrative's initiation stage. The spiritual archetype of the father figure becomes for Campbell a "priest through whom the young being passes on into the larger world."[2]

Bud has three father/mentor figures: the financial tycoon Gordon Gekko, his parental father Carl Fox, and Lou Manheim, a wise elder at Bud's workplace. Not only are these figures important for Bud's spiritual induction, but they are also cultural archetypes that are still relevant today.

Carl represents the working class and is a voice of conscience. He is both an anachronism and a moral force from another era. As well-intentioned as Carl is, he is too parochial to adequately instruct Bud about the dangers of his ambition. This leaves an opening for other father figures, including the dangerous financial executive Gordon Gekko.

The other altruistic father figure is Lou, Bud's aging co-worker, a benevolent figure who speaks in aphorisms such as "the main thing about money, Bud, is that it makes you do things you don't want to do." Bud looks confused by Lou's paternal-like observations and guidance. Lou is planting seeds of advice he hopes Bud will follow in time.

The third father figure is the charismatic and manipulative Gordon Gekko. He educates Bud by using some of the tools of a clergyman. His infamous "greed is good" speech is the equivalent of a sermon. Earlier in the film, Gekko quotes from Sun Tzu's *The Art of War*, which serves as a kind of religious text for him. He utilizes the fifth-century BCE book to persuade Bud into believing his outlook that life is essentially warfare.

At his core, Gekko is a Social Darwinist: someone who applies principles of biological natural selection to human society. Gekko endorses greed because he sees it as the "essence of evolutionary spirit." Later, Gekko claims that life itself is a zero-sum game in which the strong survive and the weak do not. Gekko believes the winners in life disassociate from any sensitivity and have utilitarian relationships with "no feelings." He tells Bud, "If you need a friend, get a dog," and says to the designer Darien that love is a "myth" and a "fiction."

Aside from the father figures, what distinguishes *Wall Street* is the terrain the hero navigates in his journey, which is a post–American Dream landscape. Gekko defines success not according the American-Dream ideology of hard work or moral values but by financial success.[3] This worldview requires breaking conventional rules and laws to prosper. There is seemingly no ethical way for Bud to elevate himself out of his working-class roots.[4] As a result, Bud ends up almost cut off from humanity when all he does is work and spend money on status symbols.[5] He is a casualty of a society that values success over integrity.[6]

BIBLE PASSAGE

"Whoever loves money never has enough; whoever loves wealth is never satisfied with their income." (Ecclesiastes 5:10 NIV)

In his "greed is good" speech, Gordon Gekko believes desire for more creates social progress. But the author of Ecclesiastes says that desire leads to vanity, meaningless, and emptiness.

DISCUSSION QUESTIONS

1. What role do the three father figures (Carl, Lou and Gordon Gekko) play in Bud's hero's journey? Have there been surrogate parental figures in your life?
2. What makes Gordon Gekko a charismatic and appealing figure? When have you ever been enticed by such a figure?

3. Has the definition of success changed since this film was made? What similarities or differences do you see?
4. What similarities exist between this movie and the Faust story? What are the key scenes that illustrate this?
5. What does the American Dream mean to you? How have you been affected by it?

WAR ROOM

2015

2 hours

CATEGORIES: Difficulty living out faith, redemption story

SUMMARY: The marriage between pharmaceutical salesman Tony Jordan (T.C. Stallings) and his wife Elizabeth (Priscilla Shirer) is disintegrating. Tony is considering having an affair and is secretly selling drug samples. Elizabeth meets the wise older widow Clara (Karen Abercrombie), who shows Elizabeth her War Room—a closet where she prays—and urges Elizabeth to deepen her spiritual life.

A brief resurgence of Christian-themed films emerged in the decade or so after the box office success of *The Passion of the Christ* (2004). Films including *The Nativity Story* (2006), *Noah* (2014), *Exodus: Gods and Kings* (2014), *Last Days in the Desert* (2015), *Risen* (2016), and *The Young Messiah* (2016) were derived from the Bible epic. However, the depiction of Biblical era stories created a void in Christian films: Christian faith in contemporary life.

Independent Christian filmmakers filled that gap by making films about living in an increasingly post-Christian culture. Some films, like *God's Not Dead* (2014) and *The Case for Christ* (2017), are partly about converting atheists. Others, like *War Room* (2015), are aimed at both casual believers as well as Christians who want to strengthen their faith.

Although secular media generally marginalizes Christian films, they have become a platform for Christians who feel ostracized. Many of these films focus on the difficulty of being a devoted Christian in an increasingly non-religious culture, depicting issues of faith largely ignored in contemporary films.

War Room falls into the spiritual film category of difficulty living out faith. However, the film is not about a direct clash with a secular institution, as in *Hacksaw Ridge* (2016). The conflict originates with what Elizabeth's friend and mentor Clara calls Elizabeth's "lukewarm" faith. This tepid spirituality is partly generated by Elizabeth and her husband Tony succumbing to the materialism and self-centeredness inherent in secular culture. The movie shows that even those who say they believe in God can fall prey to these worldly ambitions.

Tony travels frequently for his sales job, which alienates him from his family. He is tempted to have an extramarital affair and sells drug samples to support Elizabeth and Tony's affluent lifestyle. Elizabeth is resigned to being a victim of the modern anti-spiritual dilemma, engaging in busyness that makes her tepid in her faith. "I would consider myself a spiritual person," she says. "Not hot, not cold, somewhere in the middle." This casualness in faith is unacceptable to the impassioned Elizabeth. "I see in you a warrior that needs to be awakened," Clara tells Elizabeth.

The major vehicle for change in the film is prayer. Perhaps no other film in the spiritual movie genre features a narrative centered on expanding the practice of prayer. The film aims to evoke questions about prayer. What is the role of prayer? Clara says prayer is a way of seeking God. And how should one pray? The film suggests creating a private prayer space to not only pray but to review Biblical or spiritual quotes that accentuate prayer requests.

While Elizabeth works on developing her prayer life with guidance from Clara, Tony follows the three-step process of a redeemed character. In his initial flawed state, he considers an affair, ignores his family, and strays from his moral center at his job. In the second phase, he is conflicted as he realizes the mistakes he has made, but he is not sure how to correct them. Finally, he embraces a new self as he pays more attention to his family, confesses his wrongdoings to his employer, and takes on a new job with more spiritual meaning.

The film's shortcoming lies in its failure to address the dilemma and challenges of unanswered prayer. The film could give the impression that prayer is always fulfilled. Intercessory prayers are not always answered, the response can be delayed, or prayers can be responded to differently from how they are prayed. Addressing unanswered prayers would have made the film more realistic and well-rounded; yet sometimes prayers are answered, and this is a film that honors that.

BIBLE PASSAGE

"Do not be anxious about anything, but in every situation, by prayer and petition, with thanksgiving, present your requests to God." (Philippians 4:6 NIV)

Clara's insistence for prayer and petition reflects this idea as well as Jesus's suggestion in Matthew 6:6 to pray in a private place.

DISCUSSION QUESTIONS

1. How does this film make you reflect on your own prayer life? Are there any changes you will make to your prayer life?
2. What are the obstacles in modern life in the film that are barriers to prayer? What challenges do you have?
3. Why does Clara have disdain for "lukewarm" faith? Are there any areas where your faith is lukewarm?
4. Clara says that Elizabeth must recognize who the "real enemy" is? What do you think she is referring to?
5. What is the role of mentorship in the film? How do both Clara and Elizabeth benefit?

WHALE RIDER

2002

1 hour 41 minutes

CATEGORIES: Retaining Indigenous community and culture

SUMMARY: The Maori hold a tradition that their ancient ancestor Paikea rode a whale to New Zealand from Hawaiki. For generations, the eldest son of the oldest male became a chief in a line leading back to Paikea. A young girl named after Paikea (Keisha Castle-Hughes) thinks she can be a tribal leader despite opposition from her grandfather Koro (Rawiri Paratene), who believes only males can fill the role.

Whale Rider conveys a major theme in the retaining Indigenous community and culture film: modernity clashing with ancient spirituality and tradition. In other Indigenous spirituality films like *Avatar*, this conflict ignites a war between an imperialist modern army and an Indigenous tribe. However, in the quiet realism of *Whale Rider*, the threat of modernity is shown entirely within the Maori culture in a small, crumbling New Zealand village.

The town is an insular coastal community with the vastness of the outside world represented by the sea that lies beyond it.[1] The trappings of modernity and industrialization (cars, buses, and motorboats) are apparent, but, like the broken motorboat cord and the rusting cars show, technology has not solved the community's problems.[2] The community suffers from economic and social difficulties including criminality, unemployment, and substance abuse.[3]

The intergenerational clash between the tribal patriarch Koro and his son Porourangi highlights the conflict between modernism and tradition. Porourangi's solution to the disintegration of the community is to seek identity by showing his tribal-influenced art in Europe. However, Koro believes Porourangi is abandoning community and neglecting the younger generation. "Those young men you turn your back on, they've something to learn from you," he says to his son. "You've got the privileges, but you forget you've also got the obligations."

Koro embodies the trope in Indigenous religion films that separating from the tribe is a form of death.[4] Koro's identification with tradition, ancestors, and a need for a successor is increasingly urgent because of the community's problematic social situation.[5]

But Koro's adherence to tradition also makes him rigid. He refuses to allow his granddaughter Paikea to participate in his teachings about the tribe because she is a woman. Paikea's exclusion from tradition is symbolized through an important scene that revolves around a piece of frayed rope and a motorboat.[6] Koro compares the rope to the threads of their ancestors that are "joined together and strong." But after the rope breaks and Koro goes off to find a replacement, Paikea mends the rope and starts the engine herself. Koro scolds her, tells her it is dangerous, and forbids her from doing such a thing again. The recurring pattern of their relationship, then, is Paikea displaying her chiefly qualities and Koro rejecting her skills.[7]

Ultimately, Paikea convinces her grandfather of her leadership abilities. Because Paikea is in the transitional stage between childhood and adulthood, she possesses a wise innocence that, in the end, enlightens the adult world.[8] She also has a mystical connection to whales, reflecting the totemism the tribe values. Totemism comes from the bond a human tribe feels with an animal species, which represents a life force.[9]

In this worldview, the human members of the totem are responsible for the wellbeing of an animal species.[10] So when the fatigued whales wash up on the shore, the tribe rallies to help them. Because the whales are so connected to the tribe, they symbolize the same exhaustion and vital need to be revived.

In Paikea's re-enactment of the tribe's tradition of a whale rider, both species are rejuvenated. By saving the whales, Paikea saves her people as well.[11] Paikea's call for more democracy in the tribe during a speech brings the community together. "If the knowledge is given to everyone, then we can have lots of leaders," she says. "And soon, everyone will be strong, not just the ones that've been chosen." The movie concludes with union between the traditionalism that Koro represents and the flexibility and inclusivity Paikea desires.

SPIRITUAL TERM

Totemism—A human tribe is linked to an animal species or an object they consider sacred.[12] In *Whale Rider*, the Maori feel connected to the humpback whale.

DISCUSSION QUESTIONS

1. How does Paikea show leadership qualities?
2. What are Koro's strengths and weaknesses as both a leader and a grandfather?
3. Is Porourangi right to leave his hometown to be an artist? Have you had to leave your home behind to pursue your career? If so, was it the correct decision?
4. In what ways has the modern world encroached on the Maori? How do you see modernism affecting tradition and spirituality in your community?
5. What finally creates unity in the tribe at the end of the film?

WINGS OF DESIRE

1987 (Germany)

2 hour 8 minutes

CATEGORIES: Divine intervention

SUMMARY: The angel Damiel (Bruno Ganz) methodically goes through the city of Berlin, invisible to everyone except children. Weary of just observing people, Damiel wants to know what it feels like to be human. This desire intensifies as he observes the thoughtful and ethereal trapeze artist Marion (Solveig Dommartin).

Wings of Desire is a demanding spiritual film. The long ponderous takes and meandering narrative undermine conventional narrative expectations in a way similar to the films of Tarkovsky, Bresson, and other transcendental style directors. However, the innovative narrative, cinematography, and a fascinating incarnation of an angel into a human makes it one of the most distinctive movies about angels since the series of films about angels in the 1940s, including *It's a Wonderful Life* (1946) and *The Bishop's Wife* (1947).

These angels, though, are not the same gregarious guardian angels seen in *It's a Wonderful Life*. Damiel and Cassiel are stoic transients visible only to children and can only slightly console humans by a touch. The angels hear other people's thoughts, which gives them insight into the human condition. This enables them to comfort and redirect human thoughts even if they cannot affect fate more than momentarily.[1]

With several extended sequences showing the innermost feelings of humans, the film becomes a microcosm of the pains of the human condition, such as family issues, anxiety over money, and emotional conflicts.[2] The segments of the film that take place in a spacious library emphasize the human longing for knowledge to understand their condition.

Because the two angels collaboratively review what they see every day, they appear to overlook nothing, which shows that each person has significance.[3] However, Damiel realizes he is seeing humanity indistinctly and merely observing human activity from the outside.[4] To be an angel is to exist in limbo between a heavenly realm and the earthly plane.[5] "I don't want to always hover above," Damiel says. "I'd rather feel a weight within casting off this boundless freedom and tying me to earth." Within the limitations of being human, he hopes to find insight and liberation.

Although Damiel is not a Christ figure, his becoming human is an act of incarnation facilitated by his wish to learn more about what it feels like to be human. After his transformation into a human, the film moves away from a religious worldview emphasizing renunciation into curiosity about the world and a celebratory spirituality.[6] A joyfulness emerges within the restrictions of incarnation and mortality,[7] and the desire to experience the life of the body becomes a sacred impulse.[8]

However, this desire comes with a price. Like the Biblical Adam, Damiel wants to eat an apple after becoming human, a reference to the forbidden fruit in Adam's quest for knowledge.[9] He also initially experiences a stigmata-like wound, emblematic of suffering in the earthly realm, but Damiel accepts this as part of the human experience.

The trapeze artist Marion's longing for her own self-sustaining story makes her attractive to Damiel and ultimately inspires him to become human.[10] He is also drawn to her because she is more poetic and introspective than other humans. Marion embodies a loneliness that the audience members at the rock concert crowd also possess; they are together, yet alone.[11] Marion is not solely a figure of physical beauty to Damiel because he knows her thoughts and longings.[12] She represents Damiel's hunger for self-knowledge and the desire to experience love and belonging.[13]

Their spiritual love is signified by Damiel presenting a glass of wine to Marion like a communion cup when they meet face-to-face. In the film's final scene, their love appears solidified as Damiel steadies Marion's aerial rope, which shows that he is offering her strength and support.[14] Damiel's relationship with Marion shows the marriage of spirit and matter, time and eternity, and a celebration of the everyday world.[15]

BIBLE PASSAGE

"Are not all angels ministering spirits sent to serve those who will inherit salvation?" (Hebrews 1:14 NIV)

The movie shows angels as comforting entities, although their capacities are limited.

DISCUSSION QUESTIONS

1. What stood out to you most about the film style? How did the film's unconventional pacing, cinematography, and narrative affect you?
2. What are the limitations of the life of an angel/spiritual being in the film? What are the limitations of being a human in the film?
3. What do these movie angels have in common with other cinematic angels? How are they different?
4. What does Damiel and Marion's relationship say about the film's definition of romantic love? How does it match your view?

5. How does the subplot with the actor Peter Falk fit into the narrative? Did it integrate well into the narrative or was it more of a distraction? Why or why not?

THE WIZARD OF OZ

1939

1 hour 42 minutes

CATEGORIES: Hero's journey

SUMMARY: In her dream, a cyclone hurls Dorothy Gale (Judy Garland) from Kansas to the magical land of Oz. The good witch Glinda (Billy Burke) advises Dorothy to see the Wizard of Oz (Frank Morgan), who may be able to get Dorothy home. Along the way, she makes three friends (Scarecrow, the Tin Man, and the Cowardly Lion) who also need the Wizard's help.

Dorothy singing "Over the Rainbow" is an iconic call to adventure. Salman Rushdie described this awakening as "a celebration of Escape, a grand paean to the Uprooted Self, a hymn— the hymn—to Elsewhere."[1]

This comes after Dorothy's discovery that adult figures cannot help her and that she must take charge of her own destiny which pushes the call to adventure forward.[2] Dorothy's aunt and uncle capitulate to the wealthy and powerful Miss Gulch, who takes Dorothy's dog Toto away through a legal order. Aunt Em adds that, because she is a Christian woman, she cannot tell Gulch what she thinks of her. The adult domains of law and organized religion cannot support Dorothy or enact justice.

Dorothy progresses on her hero's journey by running away from home. But she refuses the call by turning back after Professor Marvel makes her believe her aunt will worry about her. In a kind of compromise, Dorothy enacts the call spiritually and psychologically through her dream.[3]

The Wizard of Oz is not only a Hero's Journey for the adolescent Dorothy Gale (Judy Garland), but also presents a dichotomy between the spirituality of the witch Glinda and the religious pomposity of The Wizard. Dorothy's journey leads to inner spiritual growth which Glinda ultimately validates. Photo courtesy MGM/Everett Collection

In the elevated state of consciousness of her dream, she crosses the threshold in the hero's journey trajectory. She is lifted in her house by a cyclone that symbolizes a disruption to her way of being.[4] During the tumultuous upheaval, she sees events and people from her life in the window. This resembles a near death experience and is the transition between one state of consciousness and another.[5]

Once in Oz, the hero's journey stages unfold to reinforce a major theme in the film: acquiring self-knowledge through trials. Scarecrow, the Tin Man, and the Cowardly Lion all help each other and Dorothy in their quests because they are insecure and feel incomplete. They focus too much on one trait they feel they lack, creating neurosis that companionship helps them to overcome.

The movie shows a divide between institutional religion, represented by the Wizard, and spirituality, signified by the witch Glinda. The Wizard symbolizes a demanding, intimidating, and distant God who instills awe and fear and wants something in return from those who ask him for help.[6] He embodies a false definition of God as a divine magician.[7] The Wizard also concocts an illusion of mystery.[8]

However, the Wizard actually aids the characters by forcing Dorothy and her new friends on a perilous journey to attain the Wicked Witch's broomstick. By doing this, the characters gain self-knowledge by discovering they already possess the traits of courage, intelligence, and compassion that they have been seeking.[9] The diplomas and medals they receive from the Wizard are symbols of no value compared to the inner virtue and abilities they have finally recognized.[10]

Although the movie deconstructs institutional religion through the defrocking of the misleading Wizard, it still upholds religion through Glinda's more placid spirituality. Glinda is the only major character in Oz who is not a projection of a character from Kansas.[11] She tells Dorothy she should not depend on external sources of power.[12]

This culminates in Glinda's instruction to Dorothy to return home by clicking her heels together. The advice illustrates that Dorothy herself possesses the power to alter her own destiny. Dorothy repeats, "There's no place like home" as if it were a prayer or mantra. If Oz represents a deepened state of consciousness and transcendent reality, it is one that she realizes cannot last.

Dorothy's quest to return home is a sacred process to feel she belongs somewhere, even in the gray reality of rural Kansas.[13] Home becomes not so much a place of refuge but a situation where all of life's sufferings and hardships are finally accepted.[14] Like George Bailey in *It's a Wonderful Life*, Dorothy ultimately realizes home and a small community are not limiting but actually the true sources of identity and happiness, although she feels no appreciation for them until they're temporarily lost.[15]

BIBLE PASSAGE

"Nor will they say, 'See here!' 'See there!' For indeed, the kingdom of God is within you." (Luke 17:21 NKJV)

The Wizard of Oz emphasizes that spiritual awareness from within is shaped by experience and trials.

DISCUSSION QUESTIONS

1. What is behind Dorothy's longing to return home to Kansas? Why doesn't she want to stay in the magical and colorful land of Oz?

2. What does home mean to you spiritually? Where is home for you?

3. How are Glinda and the Wizard both mentors and how are they not mentors?

4. How does the movie show that sometimes the journey is more important than the destination? When was a time in your life when that was true?

5. How do the characters show they have hidden strengths?

ACKNOWLEDGMENTS

As always, my deepest appreciation and love to my dear mother Virginia Zukowski for her constant example of godly living, wisdom, and kindness. I am grateful to Donald Bertram for his friendship, guidance, and spiritual mentoring. Thanks to Lou Vetri for thoughtful, meaningful, and fun conversations and so much more. I am grateful to Dave and Chizuko Walter, who have been more like family than friends for so many years. I thank Bret Talbert, whose spiritual insights always inspire me.

I thank everyone at The Pilgrim Press for believing in this project and for their hard work, advice, and support—particularly Rachel Hackenberg, Katie Martin, Adam Bresnahan, and Noah Jalango. Thanks again to Michele Hadlow at the Everett Collection for her assistance with the photos in this book.

I also thank the filmmakers who produced the films in this book. They have been an inspiration to me and to many people on their spiritual journeys.

NOTES

Introduction

1. Roger Ebert, "Ikiru," last modified September 29, 1996, https://www.rogerebert.com/reviews/great-movie-ikiru-1952.

2. William James, *The Varieties of Religious Experience* (New York: Modern Library, 1999), 61.

3. Ibid., 111.

4. Ibid., 246.

5. Mara Donaldson, "Love and Duty in Casablanca," in *Image and Likeness: Religious Visions in American Film Classics*, ed. John R. May (Mahwah: Paulist Press, 1992), 121.

6. Brian Godawa, *Hollywood Worldviews: Watching Films with Wisdom and Discernment* (Downers Grove: InterVarsity Press, 2009), 86.

7. James, *Varieties of Religious Experience*, 233.

8. Ibid., 234.

9. George Garrelts, "Citizen Kane: Descent into the Demonic," in *Image and Likeness: Religious Visions in American Film Classics*, ed. John R. May (Mahwah: Paulist Press, 1992), 55.

10. Ralph Lewis, "Spirituality, Not Just Religion, May be Declining," *Psychology Today*, February 20, 2020, https://www.psychologytoday.com/us/blog/finding-purpose/202002/spirituality-not-just-religion-may-be- declining.

11. Bruce Babington and Peter Evans, *Biblical Epics: Sacred Narrative in the Hollywood Cinema* (Manchester: Manchester University Press, 1993), 4.

12. James, *Varieties of Religious Experience*, 325.

13. Lloyd Baugh, *Imaging the Divine: Jesus and Christ-Figures in Film* (London: Sheed & Ward, 1997), 205–210.

14. Anton Kozlovic, "The Structural Characteristics of the Cinematic Christ-figure," *Journal of Religion and Popular Culture* 8, no.1 (Fall 2004), https://doi.org/10.3138/jrpc.8.1.005.

15. James, *Varieties of Religious Experience*, 231.

16. Ibid., 261.

17. Christopher Deacy, "The Christian Concept of Redemption and its Application Through the Films of Martin Scorsese," *Religious Studies and Theology* 17, no. 1 (June 1998): 48–49.

18. Christopher Deacy, *Screen Christologies: Redemption and the Medium of Film* (Cardiff: University of Wales Press, 2002), 24.

19. Godawa, *Hollywood Worldviews*, 87–89.

20. Deacy, *Religious Studies and Theology*, 53.

21. Conrad E. Ostwalt, "Visions of the End: Secular Apocalypse in Recent Hollywood Film," *Journal of Religion & Film* 2 no.1. (April 1998): 4.

22. Joseph Campbell, *The Hero with a Thousand Faces* (Novato: New World Library, 2008), 17.

23. Ibid.

24. Ibid., 28–29.

25. Victor Turner and Edith Turner, *Image and Pilgrimage in American Culture: Anthropological Structures* (New York: Columbia University Press, 1995), 2.

26. Ibid., 6.

27. Ibid., 8.

28. Jane Naomi Iwamura, "The Monk in American Popular Culture," in *Religion and Popular Culture in America*, ed. Bruce David Forbes and Jeffrey Mahan (Oakland: University of California Press, 2005), 30.

29. John Lyden, *Film as Religion, Second Edition: Myths, Morals, and Rituals* (New York: New York University Press, 2019), 253.

30. Paul Schrader, *Transcendental Style in Film: Ozu, Bresson, Dreyer* (Oakland: University of California Press, 2018), 9.

31. Ibid., 8.

32. Ibid., 88.

33. Ibid., 3.

34. Terry Lindvall, Dennis J. Bounds, and Chris Lindvall, *Divine Film Comedies: Biblical Narratives, Film Sub-Genres, and the Comic Spirit* (New York: Routledge, 2016), 196.

35. Schrader, *Transcendental Style in Film*, 2.

36. Huston Smith, *The World's Religions* (New York: Harper Collins, 1991), 377.

37. Ibid.

38. Ibid., 375.

2001: A Space Odyssey

1. Roger Ebert, "2001: A Space Odyssey," last modified March 27, 1997, https://www.rogerebert.com/reviews/great-movie-2001-a-space-odyssey-1968.

2. "Playboy Interview: Stanley Kubrick," in *The Making of 2001: A Space Odyssey*, ed. Martin Scorsese (New York: Random House, 2000), 272.

3. Philip Kuberski, "Kubrick's Odyssey: Myth, Technology, Gnosis," *The Arizona Quarterly* 64, no. 3 (Autumn 2008): 53.

4. Rhonda Burnette-Bletsch, "2001: A Space Odyssey," in *Bible and Cinema: Fifty Key Films*, ed. Adele Reinhartz (New York: Routledge, 2013), 4.

5. Kuberski, "Kubrick's Odyssey," 53.

6. Burnette-Bletsch, "2001: A Space Odyssey," 5.

7. Hans Feldmann, "Kubrick and His Discontents," *Film Quarterly* 30, no. 1 (Fall 1976): 15.

8. Ibid.

9. Burnette-Bletsch, "2001: A Space Odyssey," 4.

10. Ibid., 5.

11. Ibid.

12. Ibid.

13. Thomas Allen Nelson, *Kubrick: Inside a Film Artist's Maze* (Bloomington: Indiana University Press, 2000), 131.

14. Charlie Kobler, "Stanley Kubrick Raps," in *The Making of 2001: A Space Odyssey*, ed. Martin Scorsese. (New York: Random House, 2000), 249.

15. Ibid.

16. Feldmann, "Kubrick," 14.

17. Burnette-Bletsch, "*2001: A Space Odyssey*," 7.

18. Ibid.

19. Ibid., 8.

20. Feldmann, "Kubrick," 14.

21. Burnette-Bletsch, "*2001: A Space Odyssey*," 7.

About a Boy

1. Victor Frankl, *Man's Search for Meaning* (New York: Simon & Schuster 1984), 111.

2. Ibid., 108.

3. Ibid., 115.

The Apostle

1. Felicia Feaster, "The Apostle," *Film Quarterly 52*, no. 1 (Fall 1998): 35–36.

2. Adele Reinhartz, *Scripture on the Silver Screen* (Louisville: Westminster John Knox Press, 2003), 117.

3. Conrad Ostwalt, "The Apostle," *Church History* 68, no. 3 (Sept. 1999): 670.

4. Ibid.

5. Ibid.

6. Reinhart, *Scripture on the Silver Screen*, 120.

7. Bradley Shaw, "Baptizing Boo: Religion in the Cinematic Southern Gothic," *The Mississippi Quarterly* 63, no. 3 (Summer 2010), 473.

8. Reinhartz, *Scripture on the Silver Screen*, 121.

9. Ostwalt, "The Apostle," 669.

10. Ibid.

11. Ibid., 669–670.

12. Carl Greiner, "*The Apostle*: A Psychiatric Appraisal," *Journal of Religion and Film* 3, no. 2 (Oct. 1999), 8–9, https://digitalcommons.unomaha.edu/jrf/vol3/iss2/6.

13. Brian Godawa, *Hollywood World Views: Watching Films with Wisdom and Discernment* (Downers Grove: Intervarsity Press, 2009), 211.

Au Hasard Balthazar

1. Tony Pipolo, *Robert Bresson: A Passion for Film* (Oxford: Oxford University Press, 2010), 204.

2. Lloyd Baugh, *Imaging the Divine: Jesus and Christ Figures in Film* (Kansas City: Sheed & Ward, 1997), 199.

3. Paul Schrader, *Transcendental Style in Film* (Oakland: University of California Press, 2018), 2, 11–14.

4. Baugh, *Imaging the Divine*, 187–188.

5. James Quant, "*Au Hasard Balthazar* and *Le Diable Probablement*," in *The Hidden God*, ed. Mary Lea Bandy and Antonio Monda (New York: Museum of Modern Art, 2003), 19.

6. Ibid., 18–19.

7. Baugh, *Imaging the Divine*, 187.

8. Pipolo, *Robert Bresson*, 196.

9. Baugh, *Imaging the Divine*, 191.
10. Ibid., 193.
11. Ibid., 194.
12. Ibid., 192.

Babette's Feast

1. Lloyd Baugh, *Imaging the Divine: Jesus and Christ Figures in Film* (Kansas City: Sheed & Ward, 1997), 139.
2. Ibid., 138.
3. Wendy Wright, "*Babette's Feast*: A Religious Film," *Journal of Religion and Film* 1, no. 2 (Oct. 1997): 6, https://digitalcommons.unomaha.edu/jrf/vol1/iss2/2.
4. Thomas J. Curry, "Babette's Feast and the Goodness of God," *Journal of Religion and Film* 16, no. 2 (Oct. 2012): 35, https://digitalcommons.unomaha.edu/jrf/vol16/iss2/10.
5. Baugh, *Imaging the Divine*, 139.
6. Ibid.
7. Wright, "*Babette's Feast*," 7.
8. Curry, "*Babette's Feast* and the Goodness of God," 1.
9. Baugh, *Imaging the Divine*, 140.
10. Ibid.
11. Ibid.
12. Wright, "*Babette's Feast*," 16.
13. Ibid.
14. Daniel Loftin, "A Gift in Exile: Leadership and Creativity in *Babette's Feast*: A Film Review," *The International Journal of Servant-Leadership* 6, no. 1 (2010): 313.

Barabbas

1. Bruce Babington and Peter Evans, *Biblical Epics: Sacred Narrative in the Hollywood Cinema* (Eugene: Wipf and Stock, 1993), 186.
2. Bair Searles, *Epic! History on the Big Screen* (New York: Harry N. Abrams Inc.,1990), 58.
3. Foster Hirsch, *The Hollywood Epic* (Cranbury: A.S. Barnes & Co., 1978), 109.
4. Ibid.
5. Ibid., 111.
6. Lloyd Baugh, *Imaging the Divine: Jesus and Christ Figures in Film* (Kansas City: Sheed & Ward, 1997), 17.
7. Babington and Evans, *Biblical Epics*, 186.
8. Ibid., 187.
9. Ibid., 217.
10. Hirsch, *The Hollywood Epic*, 109.

Becket

1. Baird Searles, *Epic! History on the Big Screen* (New York: Harry N. Abrams Inc., 1990), 100.

Ben-Hur

1. Bruce Babington and Peter Evans, *Biblical Epics: Sacred Narrative in the Hollywood Cinema* (Eugene: Wipf & Stock, 1993), 171.

2. Adele Reinhartz, *Bible and Cinema: An Introduction* (New York: Routledge, 2013), 99.
3. Babington and Evans, *Biblical Epics*, 197.
4. Ibid.
5. Reinhartz, *Bible and Cinema*, 92.
6. Foster Hirsch, *Hollywood Epics* (Cranford: A. S. Barnes, 1978), 108.
7. Ibid., 111.
8. Reinhartz, *Bible and Cinema*, 100.

The Bishop's Wife

1. Peter Valenti, "The 'Film Blanc': Suggestions for a Variety of Fantasy, 1940–45," *Journal of Popular Film* 6, no. 4, 1978), 295.
2. Terry Lindvall, Dennis J. Bounds, and Chris Lindvall, *Divine Film Comedies: Biblical Narratives, Film Sub-Genres, and the Comic Spirit* (New York: Routledge, 2016), 110.
3. Valenti, "'Film Blanc,'" 296.
4. Lindvall, Bounds, and Lindvall, *Divine Film Comedies*, 111.

The Book of Eli

1. Wynn G. Hamonic, "Global Catastrophe in Motion Pictures as *Meaning and Message: The Functions of Apocalyptic Cinema in American Film*," Journal of Religion and Film 21, no. 1 (April 2017): 14.
2. Jens Bjering, "Imagining the Unheard-of in Contemporary Cinema," *Theory & Event* 21, no. 4 (Oct. 2018): 826– 827.
3. Ana Moya and Gemma López, "Looking Back: Versions of the Post-Apocalypse in *Contemporary North American Cinema*," Film Criticism 41, no. 1 (Feb. 2017).
4. Ibid.
5. David Crewe, "It's the End of the World and We Love it: Investigating the Popularity of Post-Apocalyptic Cinema," *Screen Education* 82 (2016): 36.

Bruce Almighty

1. Terry Lindvall, Dennis J. Bounds, and Chris Lindvall, *Divine Film Comedies: Biblical Narratives, Film Sub-Genres, and the Comic Spirit* (New York: Routledge, 2016), 126.
2. *Bruce Almighty*, DVD, directed by Tom Shadyac (Universal City, CA: Universal Pictures, 2011).
3. Lindvall, Bounds, and Lindvall, *Divine Film Comedies*, 137.
4. Clive Marsh, *Theology Goes to the Movies: An Introduction to Critical Christian Thinking* (New York: Routledge, 2007), 49.

Cast Away

1. Catherine Craft-Fairchild, "Castaway and *Cast Away*: Colonial, Imperial, and Religious Discourses in Daniel Defoe and Robert Zemeckis," *Journal of Religion and Film* 9, no. 1 (April 2005): 6, https://digitalcommons.unomaha.edu/jrf/vol9/iss1/4.
2. Ashleigh Hardin, "Race and Trajectories of Addiction in Robert Zemeckis's Cast Away (2000) and Flight (2012)," *The Arizona Quarterly* 72, no. 4 (Winter 2016): 142.
3. Craft-Fairchild, "Castaway and *Cast Away*," 5.
4. Hardin, "Race and Trajectories of Addiction," 149.

5. Carol Kaufman-Scarborough, "Two Perspectives on the Tyranny of Time: Polychronicity and Monochronicity as Depicted in Cast Away," *The Journal of American Culture* 26, no. 1 (2003): 93, https://doi.org/10.1111/1542- 734X.00076.

6. David LaRocca, "How to Do Slow Things with Cinema in Hollywood: Temporal Duration in the Diegetic and Non-Diegetic Worlds of *Cast Away*," in *A Critical Companion to Robert Zemeckis*, ed. Adam Barkman and Antonio Sanna, (Lanham: Lexington Books, 2020), 175.

7. Kaufman-Scarborough, "Two Perspectives," 94.

8. Hardin, "Race and Trajectories of Addiction," 147.

9. Douglas H. Ingram, "Of Time, Narrative, and Cast Away," *Journal of the American Academy of Psychoanalysis* 29, no. 4 (Winter 2001): 625.

10. Catherine Walker Bergstrom, "Searches for the Significant: Robert Zemeckis's *Cast Away* as a Late Twentieth Century Response to Daniel Defoe's *Robinson Crusoe*," *Journal of Religion and Film* 9, no. 1 (April 2005), 6, https://digitalcommons.unomaha .edu/jrf/vol9/iss1/12.

11. Craft-Fairchild, "Castaway and *Cast Away*," 13.

12. Ibid.

Chariots of Fire

1. Margaret Miles, *Seeing and Believing: Religion and Values in the Movies* (Boston: Beacon Press, 1997), 79.

2. Sophia B. Blaydes and Philip Bordinat, "Blake's Jerusalem and Popular Culture: *The Loneliness of the Long-Distance Runner* and *Chariots of Fire*," *Literature/Film Quarterly* 11, no. 4 (1983): 213.

3. Glen Jones, "Down on the Floor and Give Me Ten Sit-Ups: British Sports Feature Film," *Film & History* 35, no. 2 (2005): 34.

4. Ibid., 36.

Contact

1. Bryan Stone, "Religious Faith and Science in *Contact*," *Journal of Religion and Film* 2, no. 2 (Oct. 1998): 9, https://digitalcommons.unomaha.edu/jrf/vol2/iss2/6.

2. Marc T. Newman, "The Land of Faery as Cosmic Cheat: A Lewisian Analysis of Robert Zemeckis' *Contact*," *Journal of Religion and Popular Culture* 22, no. 1 (Spring 2010): 13.

3. Gregory Sadlek, "Robert Zemeckis' *Contact* as a Late-Twentieth Century Paradiso," *Journal of Religion and Film* 5, no. 2 (Oct. 2001): 10, https://digitalcommons .unomaha.edu/jrf/vol5/iss2/6.

4. Stone, "Religious Faith and Science in *Contact*," 6–7.

5. Ibid.

6. Sadlek, "Robert Zemeckis' *Contact*," 9.

7. Stone, "Religious Faith and Science in *Contact*," 4.

8. Sadlek, "Robert Zemeckis' *Contact*," 10.

9. Ibid.

10. Anneke Murely and Adam Barkman, "Contact from Reality, Flight from Truth: An Exploration of Objective Truth and Morality," in *A Critical Companion to Robert Zemeckis*, ed. Adam Barkman and Antonio Sanna (Lanham: Lexington Books, 2020), 146.

11. Ibid., 148.

Cool Hand Luke

1. Adele Reinhartz, "Jesus and Christ Figures," in *The Routledge Companion to Religion and Film*, ed. John Lyden (London: Routledge, 2011), 420–439.
2. David A. Davis, "'I Am a Fugitive from a Chain Gang!' and the Materiality of Southern Depravity," *The Mississippi Quarterly* 63, no. 3/4 (Summer 2010), 414.
3. Peter Malone, *Movie Christs and Antichrists* (Parish Ministry Publications, 1988), 65.
4. Nicholas Godfrey, "Against Authority: Rebellion and Religious Allegory in *Cool Hand Luke*," *Screen Education* 91, (2018), 118.
5. Neil Hurley, "Cinematic Transfigurations of Jesus," in *Religion in Film*, ed. John R. May and Michael Bird (Knoxville: University of Tennessee Press, 1982), 69.

Crimes and Misdemeanors

1. David Landry, "Faint Hope—A Theological Interpretation of Woody Allen's Crimes and Misdemeanors," *Journal of Religion and Popular Culture* 22, no. 1 (Spring 2010): 6.
2. Richard A. Blake, "Looking for God: Profane and Sacred in the Films of Woody Allen," *Journal of Popular Film & Television* 19, no. 2 (Summer 1991): 65.
3. Peter Minowitz, "Crimes and Controversies: Nihilism from Machiavelli to Woody Allen," *Literature/Film Quarterly*, 19, no. 2 (1991): 78.
4. Ibid., 80.
5. Mark Roche, "Justice and the Withdrawal of God in Woody Allen's *Crimes and Misdemeanors*," *Film & Philosophy*, (2000): 76, https://mroche.nd.edu/assets /287526/roche_crimes_and_misdemeanors_film_and_philosophy.pdf.
6. Ibid., 77.
7. Landry, "Faint Hope," 14.
8. Marat Grinberg, "The Birth of a Hebrew Tragedy: Woody Allen's Cassandra's Dream as a Morality Play," *Journal of Religion & Film* 14, no. 1 (2010): 2, https://dig-italcommons.unomaha.edu/jrf/vol14/iss1/3.
9. Sander H. Lee, *Eighteen Woody Allen Films Analyzed: Anguish, God, and Existentialism* (Jefferson: McFarland, 2002), 139.
10. Ibid., 147.
11. Ibid.
12. Landry, "Faint Hope," 7.
13. Ibid.
14. Peter Csato, "Pragmatism Goes to the Movies: Pragmatic Conceptions of Truth in Woody Allen's *Crimes and Misdemeanors*," *HJEAS: Hungarian Journal of English and American Studies* 20, no. 1 (Spring 2014): 21.
15. Roche, "Justice and the Withdrawal of God," 72.

Cry, the Beloved Country

1. Andrew Foley, "Considered as a Social Record: A Reassessment of *Cry, the Beloved Country*," *English in Africa* 25, no. 2 (Oct. 1998): 68.
2. Kemp Williams, "The Style of Paradox: Thematic and Linguistic Duality in *Cry, the Beloved Country*," *English Studies in Africa* 39, no. 2 (1996): 5, https://doi.org/10 .1080/00138399608691246.
3. Ibid., 6.

4. Foley, "Social Record," 68.
5. Ibid.
6. Williams, "Style of Paradox," 2.
7. Ibid., 1.
8. Foley, "Social Record," 79.
9. Ibid., 71.
10. Ibid., 63.
11 Ibid., 79.

Dead Man Walking

1. Maurine Sabine, *Veiled Desires: Intimate Portrayals of Nuns in Postwar Anglo-American Film* (New York: Fordham University Press, 2013), 272.
2. Ibid., 255.
3. Ibid.
4. Ibid.
5. Ibid., 255–256.
6. Lloyd Baugh, *Imaging the Divine: Jesus and Christ Figures in Film* (Kansas City: Sheed & Ward, 1997), 152.
7. Ibid., 154.
8. Ibid.
9. Sabine, Veiled Desires, 256.
10. Adele Reinhartz, *Scripture on the Silver Screen* (Louisville: Westminster John Knox Press, 2003), 53.
11. Eileen M. Condon, "Confession in the Movies: The Transmission of Sacramental Tradition through Film," *Catholic Education: A Journal of Inquiry and Practice* 4, no. 1 (Sept. 2000): 253.
12. Baugh, *Imaging the Divine*, 153.
13. Reinhartz, *Scripture*, 53.
14. Ibid., 152.

Dersu Uzala

1. John A. Schneider, "Signs and Symbols in *Dersu Uzala*," *Psychoanalytic Review* 96, no. 1 (Feb. 2009): 175.
2. Ibid., 173.
3. Ibid., 174.
4. Ma Sheng-mei, "The Myth of Nothing in Classics and Asian Indigenous Films," *CLCWeb* 15, no. 2 (June 2013): 4.
5. Donald Richie, *The Films of Akira Kurosawa* (Berkeley: University of California Press, 1996), 198.
6. Olga Solovieva, "The Erased Grave of *Dersu Uzala*: Kurosawa's Cinema of Memory and Mourning," *Journal of Japanese and Korean Cinema* 2, no. 1 (2010): 66, https://doi.org/10.1386/jjkc.2.1.63_1.
7. Ibid., 67.
8. Richie, *The Films of Akira Kurosawa*, 200.
9. Schneider, "Signs and Symbols," 178.
10. Sheng-mei, "Myth of Nothing," 4.
11. Solovieva, "Erased Grave," 64.

Diary of a Country Priest

1. Andre Bazin, *What Is Cinema?* (Berkeley: University of California Press, 1967), 135.

2. John Gerlach, "*The Diary of a Country Priest*: A Total Conversion," *Literature/Film Quarterly* 4, no. 1 (Winter 1976): 41.

3. Ibid.

4. Lloyd Baugh, *Imaging the Divine: Jesus and Christ Figures in Film* (Kansas City: Sheed & Ward, 1997), 226.

5. Ibid., 227.

6. Susan Sontag, "Spiritual Style in the Films of Robert Bresson," in *Robert Bresson*, ed. James Quandt (Toronto: Toronto Film International Group, 1998), 64.

7. Baugh, *Imaging the Divine*, 228.

8. Joseph Cunneen, *Robert Bresson: A Spiritual Style in Film* (New York: Continuum, 2003), 46.

9. R.J. Cardullo, "L'Argent and the Aesthetics of Robert Bresson, Reconsidered," *Hermeneia* 21 (2018), 247.

10. Paul Schrader, *Transcendental Style in Film* (Oakland: University of California Press, 2018), 102.

11. Bazin, *What Is Cinema?*, 136.

12. Gerlach, "*The Diary of a Country Priest*," 41.

13. John E. Keegan, "Robert Bresson's *The Diary of a Country Priest*: The Experience of God as Grace," *Sewanee Theological Review* 54, no. 1 (2010): 53.

14. Sontag, "Spiritual Style," 66.

15. Cardullo, "L'Argent," 248.

16. Sontag, "Spiritual Style," 57.

17. Ibid., 65.

18. Schrader, *Transcendental Style in Film*, 95.

19. Baugh, *Imaging the Divine*, 227.

20. Schrader, *Transcendental Style in Film*, 89.

21. Sontag, "Spiritual Style," 61.

Enlightenment Guaranteed

1. Huston Smith, *The World's Religions* (New York: Harper Collins, 1991), 99.

2. Ibid., 103.

Entertaining Angels: The Dorothy Day Story

1. Tracy Fessenden, "Worldly Madonna," in *Catholics in the Movies*, ed. Colleen McDannell (Oxford: Oxford University Press, 2008), 271.

Frankenstein

1. Jennifer Roher-Walsh, "*Frankenstein*," in *Bible and Cinema: Fifty Key Films*, ed. Adele Reinhartz (London: Routledge, 2013), 95.

2. John C. Lyden, *Film as Religion: Myths, Morals, and Rituals.* (New York: New York University Press, 2019), 206.

3. Ibid., 220.

4. Jeffrey A. Johnson, "Dr. Frankenstein, I Presume? Revising the Popular Image of Frankenstein," *Literature and Medicine* 36, no. 2 (Fall 2018): 303.

5. Elizabeth Young, "Here Comes the Bride: Wedding Gender and Race in Bride of Frankenstein," *Feminist Studies* 17, no. 3. (Autumn 1991): 424.

6. Ibid.

7. Sarah Ward, "Re-Creating the Creature: Visions of Mary Shelly's *Frankenstein*," *Screen Education* 78 (2015): 75.

8. Ibid., 74.

9. Lyden, *Film as Religion*, 219.

10. Roher-Walsh, *"Frankenstein,"* 97.

The Fugitive

1. Tag Galagher, *John Ford: The Man and His Films* (Berkeley: University of California Press, 1988), 235.

2. Scott Eyman, *Print the Legend: The Life and Times of John Ford* (New York: Simon and Schuster, 1999), 321.

3. Jim Sanderson, "American Romanticism in John Ford's the Grapes of Wrath: Horizontalness, Darkness, Christ, and F.D.R.," *Literature/Film Quarterly* 17, no. 4 (1989): 237.

4. Gallagher, *John Ford*, 237.

5. Gallagher, *John Ford*, 440.

6. Maria Elena de las Carreras Kuntz, "The Catholic Vision in Hollywood: Ford, Capra, Borzage and Hitchcock," *Film History* 14, no. 2 (2002): 132.

7. Gallagher, *John Ford*, 234.

8. Carreras Kuntz, "Catholic Vision," 219.

9. Gallagher, *John Ford*, 446.

10. Ibid., 127.

11. Ibid., 128.

12. Ibid., 132.

Gandhi

1. Darius Cooper, "Gandhi," *Film Quarterly* 37, no. 2 (Winter 1983–1984): 48, https://doi.org/10.2307/3697391.

2. Ibid., 47.

3. Ibid.

Gladiator

1. Mark Finney, *Resurrection, Hell and the Afterlife: Body and Soul in Antiquity, Judaism and Early Christianity* (New York: Routledge, 2016), 7.

2. Emily Albu, "*Gladiator* at the Millennium," *Arethusa* 41, no. 1 (2008): 192–193.

3. Jennifer Barker, "A Hero Will Rise: The Myth of the Fascist Man in *Fight Club* and *Gladiator*," *Literature/Film Quarterly* 36, no. 3 (2008): 174.

4. Elena Theodorakopoulos, *Ancient Rome at the Cinema: Story and Spectacle in Hollywood and Rome* (Liverpool: University of Liverpool Press, 2010), 104.

5. Monica Silveria Cyrino, *"Gladiator,"* in *The History on Film Reader*, ed. Marnie Hughes-Warrington (New York: Routledge, 2009), 181.

6. Darlene Juschka, "Spectacles of Gender: Enacting the Masculine in Ancient Rome and Modern Cinema," *Religious Studies and Theology* 24, no. 1 (2005): 97.

7. Ibid.

8. Ibid.

9. Barker, "A Hero Will Rise," 174.

The Gospel According to St. Matthew

1. Metello Mugnai, "Pier Paolo Pasolini's Mandatory Challenge: Jesus from *La Ricotta to The Gospel According to Saint Matthew*," Italica 91, no. 3 (2014): 444.

2. Richard Stern, Clayton Jefford, and Guerric DeBona, *Savior on the Silver Screen* (Mahwah: Paulist Press, 1999), 97.

3. William R. Telford, "Jesus Christ Movie Star: The Depiction of Jesus in the Cinema," in *Explorations in Theology and Film*, ed. Clive Marsh and Gaye Ortiz (Malden: Blackwell, 1997), 135.

4. Lloyd Baugh, *Imaging the Divine: Jesus and Christ Figures in Film* (Kansas City: Sheed & Ward, 1997), 94.

5. Stern, Clayton, and DeBona, *Savior on the Silver Screen*, 103.

6. Ibid., 111.

7. Ibid., 101.

8. Ibid., 111.

9. Ibid., 102.

10. Stern, Clayton, and DeBona, *Savior on the Silver Screen*, 102.

11. Ibid., 101.

12. Ibid., 124.

Gran Torino

1. Stacy Torres, "Aging, *Gran Torino*-Style: Understanding People in their Social Worlds," *Contexts* 9, no. 1 (2010): 68.

2. Ibid., 66.

3. Ibid.

4. Annalee R. Ward, "*Gran Torino* and Moral Order," *Christian Scholar's Review* 40, no. 4 (2011): 391.

5. Diane Corkey, "Walt Kowalski A Christ Figure? Christic Resonances in *Gran Torino*," *Journal of Religion and Film* 15, no. 2 (Oct. 2011): 12, https://digitalcommons .unomaha.edu/jrf/vol15/iss2/5.

6. Umberto Curi and Mario Pezzella, "Clint Eastwood's *Gran Torino*," Iris 1, no. 2 (Oct. 2009): 533.

7. Ibid.

8. Ward, "*Gran Torino* and Moral Order," 384.

9. Curi and Pezzella, "Clint Eastwood's *Gran Torino*," 535.

10. Corkey, "Walt Kowalski," 6.

11. Curi and Pezzella, "Clint Eastwood's *Gran Torino*," 534.

Grand Canyon

1. Charles Ramírez Berg, "A Taxonomy of Alternative Plots in Recent Films: Classifying the 'Tarantino Effect,'" *Film Criticism* 31, no. 1 (2006): 6.

2. Ibid., 14, 18.

3. Hsuan L. Hsu, "Racial Privacy, the L.A. Ensemble Film, and Paul Haggis's *Crash*," *Film Criticism* 31, no. 1/2 (Fall 2006): 135.

4. Wallace Katz, "*Crash*: Film Noir in Post-Modern L.A.," *New Labor Forum* 15, no. 1 (Spring 2006): 124.

5. Ibid.
6. Ibid., 125.
7. Hsu, "Racial Privacy," 136.
8. David Denby, "Lost Angels," *New York*, January 13, 1992, 46.
9. Hsu, "Racial Privacy," 139–140.

Groundhog Day

1. Alex Kuczynski, "Groundhog Almighty," *The New York Times*, December 7, 2003, https://www.nytimes.com/2003/12/07/style/groundhog-almighty.html.
2. Wayne Glausser, "*Groundhog Day* at 25: Conflict and Inspiration at the Tipping Point of Seasonal Genres," *Journal of Religion and Film* 23, no. 1 (April 2019): 18.
3. Robert Jewett, "Stuck in Time: Kairos, Chronos, and the Flesh in *Groundhog Day*," in *Explorations in Theology and Film*, ed. Clive Marsh and Gaye Ortiz (Malden: Wiley-Blackwell, 1997), 162.
4. Joseph H. Kupfer, *Visions of Virtue in Popular Film* (Boulder: Westview Press, 1999), 55.
5. Mario Sesti, "*Groundhog Day*," in *The Hidden God*, ed. Mary Lea Bandy and Antonio Monda (New York: The Museum of Modern Art, 2003), 206.
6. Ibid., 211.

Hacksaw Ridge

1. Duane Cady, *From Warism to Pacifism: A Moral Continuum* (Philadelphia: Temple University Press, 2010), xvii.

Harry Potter

1. John Granger, *Looking for God in Harry Potter* (Carol Stream: Tyndale, 2004), 4.
2. Ibid.
3. Roni Natov, "*Harry Potter* and the Extraordinariness of the Ordinary," *The Lion and the Unicorn* 25, no.2 (April 2001): 319.
4. Gary Simmons and Christine Evely, "*Harry Potter and the Philosopher's Stone*," *Screen Education* 37, (2004): 71.
5. Ibid.
6. Natov, "*Harry Potter* and the Extraordinariness of the Ordinary," 319.
7. Francis Bridger, *A Charmed Life: The Spirituality of Potterworld* (New York: Image Books/Doubleday, 2002), 99.
8. Andrea Stojiklov, "Life and Death in *Harry Potter*: The Immortality of Love and Soul," *Mosaic: An Interdisciplinary Critical Journal* 48, no. 2 (June 2015): 135–137.

The Hunger Games

1. Ildiko Limpar, "*The Hunger Games* Trilogy as a Text for Education," *HJEAS: Hungarian Journal of English and American Studies* 23, no. 2 (2017): 394.
2. Ibid.

I Can Only Imagine

1. Matthew Ryan, "Art, Utopia and the Aestheticized Self," *Arena Journal* 39/40 (2012–2013): 263.
2. Ibid., 264.
3. Ibid.

I Origins

1. Nathan Rabin, "The Bataan Death March of Whimsy Case File #1: Elizabeth-town," https://film.avclub.com/the- bataan-death-march-of-whimsy-case-file-1-elizabet-1798210595.

2. Michael Behe, *Darwin's Black Box: The Biochemical Challenge to Evolution* (New York: Free Press, 2006), 257.

3. Ibid.

Ida

1. Steven Vredenburgh, "Finding God in Pawlikowski's *Ida*," *Religions* 7, no. 6 (2016): 4.

2. Ibid.

3. Ibid., 8.

4. Maureen Sabine, *Veiled Desires: Intimate Portrayals of Nuns in Postwar Anglo-American Film* (New York: Fordham University Press, 2013), 2.

5. A.O. Scott, "An Innocent Awakened," *New York Times*, May 1, 2014, https://www.nytimes.com/2014/05/02/movies/ida-about-an-excavation-of-truth-in-postwar-poland.html. 6 Vredenburgh, "Finding God," 4.

Ikiru

1. Peter L. Doebler, "Jest in Time: The Problems and Promises of the Holy Fool in Francesco, Giullare Di Dio, Ordet, and Ikiru," *Journal of Religion and Film* 17, no. 1 (2013), 25, https://digitalcommons.unomaha.edu/jrf/vol17/iss1/35.

2. Ibid., 26.

3. Jeanine Young-Mason, "Understanding Suffering and Compassion," *Cross Currents* 51, no. 3 (Fall 2001): 355.

4. Ernest Ferlita and John R. May, *Film Odyssey: The Art of Film as Search for Meaning* (Mahwah: Paulist Press, 1976), 41.

5. Donald Richie, *The Films of Akira Kurosawa* (Berkeley: University of California Press, 1965), 93.

6. Doebler, "Jest in Time," 41.

7. Edward Murray, *Ten Film Classics: A Re-Viewing* (New York: Frederick Ungar Publishing, 1965), 58.

8. Ibid.

9. Jeanine Young-Mason, *States of Exile: Correspondences Between Art, Literature, and Nursing* (New York: National League for Nursing Press, 1995), xi.

10. R. T. Simone, "The Mythos of the Sickness unto Death: Kurosawa's *Ikiru* and Tolstoy's *The Death of Ivan Ilych*," Literature/Film Quarterly 3, no. 1 (1975): 12.

11. Neil P. Hurley, *Theology Through Film* (New York: Harper & Row, 1970), 136.

12. Doebler, "Jest in Time," 38.

13. Ibid., 41.

14. Jeffrey Gordon, "Kurosawa's Existential Masterpiece: A Meditation on the Meaning of Life," *Human Studies* 20, no. 2 (April 1997): 138.

Into the Wild

1. Laura I. H. Beattie, "Wilderness, the West and the Myth of the Frontier in Sean Penn's *Into the Wild*," Forum 16, (2013): 2.

2. Ibid., 4.

3. David Laderman, *Driving Visions: Exploring the Road Movie* (Austin: University of Texas Press, 2002), 1.

4. Ibid., 18.

5. Charles McGrath, "Mother Nature's Restless Sons," *New York Times*, September 16, 2007, https://www.nytimes.com/2007/09/16/movies/16mcgr.html.

6. Susan Bye, "Flight from Destiny: *Into the Wild* and the Getting of Wisdom," *Screen Education* 85 (2017): 125.

It's a Wonderful Life

1. Daniel J. Sullivan, "Sentimental Hogwash? On Capra's *It's a Wonderful Life*," *Humanitas* 18, no. 1/2 (2005): 121.

2. Ibid.

3. Ibid.

4. Robert E. Lauder, "*It's a Wonderful Life*: Divine Benevolence," in *Image and Likeness: Religious Visions in American Film Classics*, ed. John R. May (Mahwah: Paulist Press, 1992), 141.

5. Robert B. Ray, *A Certain Tendency of the Hollywood Cinema 1930–1980* (Princeton: Princeton University Press, 1985), 196.

6. Ibid., 198.

7. Ibid., 193.

8. Ibid., 186.

9. Ibid.

10. Ibid., 193.

11. Sullivan, "Sentimental Hogwash?", 117.

12. Ibid., 132.

13. Ibid.

14. Robin Wood, "Ideology, Genre, Auteur," *Film Comment* 13, no. 1 (Jan.–Feb. 1977), 49.

15. Ray, *Certain Tendency*, 201.

16. Sullivan, "Sentimental Hogwash?", 117.

17. Ibid., 120.

18. Ibid., 123.

19. Ibid., 137.

Jesus of Montreal

1. Lloyd Baugh, *Imaging the Divine: Jesus and Christ Figures in Film* (Kansas City: Sheed & Ward, 1997), 125.

2. Margaret Miles, *Seeing and Believing: Religion and Values in the Movies* (Boston: Beacon Press, 1996), 41.

3. Baugh, *Imaging the Divine*, 122.

4. Ibid., 117–118.

5. Ibid., 119.

6. Ibid., 114.

7. Roberta Imboden, "The Barbarian Invasions," *Film Quarterly* 58, no. 3 (Spring 2005): 48.

Joan the Maid (Jeanne la Pucelle)

1. Robin Blaetz, *Visions of the Maid: Joan of Arc in American Culture and Film* (Charlottesville: University of Virginia Press, 2001), 4.

2. Ibid., 9.

3. Pamela Grace, "*Joan the Maid*: The Battles/The Prisons," in *Bible and Cinema: Fifty Key Films*, ed. Adele Reinhartz (New York: Routledge, 2013), 157.

4. Ibid., 156.

5. Joan Hinde Stewart, "The Maid and the Milkmaid: Joan of Arc and Marie Antoinette," *The French Review* 93, no. 4 (May 2020): 22.

6. Grace, "*Joan the Maid*," 160.

7. Ibid.

Journey to Italy

1. Peter Brunette, *Roberto Rossellini* (Berkeley: University of California Press, 1996), 164.

2. Tag Gallagher, *The Adventures of Roberto Rossellini* (New York: Da Capo Press, 1998), 406.

3. Joseph Luzzi, "The End of the Affair: Rossellini and Antonioni after Neorealism," *Raritan* 33, no. 1 (Summer 2013): 118.

4. Peter Bondanella, *The Films of Roberto Rossellini* (Cambridge: Cambridge University Press, 1993), 111.

5. Virgilio Fantuzi, "Voyage to Italy," in *The Hidden God: Film and Faith*, ed. Mary Lea Bandy and Antonio Monda (New York: Museum of Modern Art, 2003) 81.

6. Ibid., 82.

7. Ibid.

8. Brunette, *Roberto Rossellini*, 164.

9. Ibid., 156.

10. Ibid., 162.

11. Ibid.

12. Barbara Kellum, "The Archeology of a Relationship: Journeying to Italy with Roberto Rossellini," *The Massachusetts Review* 55, no. 4 (Winter 2014): 83.

13. Ibid., 78.

14. Ibid.

15. Brunette, *Roberto Rossellini*, 168.

The Keys of the Kingdom

1. David Parkinson, "Gregory Peck: 10 Essential Films," last modified April 5, 2016, https://www.bfi.org.uk/news- opinion/news-bfi/lists/gregory-peck-10-essential -films.

King of Kings

1. Richard Stern, Clayton Jefford, and Guerric DeBona, *Savior on the Silver Screen* (Mahwah: Paulist Press, 1999), 43.

2. Ibid., 49.

3. W. Barnes Tatum, *Jesus at the Movies: A Guide to the First Hundred Years and Beyond* (Salem: Polebridge Press, 2013), 56.

4. Bruce Babington and Peter Evans, *Biblical Epics: Sacred Narrative in the Hollywood Cinema* (Eugene: Wipf & Stock, 1993), 111.

5. Ibid., 119.

6. Ibid., 122.

7. Ibid., 121.

8. Stern, Jefford, and DeBona, *Savior on the Silver Screen*, 44.
9. Babington and Evans, *Biblical Epics*, 122.
10. Stern, Jefford, and DeBona, *Savior on the Silver Screen*, 30.
11. Tatum, *Jesus at the Movies*, 55.

Kundun

1. Ben Nyce, *Scorsese Up Close: A Discussion of His Films* (Lanham: Scarecrow Press, 2004), 148.
2. Robert Casillo, "Scorsese in the Land of Snows: The Splendor of *Kundun*," *Italian Americana* 17, no. 1 (1999): 19.
3. Ibid., 17.
4. Gavin Smith, "The Art of Vision: Martin Scorsese's *Kundun*," in *Martin Scorsese Interviews*, ed. Peter Brunette (Jackson: University Press of Mississippi, 1999), 236.
5. Felicia Chan, "Politics into Aesthetics: Cultural Translation in *Kundun*, *Seven Years in Tibet*, and *The Cup*," in *Buddhism and American Cinema*, ed. John Whalen-Bridge and Gary Storhoff (Albany: SUNY Press, 2014), 104.
6. Ibid., 101.
7. Judith Barad, "The Ethical Underpinnings of *Kundun*," in *The Philosophy of Martin Scorsese*, ed. Mark T. Conrad (Lexington: University Press of Kentucky, 2007), 213.
8. Paul Duncan, *The Pocket Essential Martin Scorsese* (Reading: Cox & Wyman, 2004), 14.
9. Nyce, *Scorsese Up Close*, 148, 153.
10. Duncan, *The Pocket Essential Martin Scorsese*, 139.
11. Ibid., 58.

Les Miserables

1. Kathryn M. Grossman, *Les Miserables: Conversion, Revolution, Redemption* (New York: Twayne Publishers, 1996), 29.
2. Ibid.
3. Ibid., 28.
4. Lisa Gasbarrone, "Restoring the Sacred in Les Miserables," *Religion & Literature* 40, no. 2 (2008): 14–15.
5. Grossman, *Les Miserables*, 117.
6. Victor Brombert, "*Les Miserables*: Salvation from Below," in *Victor Hugo: Modern Critical Views*, ed. Harold Bloom (New York: Chelsea House, 1988), 217.
7. Ibid.
8. Gasbarrone, "Restoring the Sacred," 12.

Life of Pi

1. Rebecca Duncan, "*Life of Pi* as Postmodern Survivor Narrative," *Mosaic: A Journal for the Interdisciplinary Study of Literature* 41, no. 2 (June 2008): 167.
2. John Kuriakose, "Religious Pluralism in Yan Martel's *Life of Pi*: A Case of Intertextual Correspondence with Swami Vivekananda's Religious Philosophy," *Advances in Language and Literary Studies* 9, no. 2 (2018): 139.
3. Chad Bolton, "*Life of Pi*," *Journal of Religion and Film* 17, no. 1 (2013): 3.
4. Jean-Christophe Castelli, *The Making of Life of Pi: A Film, A Journey* (New York: Harper Design, 2012), 9.

5. Ibid., 158.
6. Bolton, *"Life of Pi,"* 4.
7. Castelli, *The Making of Life of Pi*, 128.
8. Duncan, *"Life of Pi* as Postmodern Survivor Narrative," 170.
9. Rachel Wagner, "Screening Belief: *The Life of Pi*, Computer Generated Imagery, and Religious Imagination," *Religions* 7, no. 8 (2016): 19.
10. Nancy J. Moules, "Postmodernism and the Sacred: Reclaiming Connection in our Greater-than-Human Worlds," *Journal of Marital and Family Therapy* 26, no. 2 (2000): 229–230, https://doi.org/10.1111/j.1752- 0606.2000.tb00292.x.
11. Ibid., 230.
12. Ibid.

The Lion King

1. Analee Ward, *Mouse Morality: The Rhetoric of Disney Animated Film* (Austin: University of Texas Press, 2002), 22.
2. Ibid.
3. Annalee Ward, "*The Lion King*'s Mythic Narrative," *Journal of Popular Film & Television* 23, no. 4 (Winter 1996): 173.
4. Kim Edwards, "Coming Full Circle: A Study Guide to *The Lion King*," *Screen Education* 88, (2018): 11.
5. Ward, "*The Lion King*'s Mythic Narrative," 173.
6. Ibid.
7. Ibid.
8. Ward, *Mouse Morality*, 20.
9. Marc Demont, "Of Male Friendships and Spirals in *The Lion King*, Vertigo and the American Pie Saga," *Gender Forum* 47, (2014): 2.
10. Ward, *Mouse Morality*, 23.
11. Edwards, "Coming Full Circle," 10.
12. Ibid.
13. Ibid.
14. Ward, "*The Lion King*'s Mythic Narrative," 175–176.
15. Ibid., 176.
16. Susan Mackey-Kallis, *The Hero and the Perennial Journey Home in American Film* (Philadelphia: University of Pennsylvania Press, 2001), 100.
17. Ibid., 99.
18. Ward, *Mouse Morality*, 23.

The Lion, the Witch, and the Wardrobe

1. Mark Worthing, *Narnia, Middle-Earth and The Kingdom of God: A History of Fantasy Literature and the Christian Tradition* (Eugene: Wipf and Stock, 2016), 19.
2. Ibid., 26.
3. Ibid., 10.
4. Ibid., 17.
5. David Downing, *Into the Wardrobe: C.S. Lewis and the Narnia Chronicles* (San Francisco: John Wiley & Sons, 2005), 121.
6. Martin Hinten, *The Keys to the Chronicles: Unlocking the Symbols of C. S. Lewis's Narnia* (Nashville: Broadman & Holman, 2005), 12.
7. Downing, *Into the Wardrobe*, 70.

8. Paul F. Ford, *Companion to Narnia: A Complete Guide to the Magical World of C.S. Lewis's The Chronicles of Narnia*, rev. ed. (New York: Harper Collins, 2005), 6.

9. Kathryn Walls, "An Analogous Adversary: The Old Dispensation in *The Lion, The Witch and the Wardrobe*," *Journal of the Fantastic in the Arts* 28, no. 2 (2017): 213, JSTOR.

10. Ibid., 205.

11. Ibid., 206.

12. Ibid., 208.

13. Bryan Dove, "Wanting the White Witch," in *Vader, Voldemort and Other Villains: Essays on Evil in Popular Media*, ed. Jamey Heit (Jefferson: McFarland, 2011), 121.

14. Ford, *Companion to Narnia*, 92.

The Lord of the Rings

1. John Rosegrant, "J.R.R. Tolkien and Creativity II: Symbols of Transitionality and the Fetish in *The Lord of the Rings*," *American Imago* 76, no. 2 (Summer 2019): 168.

2. Eric Katz, "The Rings of Tolkien and Plato: Lessons in Power, Choice, and Morality," in *The Lord of the Rings and Philosophy: One Book to Rule Them All* (Chicago: Open Court Publishing, 2003), 10.

3. Ibid., 19.

4. Douglas Blount, "Uberhobbits: Tolkien, Nietzsche, and the Will to Power," in *The Lord of the Rings and Philosophy: One Book to Rule Them All*, ed. Gregory Bassham and Eric Bronson (Chicago: Open Court Publishing, 2003), 98.

5. Kathleen O'Neill, "Tolkien's *The Lord of the Rings*: A Cistercian Perspective," *Cistercian Studies Quarterly* 40, no. 3, (2005): 307.

6. Scott Davison, "Tolkien and the Nature of Evil," in Bassham and Bronson, *The Lord of the Rings and Philosophy*, 103.

7. Rosegrant, "J.R.R. Tolkien and Creativity II," 169.

8. Ibid.

9. Ibid.

10. Ibid., 168.

Malcolm X

1. Kameron J. Copeland, "I Do Feel the Fire!: The Transformations of Prison-Based Black Male Converts to Islam in *South Central*, *Malcolm X*, and *Oz*," *Journal of Religion and Film* 21, no. 1 (April 2017): 42.

2. Ibid., 45.

3. Ibid., 14.

4. Ibid., 42.

5. Ibid., 29.

A Man Called Ove

1. Anders Marklund, "No Country for Old Men: Utopian Stories of Welfare Society's Shortcomings in *A Man Called Ove* and *The 100-Year-Old Man*," *Journal of Aesthetics and Culture* 10, no. 2 (2018): 51.

2. Ibid., 51.

3. Clara Neupert, "*A Man Called Ove* in Review," *University Wire*, September 18, 2017, https://search.proquest.com/wire-feeds/man-called-ove-review/docview/193997 2292/se-2?accountid=3588.

4. Marklund, "No Country for Old Men," 53.
5. Ibid., 51.
6. Neupert, "*A Man Called Ove* in Review."
7. Marklund, "No Country for Old Men," 49.
8. Ibid., 48–49.
9. Ibid., 54.

The Matrix

1. David J. Gunkel, "The Virtual Dialectic: Rethinking *The Matrix* and its Significance," *Configurations* 14, no. 3 (Fall 2006): 195.
2. Frances Flannery-Dailey and Rachel Wagner, "Wake Up! Gnosticism and Buddhism in The Matrix," *Journal of Religion and Film* 5, no. 2 (Oct. 2001): 2, https://digital commons.unomaha.edu/jrf/vol5/iss2/4.
3. Ibid.
4. Paul Fontana, "Finding God in *The Matrix*," in *Taking the Red Pill: Science, Philosophy and the Religion in the Matrix*, ed. Glenn Yeffeth (Dallas: BenBella Books, 2003), 165.
5. Ibid., 166.
6. Ibid., 164.
7. Gunkel, "The Virtual Dialectic," 197.
8. Flannerey-Dailey and Wagner, "Wake Up!", 14.
9. Gunkel, "Virtual Dialectic," 197–198.
10. Flannerey-Dailey and Wagner, "Wake Up!", 7.
11. Ibid., 1.
12. Ibid., 13.
13. G. C. Williams, "Mastering the Real: Trinity as the Real Hero of The Matrix," *Film Criticism* 27, no. 3 (Spring 2003): 13.
14. Gregory Grieve, "There Is No Spoon? Teaching *The Matrix*, Postperennialism, and the Spiritual Logic of Late Capitalism," in *Teaching Religion and Film*, ed. Gregory Watkins (Oxford: Oxford University Press, 2008), 197.
15. *Karen Armstrong, A History of God: The 4,000-Year Quest of Judaism, Christianity and Islam* (New York: Albert Knopf, 1993), 95–96.

The Mission

1. David J. Farmer, "Talking About Religion," *Administrative Theory & Praxis* 27, no. 1 (March 2005): 190.
2. John McInerney, "*The Mission* and Robert Bolt's Drama of Revolution," *Literature/Film Quarterly* 15, no. 2 (1987): 72.
3. Michael Dempsey, "Light Shining in Darkness: Roland Joffe on *The Mission*," *Film Quarterly* 40, no. 4 (Summer 1987): 6.
4. Roy Anker, *Catching Light: Looking for God in the Movies* (Grand Rapids: William Eerdmans, 2004), 189.
5. Bryan Stone, *Faith and Film: Theological Themes at the Cinema* (St. Louis: Chalice Press, 2000), 144.
6. McInerney, "*The Mission*," 74.
7. Anker, *Catching Light*, 170.
8. Sylvain DeBleeckere, "The Religious Dimension of Cinematic Consciousness in Postmodern Culture," in *New Image of Religious Film*, ed. John R. May (Kansas City: Sheed & Ward, 1997), 101.

Night of the Hunter

1. Tom Aitken, "Pervasion and Fulfilment: Revivalist Christianity in *The Night of the Hunter*," in *Cinema Divinite: Religion, Theology and the Bible in Film*, ed. Eric S. Christianson, Peter Francis, and William R. Telford (London: SCM Press, 2005), 255.

2. Elizabeth McCarthy, "*The Night of the Hunter*," *The Irish Journal of Gothic and Horror Studies*, no. 10 (October 2011): 82.

3. Ibid.

4. Aitken, "Pervasion and Fulfilment," 255.

5. Ibid.

6. Ibid., 256–257.

7. Tom Aitken, "*Night of the Hunter*," in *Bible and Cinema: Fifty Key Films*, ed. Adele Reinhartz (New York: Routledge, 2012), 192.

8. McCarthy, "*The Night of the Hunter*," 82.

Noah

1. Lindsay Macumber and Abdul-Masih Magi, "A Journey into the Heart of God: Darren Aronofsky's *Noah* as a Subversive Kabbalistic Text," *Journal of Religion and Film* 22, no. 3 (2018): 2, https://digitalcommons.unomaha.edu/jrf/vol22/iss3/5.

2. Ibid., 13.

3. Ibid., 14–15.

4. Robert K. Johnston, "Retelling the Biblical Story of Noah: Jewish and Christian Perspectives," in *Noah as Anti- Hero: Darren Aronofsky's Cinematic Deluge*, ed. Rhonda Burnette-Bletsch and Jon Morgan (New York: Routledge, New York, 2017), 57.

5. Rhonda Burnette-Bletsch, "Real Women and Multiple Masculinities," in *Noah as Anti-Hero: Darren Aronofsky's Cinematic Deluge*, ed. Rhonda Burnette-Bletsch and Jon Morgan (New York: Routledge, 2017), 173.

6. Ibid., 177.

7. Marianna R. Shapiro and Lila Moore, "Not Your Grandmother's Bible—A Comparative Study of the Biblical Deluge Myth in Film," *Religions* 10, no. 10 (October 2019): 14.

8. Richard Walsh, "Aronofsky's Nuancing of the Biblical Epic," in *Noah as Anti-Hero: Darren Aronofsky's Cinematic Deluge*, ed. Rhonda Burnette-Bletsch and Jon Morgan (New York: Routledge, 2017), 126.

9. Burnette-Bletsch, "Real Women and Multiple Masculinities," 164.

10. Walsh, "Aronofsky's Nuancing," 127.

11. Shapiro and Moore, "Not Your Grandmother's Bible," 10.

The Nun's Story

1. Saint Ignatius, *The Spiritual Exercises* (New York: Image Books, 1964), 53.

2. Arthur Nolletti, "Spirituality and Style in The Nun's Story," *Film Criticism* 18/19, no. 3/1 (Spring/Fall 1994): 85.

3. Ibid., 84.

4. Mary Ann Janosik, "Madonnas in Our Midst: Representations of Women Religious in Hollywood Film," *U.S. Catholic Historian* 15, no. 3 (Summer 1997): 91.

5. Nolletti, "Spirituality and Style," 95.

6. Maureen Sabine, *Veiled Desires: Intimate Portrayals of Nuns in Postwar Anglo-American Film* (New York: Fordham University Press, 2013), 110.

7. Ibid., 112.

8. Nolletti, "Spirituality and Style," 83.

Office Space

1. Robert T. Schultz, *Soured on the System: Disaffected Men in 20th Century American Film* (Jefferson: McFarland, 2012), 164.

2. Willy Staley, "Mike Judge, the Bard of Suck," *The New York Times Magazine*, April 13, 2017.

3. Latham Hunter, "The Celluloid Cubicle: Regressive Constructions of Masculinity in 1990s Office Movies," *The Journal of American Culture* 26 no. 1 (March 2003): 84.

4. Doyle Green, *The American Worker on Film: A Critical History 1909–1999* (Jefferson: McFarland, 2010), 91.

5. Hunter, 84.

6. Ibid., 84.

7. Ibid., 72

8. Ibid., 72.

9. Schultz, *Soured on the System*, 12.

10. Ibid., 113.

Of Gods and Men

1. Andrea Sabbadini and Giovanna Di Ceglie, "A Camera Inside a Monastery: Reflections on *Of Gods and Men*," *International Journal of Psychoanalysis* 92, no. 3 (June 2011): 747.

2. Ibid.

3. Ibid.

4. Anne Thurston, "The Eucharist: Passion for Life: A Reflection on *Of Gods and Men*," *The Furrow* 62, no. 5 (May 2011), 261.

5. "*Of Gods and Men*," filmed April 8, 2011 for *Religious and News Ethics Weekly*, video, https://www.pbs.org/wnet/religionandethics/2011/04/08/father-james-martin-sj-of-gods-and-men/8533/.

6. Ibid.

7. Sabbadini and Di Ceglie, "A Camera Inside a Monastery," 746.

8. Peter Bradshaw, "Grace Under Fire: Severe, Austere and Deeply Moving, this True Story is One of the Year's Highlights: *Of Gods and Men*," *The Guardian*, December 3, 2010, 12.

9. Thurston, "The Eucharist: Passion for Life," 262.

10. Sabbadini and Di Ceglie, "A Camera Inside a Monastery," 750.

11. Ibid., 751.

12. Ibid.

13. Bradshaw, "Grace Under Fire," 12.

14. Ibid.

15. *Religious and News Ethics Weekly* video.

On The Waterfront

1. Peter Biskind, "The Politics of Power in *On the Waterfront*," *Film Quarterly* 29, no. 1 (1975): 29.

2. Gary Simmons, "Back to the Waterfront: A Close Reading of *On the Waterfront*," *Screen Education* 57 (2010): 140.

3. Ibid.
4. Gary Simmons, "Conscience, Confessions, and Context in *On the Waterfront*," *Screen Education* 56 (2009): 94.
5. Simmons, "Back to the Waterfront," 139.
6. Ibid.
7. Ibid.

Ordet

1. Peter L. Doebler, "Jest in Time: The Problems and Promises of the Holy Fool in *Francesco, Giullare Di Dio, Ordet*, and *Ikiru*," *Journal of Religion and Film* 17, no. 1 (April 2013): 21.
2. Ibid., 21.
3. Paul Schrader, *Transcendental Style in Film* (Oakland: University of California Press, 2018), 153.
4. Ibid.
5. Daniel Watts, "The Fullness of Time: Kierkegaardian Themes in Dreyer's *Ordet*," Religions 10, no. 1 (Jan. 2019): 2.
6. Doeber, "Jest in Time," 18.
7. Raymond Carney, *Speaking the Language of Desire: The Films of Carl Dreyer* (Cambridge: Cambridge University Press, 1989), 255.
8. Mike King, *Luminous: The Spiritual Life on Film* (London: Stochastic Press, 2018), 129.
9. Watts, "The Fullness of Time," 1.
10. Schrader, *Transcendental Style in Film*, 154.
11. Ibid.
12. Ibid.
13. Richard V. Goodwin, "An Old Film in a New Light: Lighting as the Key to Johannine Identity in *Ordet*," *Journal of Religion and Film* 22, no. 2 (2018): 10.
14. Doebler, 3–4.
15. Ibid., 5.
16. Ibid.
17. Ibid., 7–8.
18. Ibid.

Pale Rider

1. John Lyden, *Film as Religion: Myths, Morals, and Rituals* (New York: New York University Press, 2019), 119.
2. Ibid., 122.
3. Robert Jewett, "The Disguise of Vengeance in *Pale Rider*," in *Religion and Popular Culture in America*, ed. Bruce Forbes and Jeffrey Mahan (Oakland: University of California Press, 2005), 238.
4. Lloyd Baugh, *Imaging the Divine: Jesus and Christ Figures in Film* (Kansas City: Sheed & Ward, 1997), 160.
5. Ibid., 157.
6. Lyden, *Film as Religion*, 121.
7. Adele Reinhartz, *Scripture on the Silver Screen* (Louisville: Westminster John Knox Press, 2003), 173.
8. David Lusted, *The Western* (Harlow: Pearson Education, 2003), 192.
9. Reinhartz, *Scripture on the Silver Screen*, 173.

10. Andrew M. Bergesen and Albert J. Greeley, *God in the Movies* (New York: Routledge, 2000), 73.
11. Jim Kitses, *Horizons West: Directing the Western from John Ford to Clint Eastwood* (London: British Film Institute, 2004), 301.
12. Bergesen and Greeley, *God in the Movies*, 77.
13. Ibid.
14. Baugh, *Imaging the Divine*, 157.
15. Bergesen and Greeley, *God in the Movies*, 76.
16. Reinhartz, *Scripture on the Silver Screen*, 172.
17. Kitses, *Horizons West*, 301.
18. Ibid., 302.

The Passion of the Christ

1. Eric S. Christianson, Peter Francis, and William R. Telford, *Cinema Divinite: Religion, Theology, and the Bible in Film* (London: SCM Press, 2005), 314.
2. Ibid.
3. Robert. K. Johnston, "The Passion as Dynamic Icon," in *Re-Viewing The Passion: Mel Gibson's Film and its Critics*, ed. S. Brent Plate (New York: St. Martin's Griffin, 2004), 56.
4. Paul Flesher and Robert Torry, *Film and Religion: An Introduction* (Nashville: Abington Press, 2007), 159.
5. Ibid., 167.
6. Ibid.
7. Ibid.
8. Ibid., 173.
9. Hal Childs, "The Eye of Suffering: Reflections on *The Passion of the Christ*," *Pastoral Psychology*, 53, no. 4 (March 2005): 334.
10. Dennis Morgan, "Catholic Visual Piety and *The Passion of the Christ*," in Plate, *Re-Viewing The Passion*, 87.
11. Flesher and Torry, *Film and Religion*, 165.
12. Ibid.
13. Ibid.
14. Ibid., 166.
15. Ibid.
16. Christianson, Francis, and Telford, *Cinema Divinite*, 313.
17. Childs, "The Eye of Suffering," 333.
18. Ibid.
19. Flesher and Torry, *Film and Religion*, 173.

Peaceful Warrior

1. Jane Naomi Iwamura, "The Oriental Monk in American Popular Culture," in *Religion and Popular Culture in America*, ed. Bruce David Forbes and Jeffrey Mahan (Oakland: University of California Press, 2005), 30.
2. Huston Smith, *The World's Religions* (New York: Harper Collins, 1991), 136.

Pinocchio

1. Thomas A. Nelson, "Darkness in the Disney Look," *Literature/Film Quarterly* 6, no. 2 (Spring 1978): 97.
2. David Bosworth, "From Wariness to Wishfulness: Disney's Emasculation of Pinocchio's Conscience," *The Georgia Review* 65, no. 3 (Fall 2011): 596.

Princess Mononoke

1. Yuan Pan, "Human–Nature Relationships in East Asian Animated Films," *Societies* 10, no. 2 (2020): 9.

2. Shinobu Price, "Cartoons from Another Planet: Japanese Animation as Cross-Cultural Communication," *Journal of American and Comparative Cultures* 24, no. 1/2 (Spring 2001): 166.

3. Sema Mumcu and Serap Yılmaz, "Anime Landscapes as a Tool for Analyzing the Human–Environment Relationship: Hayao Miyazaki Films," *Arts* 7, no. 2 (June 2018): 7.

4. Susan J. Napier, *Anime from Akira to Princess Mononoke: Experiencing Contemporary Japanese Animation* (New York: Palgrave, 2000), 178.

5. Pan, "Human–Nature Relationships," 10.

6. Ibid.

7. Mumcu and Yilmaz, "Anime Landscapes," 11.

8. Ibid.

9. Adam Barkman, "The Earth Speaks to Us All: A Critical Appreciation of Filmmaker Hayao Miyazaki's Shinto Environmental Philosophy," *Christian Scholar's Review* 48, no. 4 (Summer 2019), 330.

10. Pan, "Human–Nature Relationships," 6.

11. Ibid.

12. Tara Judah, "Princess Mononoke: Transgressing the Binaries that Bind," *Screen Education* 74 (2014): 59.

13. Ibid., 57–58.

14. Ibid.

15. Price, "Cartoons from Another Planet," 157.

16. Mumcu and Yilmaz, "Anime Landscapes," 7–8.

17. Napier, *Anime from Akira*, 177.

18. Ibid.

The Razor's Edge

1. Robert Calder, *W. Somerset Maugham and the Quest for Freedom* (New York: Doubleday, 1973), 129.

2. Ibid., 244.

3. Ibid.

4. Ibid.

5. Ibid., 245.

6. Ibid.

7. William James, *The Varieties of Religious Experience* (New York: Modern Library, 1999), 414–415.

Revenge of the Sith

1. Nick Jamilla, "Defining the Jedi Order: *Star Wars*' Narrative and the Real World," in *Sex, Politics, and Religion in Star Wars: An Anthology*, ed. Douglas Brode and Leah Deyneka (Lanham: Scarecrow Press, 2012), 157.

2. Tony Vinci, "Fall of the Rebellion; Or Defiant and Obedient Villains in a Galaxy Far, Far Away," in *Culture, Identities and Technology in the Star Wars Films: Essays on the Two Trilogies*, ed. Carl Silvio and Tony M. Vinci (Jefferson: McFarland, 2007), 2.

3. Jason T. Eberl, "Know the Dark Side: A Theodicy of the Force," in *The Ultimate Star Wars and Philosophy: You Must Unlearn What You Have Learned*, ed. Jason T. Eberl and Kevin S. Decker (Malden: John Wiley & Sons, 2015), 104.

4. Ibid.

5. Payal Doctor, "The Force Awakens: The Individualistic and Contemporary Heroine," *NANO: New American Notes Online* 12 (Dec. 2017), https://www.proquest.com/scholarly-journals/force-awakens-individualistic-contemporary/docview/23221 58831/se-2.

6. Ibid.

The River

1. Christopher Faulkner, *The Social Cinema of Jean Renoir* (Princeton: Princeton University Press, 1986), 168.

2. Ibid., 172.

3. Ibid., 168–169.

4. Ibid., 168.

5. Ibid., 172.

6. Raymond Durgnat, *Jean Renoir* (Berkeley: University of California Press, 1974), 280.

7. Katherine Golsan, "Desperately Seeking Radha: Renoir's *The River* and its Reincarnation," *South Central Review* 28, no. 3 (Fall 2011): 108.

8. Faulkner, *The Social Cinema of Jean Renoir*, 178.

9. Golsan, "Desperately Seeking Radha," 114.

10. Ibid.

11. Ibid., 115.

12. Ibid., 114.

13. Ibid.

14. Ibid., 111.

The Robe

1. Martin Winkler, "The Roman Empire in Cinema After 1945," in *Imperial Projections: Ancient Rome in Modern Popular Culture*, ed. Sandra R. Joshel, Margaret Malamud, and Donald T. McGuire Jr. (Baltimore: Johns Hopkins University Press, 2001), 51.

2. Bruce Francis Babington and Peter William Evans, *Biblical Epics: Sacred Narrative in the Hollywood Cinema* (Eugene: Wipf and Stock, 1993), 206.

3. Adele Reinhartz, *Bible and Cinema: An Introduction* (New York: Routledge, 2013), 94–95.

4. Forest Hirsch, *The Hollywood Epic* (Cranbury: A.S. Barnes & Co., 1978), 73.

5. Ibid., 109.

6. Babington and Evans, *Biblical Epics*, 213.

7. Ibid., 207.

8. Paul Flesher and Robert Torrey, *Film and Religion: An Introduction* (Nashville: Abingdon Press, 2007), 62–63.

9. Ibid.

10. Reinhartz, *Bible and Cinema*, 103.

11. Babington and Evans, *Biblical Epics*, 213.

Romero

1. Bryan P. Stone, *Faith and Film: Theological Themes at the Cinema* (St. Louis: Chalice Press, 2000), 89.
2. Ibid., 85.
3. Gustavo Gutierrez, *A Theology of Liberation: History, Politics, and Salvation* (New York: Orbis Books, 1988), 165.
4. Ibid., 127.
5. Margaret Miles, *Seeing and Believing: Religion and Values in the Movies* (Boston: Beacon Press, 1996), 51.
6. Stone, *Faith and Film*, 88.
7. Ibid., 24.
8. Ibid., 103.

Run Lola Run

1. Charles Ramírez Berg, "A Taxonomy of Alternative Plots in Recent Films: Classifying the Tarantino Effect," *Film Criticism* 31, no. 1/2 (Fall 2006), 30.
2. Ibid.
3. Ibid., 31.
4. David Clarke, "In Search of Home: Filming Post-Unification Berlin," in *German Cinema Since Unification*, ed. David Clarke (London: Continuum, 1996), 174.
5. Berg, "A Taxonomy," 31.
6. Catherine Wood, "Sometimes You Need the Help of the Universe: *Run Lola Run*," *Screen Education* 42 (2006): 110.
7. Ibid.
8. Ibid.
9. Kate Matthews, "Running in Circles: Form in *Run Lola Run*," *Screen Education* 45 (2007): 156.
10. Ibid.
11. Tom Whalen, "*Run Lola Run*," *Film Quarterly* 53, no. 3 (2000): 38.
12. Wood, "Sometimes You Need," 109.

The Sacrifice

1. Paul Schrader, *Transcendental Style in Film* (Oakland: University of California Press, 2018), 21.
2. Ibid., 10, 17, 22.
3. Ibid., 23.
4. Thomas Odde, "Time Sickness in Andre Tarkovsky's *The Sacrifice*," *Canadian Journal of Film Studies* 18, no. 2 (Fall 2009): 67.
5. Susan Bye, "Andrei Tarkovsky," *Screen Education* 97 (2020): 72.
6. Odde, "Time Sickness," 68.
7. Ibid.
8. Ibid.
9. Ibid.
10. Lloyd Baugh, *Imaging the Divine: Jesus and Christ-Figures in Film* (Kansas City: Sheed & Ward, 1997), 233.
11. Gabriel F. Giralt, "Andrei Tarkovsky's Adaptation of Motifs Embedded in Leonardo da Vinci's 'The Adoration of the Magi,'" *Canadian Journal of Film Studies* 14, no. 2 (Fall 2005): 74.
12. Bye, "Andrei Tarkovsky," 71.
13. Giralt, "Andrei Tarkovsky's Adaptation," 79.

14. Ibid.
15. Ibid.
16. Ibid., 78.
17. Ibid.
18. Ibid., 78–79.

Schindler's List

1. Clifford J. Marks and Robert Torry, "Herr Direktor: Biography and Autobiography in *Schindler's List*," *Biography*, 23, no. 1 (Winter 2000): 51.
2. Ibid., 52.
3. Garry Schmidt, "Spirituality and Justice in *Schindler's List*: A Case Study Informed by Karl Barth and Gustav Gutierrez," *Pastoral Psychology* 54, no. 3 (Jan. 2006): 262.
4. Marks and Torry, "Herr Direktor," 59–60.
5. Schmidt, "Spirituality and Justice," 265.
6. Ibid., 259.
7. Ibid., 272.
8. Keith W. Carpenter, "Oskar Schindler: A Sheep in Wolf's Clothing," *The International Journal of Servant-Leadership* 8/9, no. 1 (2012/2013): 482.
9. Jose Diaz-Cuesta Galian, "Man as Rescuer and Monster in Steven Spielberg's Film *Schindler's List*," *Journal of English Studies* 5–6 (2005–2008): 67, https://doi.org/10.18172/jes.121.

The Shack

1. Kenneth Paradis, "Typological Realism in Contemporary Evangelical Fiction: Tragedy, Eternity, and The Shack," *English Studies in Canada* 37, no. 1 (2011): 115.
2. Ibid., 124.
3. Ibid.
4. Larry Poston, "*The Shack*: A Novel," *Christian Scholar's Review* 38, no. 4 (2009): 492.
5. Ibid., 490.

Shadowlands

1. Carlos Villar Flor, "Intertextuality in *Shadowlands*: From the Essay to the Love Story," *Literature/Film Quarterly* 27, no. 2 (1999): 98.
2. Ibid.
3. Ibid.
4. W. M. Hagen, "*Shadowlands* and the Redemption of Light," *Literature/Film Quarterly* 26, no. 1 (1998): 10.
5. Villar Flor, "Intertextuality in *Shadowlands*," 101.
6. David Baggett, "Rats in God's Laboratory: *Shadowlands* and the Problem of Evil," in *Movies and the Meaning of Life: Philosophers Take on Hollywood*, ed. Kimberly A. Blessing and Paul J. Tudico (Chicago: Open Court, 2005), 134.
7. Ibid.

Shane

1. Lloyd Baugh, *Imaging the Divine: Jesus and Christ Figures in Film* (Kansas City: Sheed & Ward, 1997), 157.
2. Will Wright, *Sixguns and Society: A Structural Study of the Western* (Berkeley: University of California Press, 1975), 48–49.

3. Eric Michael Mazur, *Encyclopedia of Religion and Film* (Santa Barbara: ABC-CLIO, 2011), 463.

4. Patrick McGee, *From Shane to Kill Bill: Rethinking the Western* (Malden: Blackwell Publishing, 2007), 6.

5. Ibid., 5.

6. Baugh, *Imaging the Divine*, 170.

7. Robert Banks, "Salvation in George Stevens' *Shane*," in *Explorations in Theology and Film*, ed. Clive Marsh and Gaye Ortiz (Malden: Blackwell Publishing, 1997), 61.

8. Baugh, *Imaging the Divine*, 170.

9. Banks, "Salvation," 61.

10. Baugh, *Imaging the Divine*, 162

11. Ibid., 161.

12. David Desser, "Kurosawa's Eastern Western: *Sanjuro* and the Influence of *Shane*," *Film Criticism* 8, no. 1 (Fall 1983): 58, JSTOR.

13. Baugh, *Imaging the Divine*, 161.

14. Peter Francis, "*Shane*," in *Bible and Cinema: 50 Key Films*, ed. Adele Reinhartz (London: Routledge, 2013), 234.

15. Banks, "Salvation," 65.

16. McGee, *From Shane to Kill Bill*, 9.

17. Banks, "Salvation," 65.

The Shawshank Redemption

1. Mark Kermonde, "Hope Springs Eternal," *The Guardian*, August 21, 2004, https://www.theguardian.com/film/2004/aug/22/film.

2. Kevin Kehrwald, *Prison Movies: Cinema Behind Bars* (New York: Wallflower Press, 2017), 8.

3. Kermode, "Hope Springs Eternal."

4. Adele Reinhartz, *Scripture on the Silver Screen* (Louisville: Westminster John Knox Press, 2003), 135.

5. Ibid., 139.

6. William Young, "*The Shawshank Redemption* and the Hope for Escape," in *Movies and the Meaning of Life: Philosophers Take on Hollywood*, ed. Kimberly A. Blessing and Paul J. Tudico (Chicago: Open Court, 2005), 191.

7. Kehrwald, *Prison Movies*, 19.

8. Peter Gutierrez, "Redeeming the Myth of Upward Mobility: *The Shawshank Redemption*," *Screen Education* 70, (2013): 102.

9. Reinhartz, *Scripture on the Silver Screen*, 139.

10. Kermode, "Hope Springs Eternal."

Sleeping Beauty

1. Rebecca-Anne, C. Do Rozario, "The Princess and the Magic Kingdom: Beyond Nostalgia, the Function of the Disney Princess," *Women's Studies in Communication* 27, no. 1 (Spring 2004): 40.

2. Ibid.

3. Elizabeth Bell, "Somataxts at the Disney Shop: Constructing the Pentimentos of Women's Animated Bodies," in *From Mouse to Mermaid: The Politics of Film, Gender, and Culture*, ed. Elizabeth Bell, Lynda Haas, and Laura Sells (Bloomington: Indiana University Press, 1995), 119.

Smoke Signals

1. Dennis West and Joan M. West, "Sending Cinematic Smoke Signals: An Interview with Sherman Alexie," *Cineaste* 23, no. 4 (1998), 28.

2. Jim Charles, "Contemporary American Indian Life in *The Owl's Song* and *Smoke Signals*," *English Journal* 90, no. 3 (Jan. 2001): 141.

3. Julien R. Fielding, "Native Religion and Film: Interviews with Chris Eyre and Sherman Alexie," *Journal of Religion and Film* 7, no. 1 (April 2003): 1, https://digital-commons.unomaha.edu/jrf/vol7/iss1/5.

4. Ibid., 8–9.

5. Gordon E. Slethaug, "Hurricanes and Fires: Chaotics in Sherman Alexie's *Smoke Signals* and the Lone Ranger and Tonto Fistfight in *Heaven*," *Literature/Film Quarterly* 31, no. 2 (2003): 136.

6. Andrea Baltazar, "Native Voices: Or, Vehicle as Symbol in Smoke Signals," *Americana: The Journal of American Popular Culture*, 1900 to Present 15, no. 1 (Spring 2016).

7. Slethaug, "Hurricanes and Fires," 138.

8. Ibid.

9. Wendy G. Pearson, "Detours Homeward: Indigenizing the Road Movie," *The Canadian Journal of Native Studies*, 31, no. 1 (2011): 55.

10. Anjelica Lawson, "Native Sensibility and the Significance of Woman in *Smoke Signals*," in *Sherman Alexie: A Collection of Critical Essays*, ed. Jeff Berglund and Jan Roush (Salt Lake City: University of Utah Press, 2010), 103.

11. Slethaug, "Hurricanes and Fires," 138.

12. Ibid., 4.

13. Ibid.

14. Ibid., 137.

15. Baltazar, "Native Voices."

The Song of Bernadette

1. Paula M. Kane, "Jews and Catholics Converge: The Song of Bernadette," in *Catholics in the Movies*, ed. Colleen McDannell (Oxford: Oxford University Press, 2008), 85.

2. William James, *The Varieties of Religious Experience* (New York: Modern Library, 1999), 286.

3. Ann W. Astell, "Artful Dogma: The Immaculate Conception and Franz Werfel's *Song of Bernadette*," *Christianity & Literature* 62, no. 1 (Autumn 2012): 20.

4. Kane, "Jews and Catholics Converge," 89.

5. Astell, "Artful Dogma," 11–12.

6. Kane, "Jews and Catholics Converge," 87.

7. Ibid., 102.

8. Astell, "Artful Dogma," 11.

9. Ibid., 19.

10. Kane, "Jews and Catholics Converge," 90.

11. Ibid., 101.

Soul

1. Benjamin Resnick, "How Pixar's 'Soul' Borrows from an Ancient Jewish Idea," last modified December 30, 2020, https://www.jpost.com/judaism/how-pixars-soul-borrows-from-an-ancient-jewish-idea-653682.

Spirited Away

1. Jolyon Baraka Thomas, "Religion in Japanese Film: Focus on Anime," in *The Routledge Companion to Religion and Film*, ed. John Lyden (London: Routledge, 2011), 197.
2. Kate Matthews, "Logic and Narrative in *Spirited Away*," *Screen Education* 43 (2006): 139.
3. Noriko T. Reider, "*Spirited Away*: Film of the Fantastic and Evolving Japanese Folk Symbols," *Film Criticism* 29, no. 3 (Spring 2005): 9.
4. James Boyd and Tetsuya Nishimura, "Shinto Perspectives in Miyazaki's Anime Film *Spirited Away*," *Journal of Religion & Film* 8, no. 3 (October 2004): 6, https://digitalcommons.unomaha.edu/jrf/vol8/iss3/4.
5. Reider, "*Spirited Away*," 10.
6. Thomas, "Religion in Japanese Film," 197.
7. Yuan Pan, "Human–Nature Relationships in East Asian Animated Films," *Societies* 10, no. 2 (2020): 11.
8. Boyd and Nishimura, "Shinto Perspectives," 6.
9. Ibid.
10. Matthews, "Logic and Narrative," 140.
11. Susan Bye, "Spirits of Times Past: Fantasy, Tradition and Identity in *Spirited Away*," *Screen Education* 67 (2012): 126.
12. Ibid., 125.
13. Ando Satoshi, "Regaining Continuity with the Past: *Spirited Away* and *Alice's Adventures in Wonderland*," *Bookbird* 46, no. 1 (2008): 26.
14. Matthews, "Logic and Narrative," 138.
15. Boyd and Nishimura, "Shinto Perspectives," 9.
16. Ibid., 6.
17. Ibid., 9.
18. Bye, "Spirits of Times Past," 125.
19. Matthews, "Logic and Narrative," 138.
20. Ibid., 138–139.
21. Boyd and Nishimura, "Shinto Perspectives," 9–10.
22. Chris Muir, "Strangers in the Night Spirited Away," *Screen Education* 74 (2014): 31.
23. Bye, "Spirits of Times Past," 123.
24. Pan, "Human–Nature Relationships," 8.

Stars Wars Trilogy

1. John C. Lyden, *Film as Religion: Myths, Morals, and Rituals* (New York: New York University Press, 2003), 218.
2. Ibid., 217.
3. Ibid., 220.
4. Ibid., 222.
5. Susan Markey-Kallis, *The Hero and the Perennial Journey Home in American Film* (Philadelphia: University of Pennsylvania, 2001), 218.
6. Ibid., 221.
7. Huston Smith, *The World's Religions* (New York: Harper Collins, 1991), 201.

The Straight Story

1. Tim Kreider and Rob Content, "The Straight Story," *Film Quarterly* 54, no. 1 (Fall 2000): 32.

2. Colin Odell and Michelle LeBlanc, *David Lynch* (Harpenden: Kamera Books, 2007), 105.

3. Kreider and Content, "The Straight Story," 33.

4. Ibid., 26.

5. Devin Orgeron, "Revising the Postmodern American Road Movie: David Lynch's *The Straight Story*," *Journal of Film and Video* 54, no. 4 (Winter 2002): 40.

6. Ibid., 38.

7. Ibid., 43.

The Ten Commandments

1. Gerald Forshey, *American Religious and Biblical Spectaculars* (Westport: Praeger, 1992), 1.

2. Bruce Babington and Peter Evans, *Biblical Epics: Sacred Narrative in the Hollywood Cinema* (Eugene: Wipf & Stock, 1993), 50.

3. Brian Baker, "Key Concepts in Film Studies," in *Cinema Divinite: Religion, Theology, and the Bible in Film*, ed. Eric Christianson, Eric, Peter Francis, and William Telford (London: SCM Press, 2005), 47.

4. Alicia Ostriker, "Whither Exodus? Movies as Midrash," *Michigan Quarterly Review* 42, no. 1 (Winter 2003): 144- 145.

5. Forshey, *American Religious*, 133.

6. Ibid.

7. Adele Reinhartz, *Bible and Cinema: An Introduction* (New York: Routledge, 2013), 40.

8. Forshey, *American Religious*, 127.

9. Ibid., 128.

10. Ostriker, "Whither Exodus?", 149–150.

11. Foshey, *American Religious*, 130.

Tender Mercies

1. *Tender Mercies*, 2009, DVD, dir. Bruce Beresford (Santa Monica, CA: Lionsgate).

2. Robert Jewett, *Saint Paul at the Movies: The Apostle's Dialogue with American Culture* (Louisville: Westminster John Knox Press, 1993), 63.

3. Roy Anker, *Catching Light: Looking for God in the Movies* (Grand Rapids, Wm. B. Eerdmans Publishing Co., 2004), 124.

4. Jewett, *Saint Paul at the Movies*, 62.

5. Anker, *Catching Light*, 133.

6. Maxine Grossman, "Jesus, Mama, and the Constraints on Salvific Love in Contemporary Country Music," *Journal of the American Academy of Religion* 70, no. 1 (March 2002): 88.

7. Anker, *Catching Light*, 137.

8. Jewett, *Saint Paul at the Movies*, 62.

9. David Desser, "Transcendental Style in *Tender Mercies*," *Religious Communication Today* 8 (Sept. 1985): 25.

10. Ibid., 24.

Three Godfathers

1. Jim Kitses, *Horizons West: Directing the Western from John Ford to Clint Eastwood* (London: British Film Institute, 2004), 13.

2. Ibid., 76.

3. Maria Elena de las Carreras Kuntz, "The Catholic Vision in Hollywood: Ford, Capra, Borzage and Hitchcock," *Film History* 14, no. 2 (2002): 130.

4. Ibid., 130.

5. Ibid., 132.

6. Charles Silver, "3 Godfathers," in *The Hidden God: Film and Faith*, ed. Mary Lea Bandy and Antonio Monda (New York: The Museum of Modern Art, 2003), 59–60.

7. Kitses, *Horizons West*, 71.

8. Ibid.

9. Ibid.

10. Kitses, *Horizons West*, 75.

11. J.A. Place, *The Western Films of John Ford* (Secaucus: Citadel Press, 1974), 105.

12. Ibid.

13. Ibid.

14. Ibid., 106.

15. Ibid., 105.

Tokyo Story

1. "The 100 Greatest Films of All Time," June 28, 2021, https://www.bfi.org.uk/sight-and-sound/greatest-films-all- time.

2. Donald Richie, *Ozu* (Berkeley: University of California Press, 1974), 1.

3. Paul Schrader, *Transcendental Style in Film* (Oakland: University of California Press, 2018), 49.

4. Richie, *Ozu*, 4.

5. Schrader, *Transcendental Style in Film*, 64.

6. Linda Ehrlich, "Travel Toward and Away: Furusato and Journey in Tokyo Story," in *Ozu's Tokyo Story*, ed. David Desser (Cambridge: Cambridge University Press, 1997), 69.

7. Ehrlich, "Travel Toward and Away," 69.

8. Kathe Geist, "Buddhism in *Tokyo Story*," in *Ozu's Tokyo Story*, ed. David Desser (Cambridge: Cambridge University Press, 1997), 107.

9. Ibid., 115.

10. Schrader, *Transcendental Style in Film*, 45.

11. Ibid., 72.

12. Ibid.

13. Ibid., 51.

14. David Bordwell, "*Tokyo Story*: Compassionate Detachment," last modified November 18, 2013, https://www.criterion.com/current/posts/301-tokyo-story-compassionate-detachment.

15. Schrader, *Transcendental Style in Film*, 57.

16. Geist, "Buddhism in *Tokyo Story*," 109.

17. Schrader, *Transcendental Style in Film*, 75.

18. Ibid., 82.

19. Ibid.

20. Ibid.

21. Huston Smith, *The World's Religions* (New York: Harper Collins, 1991), 116.

The Treasure of the Sierra Madre

1. John Engell, "*The Treasure of Sierra Madre*: B. Traven, John Huston and Ideology in Film Adaptation," *Literature/Film Quarterly* 17, no. 4 (1989): 246.
2. Ibid.
3. William Graebner, "Fathers and Sons: An Exploration of *The Treasure of the Sierra Madre*," *Literature/Film Quarterly* 32, no. 1 (2004): 32.
4. Peter Valenti, "*The Treasure of the Sierra Madre*: Spiritual Quest," in *Image and Likeness: Religious Visions in American Film Classics*, ed. John R. May (Mahwah: Paulist Press, 1992), 88.
5. Graebner, "Fathers and Sons," 32.
6. Valenti, "*The Treasure of the Sierra Madre*," 88.
7. Leslie Brill, *John Huston's Filmmaking* (Cambridge: Cambridge University Press, 1997), 21–22.
8. Graebner, "Fathers and Sons," 32.
9. Brill, *John Huston's Filmmaking*, 22.
10. Ibid., 19.
11. Ibid., 18.
12. Engell, "*The Treasure of Sierra Madre*," 246.
13. Brill, *John Huston's Filmmaking*, 18–19.
14. Ibid., 29.
15. Ibid., 18.
16. Graebner, "Fathers and Sons," 31.
17. Ibid.
18. Brill, *John Huston's Filmmaking*, 31.

The Tree of Life

1. Christopher B. Barnett, "Spirituality in the Films of Terrence Malick," *Journal of Religion and Film* 17, no. 1 (2013): 1.
2. Bertha A. Manninen, "The Problem of Evil and Humans' Relationship with God in Terrence Malick's *The Tree of Life*," *Journal of Religion and Film* 17, no. 1 (April 2013): 13.
3. Ibid., 14.
4. Ibid.
5. Ibid., 1–2.
6. Ibid., 13.
7. Ibid., 11.
8. Pablo A. Cerero, "Standing at God's Threshold: Film Viewing as Dwelling in Terrence Malick's *Tree of Life*," *Communication and Culture* 4, no. 2 (Aug. 2019): 157.
9. Elisa Zocchi, "Terrence Malick Beyond Nature and Grace: Song to Song and the Experience of Forgiveness," *Journal of Religion and Film* 22, no. 2 (Oct. 2018): 5.
10. Ibid., 5.
11. Ibid.
12. Ibid., 3.
13. Ibid.
14. Peter Leitart, *Shining Glory: Theological Reflections on the Tree of Life* (Eugene: Cascade Books, 2013), 75.
15. Ibid., 86
16. Cerero, "Standing at God's Threshold," 164.

V for Vendetta

1. Rjurik Davidson, "Vagaries & Violence in *V for Vendetta*," *Screen Education* 46 (2007): 160.

2. Ibid.

Voyage of the Dawn Treader

1. Paul F. Ford, *Companion to Narnia: A Complete Guide to the Magical World of C.S. Lewis's The Chronicles of Narnia* (San Francisco: Harper, 2005), 6.

2. Jameela Lares, "The Reception of Ancient Greece and Rome in Children's Literature: Heroes and Eagles, ed. by Lisa Maurice (review)," *Children's Literature* 45 (2017): 199.

3. Mark Worthing, *Narnia, Middle Earth, and the Kingdom of God: A History of Fantasy Literature and the Christian Tradition* (Eugene: Wipf & Stock, 2016), 82.

4. Ford, *Companion to Narnia*, 447.

5. Ibid., 148.

6. Ibid.

7. Dianne Shober, "Leonine Imagery in C.S. Lewis's Series *The Chronicles of Narnia*," *Literator* 40, no. 1 (2019): 6.

8. Peter J. Schake, "Hidden Images of Christ in the Fiction of C.S. Lewis," *Studies in the Literary Imagination*, 46, no. 2 (Fall 2013): 9.

9. Ibid.

Wall Street

1. Frank Beaver, *Oliver Stone: Wakeup Cinema* (Woodbridge: Twayne Publishers, 1994), 104.

2. Joseph Campbell, *The Hero with a Thousand Faces* (Novato: New World Library, 2008), 115.

3. Emmett J. Winn, "Every Dream Has Its Price: Personal Failure and the American Dream in *Wall Street* and *The Firm*," *The Southern Communication Journal* 68, no. 4 (Summer 2003): 313.

4. Ibid., 308.

5. Norman Kagan, *The Cinema of Oliver Stone* (New York, Continuum, 1995), 123.

6. Susan Mackey-Kallis, *Oliver Stone's America: Dreaming the Myth Outward* (New York: Routledge, 2019), 124.

Whale Rider

1. Brendan Hokowhitu, "The Death of Koro Paka: 'Traditional' Maori Patriarchy," *Contemporary Pacific* 20, no. 1, (2008): 131–132.

2. Ibid., 132.

3. Irene Visser, "Exclusion and Revolt in Witi Ihimaera's *Whale Rider*," *Commonwealth: Essays and Studies* 30, no. 2 (Spring 2008): 67.

4. Huston Smith, *The World's Religions* (New York: Harper Collins, 1991), 374.

5. Visser, "Exclusion and Revolt," 67.

6. Ibid.

7. Ibid., 67–68.

8. Hokowhitu, "The Death of Koro Paka," 132.

9. Smith, *The World's Religions*, 374.

10. Ibid.

11. Kevin Dodd, "*Whale Rider*: The Re-enactment of Myth and the Empowerment of Women," *Journal of Religion & Film* 16, no. 2 (Oct. 2012): 6, https://digitalcommons .unomaha.edu/jrf/vol16/iss2/9.

12. Smith, *The World's Religions*, 375.

Wings of Desire

1. Linda C. Ehrlich, "Meditations on Wim Wenders's *Wings of Desire*," *Literature/Film Quarterly* 19, no. 4 (1991): 243.

2. Les Caltvedt, "Berlin Poetry: Archaic Cultural Patterns in Wenders's *Wings of Desire*," *Literature/Film Quarterly* 20, no. 2 (1992): 122.

3. Mike King, *Luminous: The Spiritual Life on Film* (London: Stochastic Press, 2018), 88.

4. Charles H. Helmetag, "'. . . of Men and of Angels': Literary Allusions in Wim Wenders's 'Wings of Desire,'" *Literature/Film Quarterly* 18, no. 4, (1990): 252.

5. Ibid., 253.

6. King, *Luminous*, 89.

7. Cathleen Rountree, "The Divine Pilgrimage to Love by a Poet and an Angel, Dante and Damiel: A Psychological Study Comparing the *Divine Comedy* and *Wings of Desire*," *Jung Journal* 1, no. 1 (Winter 2007): 56.

8. King, *Luminous*, 89.

9. Ehrlich, "Meditations," 243.

10. Roger Cook, "Angels, Fiction and History in Berlin: Wim Wenders' *Wings of Desire*," *The Germanic Review* 66, no. 1 (Winter 1991): 41.

11. Ehrlich, "Meditations," 243–244.

12. Cook, "Angels, Fiction and History," 41.

13. Rountree, "The Divine Pilgrimage," 56.

14. Ibid., 58.

15. Ibid.

The Wizard of Oz

1. Salman Rushdie, "Out of Kansas," *New Yorker*, May 11, 1992.

2. Ibid.

3. Sat Yoga Institute, "The Hidden Meaning of *The Wizard of Oz*: An Esoteric Allegory," YouTube video, December 25, 2019, https://www.youtube.com/watch?v= oWi5fF-lhpk.

4. Ibid.

5. Ibid.

6. Scott J. Cochrane, "The Wizard of Oz and Rites of Passage," in *Image and Likeness: Religious Visions in American Film Classics*, ed. John R. May (Mahwah: Paulist Press, 1992), 84.

7. Ibid., 85.

8. Maria Tatar, "Why Fairy Tales Matter: The Performative and the Transformative," *Western Folklore* 69, no. 1 (Winter 2010): 62.

9. Susan Mackey-Kallis, *The Hero and the Perennial Journey Home in American Film* (Philadelphia: University of Pennsylvania Press, 2001), 133.

10. Russel Nye, "An Appreciation," in *The Wizard of Oz and Who He Was*, ed. Martin Gardner and Russel Nye (East Lansing: Michigan State University Press, 1957), 5.

11. Paul Nathanson, "Over the Rainbow: *The Wizard of Oz* as a Secular Myth of America" (Albany: State University of New York, 1991), 13.

12. Ibid., 11–13.

13. Linda Hansen, "Experiencing the World as Home: Reflections on Dorothy's Quest in 'The Wizard of Oz,'" *Soundings: An Interdisciplinary Journal* 67, no. 1 (Spring 1988): 98–99.

14. Ibid., 101–102.

15. Mackey-Kallis, *The Hero and the Perennial Journey Home*, 130.